The Seven-Sealed Book

By

David Lawrence

Copyright © 2025 self published by David Lawrence

All rights reserved.

Second Edition proofread by editGTP

To the church at Philadelphia

To the ones I've lost...

Introduction	7
The 70 Weeks of Daniel & The Church	14
Prophecy of the Seven-Sealed Book	22
The Throne Room of Heaven	23
The Seals	29
Birth Pangs	30
The Four Horsemen	31
The White Horse	36
The Red Horse	51
A Great Sword	61
The Black Horse	64
The Pale Horse	83
The Fifth Seal	90
The Sixth Seal	96
Interlude	99
The Seventh Seal: Silence in Heaven	102
The First Four Trumpets	106
The Fifth Trumpet	120
The Sixth Trumpet	132
The Seven Thunders, the Angel and the Little Book	139
The Two Witnesses	143
The Seventh Trumpet	155
Practical Tips	158
Appendix A: 70 Weeks of Daniel	162
Appendix B: Of Monkeys, Typewriters & the Creator	163
Appendix C The Age of Grace	167
Appendix D Qualitative Juxtaposition	171
Appendix E The Parable of the Rich Young Man	176
Appendix F The Church Clock	180
Appendix G The Great Falling Away	207

Introduction

I was listening to a YouTube video of the late Dr. Chuck Missler a few years ago when he made a statement that piqued my curiosity. He basically made the case that the book of Revelation is written in code, and that the rest of the Bible can be used as source material to decrypt the message hidden within. Intrigued, I started looking up Old Testament references listed next to the text in my NASB Study Bible to see if there was anything to this idea. Having grown up in the church, I knew there was some correlation to be discovered, but I was cautiously skeptical about being able to find out anything new. Of course, I should have known better, as the Bible seems to always contain deeper layers of meaning every time you come back to it. Perhaps what was different this time is that, in order to effectively pursue the idea of using the rest of the Bible as a decoder ring, this raises the bar on what I thought my beliefs were about the inerrancy of Scripture.

So, for the time that you spend reading this book, I want you to go on a journey with me. I want you to join me in a thought experiment. Whether you believe in God or the Bible or not, I want you to assume, just for a little while, that the Bible is not only one hundred percent true in its original languages, but that, to paraphrase Dr. Missler, the Bible is a highly complex, encoded communication from the God of the universe to all mankind. For some of you, this will not be much different than when Albert Einstein proposed what it might be like to hitch a ride on a beam of light. That's okay.

What this means practically is that when we come across apparent contradictions or inconsistencies, for the sake of our experiment, we take this as a clue that there is some hidden meaning to be discovered. In other words, for the time that it takes for you to read this book, I want you to assume with me that the Bible is such a supernaturally perfect document, that its accuracy is precisely the thing which makes it so hard to understand, as it requires our knowledge of history and culture to be up to the same standard. Granted, this could quickly lead to a host of divergent, unrelated contradictions, so I propose that the test for this experiment be the opposite. As a part of this experiment, you should prepare by reading the Revelation in its entirety (or at least chapters 4-11). Then, after you finish *The Seven-Sealed Book*, you should ask yourself:

Does this interpretation bring clarity as opposed to more confusion? Hopefully by the end, if I've done a good job, you will have a clear answer.

In keeping with our experiment, we will say John did not compose the content of The Revelation, so much as he had it *shown* to him:

> The Revelation of Jesus Christ, which God gave Him to show His bond-servants, the things which must soon take place; and He sent and communicated it by His angel to His bond-servant John, who testified to the word of God and to the testimony of Jesus Christ, even to all that he saw.[a]

This verse basically says that God (the Father) gave the Revelation to the Son (Him/Jesus Christ), and that it was communicated by way of a messenger (His angel) to John. Right from the first, the claim is made that John did not create the content of Revelation; it was *given* to him. John wrote down 'all that he saw'.[b] However, before Jesus gave the revelation to John, He *changed* it. The word translated as 'communicated' above, *sémainó*,[1] can be defined as 'I signify, indicate, give a sign, make known'[2] or simply to signify, or render in signs and symbols. What this means is that the book of Revelation has been biblically encoded, and this makes it much harder to understand. Why would Jesus do such a thing? If I were to hazard a guess, perhaps it is so that all things would be understood in their proper time.

Writing is a linear process; once you undertake the task to write things down, the structure of building words into sentences and arranging paragraphs forces your story to be told one subject, one idea, or one item at a time. This creates the basis for a subjective viewpoint with respect to John. This simply means that we see the Revelation of Jesus Christ through the eyes of John. Not that he embellished or added to it, but that he presents it to us in just the same manner as it was presented to him. As such, I would propose that what we read is the order in which John saw what was revealed to him, not necessarily the order in which prophecy will come true. The book of Revelation spans the whole of biblical time, from the fall of the angels from heaven[c] until the end of

---

[a] Revelation 1:1-2

[b] For the most part, John was not composing when he wrote the book of Revelation. Obviously, when he saw things that he did not understand, he had to invent comparisons and descriptions to try to effectively convey what he was witnessing, presumably as directed by the Holy Spirit.

days,[a] and I see it unfolding as a set of twelve independent yet highly correlated prophecies, each with its own storyline. These narratives are generally arranged in chronological order, though many overlap, timewise. As such, the structure of the book of Revelation would be:

Introduction (Chapter 1)
I. The Seven Letters to the Seven Churches[b] (Chapters 2-3)
    II. The Seven-Sealed Book (Chapters 4-11)
    III. The Woman (Chapter 12)
    IV. The Two Beasts (Chapter 13)
        V. The 144,000 (Chapter 14:1-5)
        VI. The Eternal Gospel (Chapter 14: 6-8)
        VII. The Mark of the Beast (Chapter 14: 9-13)
        VIII. The Reapers (Chapter 14:14-20)
    IX. The Seven Bowls of Wrath (Chapters 15-16)
    X. The Judgment of Babylon (Chapters 17-18)
    XI. The Coming of Christ (Chapters 19-20)
XII. New Jerusalem (Chapters 21-22:9)
Conclusion (Chapter 22:10-21)

This reveals a general order to the book that starts to make sense. The letters to the Seven Churches prophesy or foretell church history up until the time of judgment and can be considered as *pre*-judgment prophecy. Then follow six major judgment prophecies (chapters 4-13 and 15-20), with four minor judgment prophecies sandwiched in the middle (chapter 14). Then we wrap up with the prophecy of New Jerusalem, which tells of a time after the judgment of mankind has been completed; that is, we could view it as a *post*-judgment prophecy.

---

[c] Revelation 12:4
[a] Revelation 21:1
[b] I am making the assumption that the Seven Letters to the Seven Churches are prophetic in nature, that is, they foretell church history. The reader should be aware that this is not a universally accepted interpretation. See Appendix F, *The Church Clock*.

Prophecy is multi-dimensional and highly integrated. To try to squash it into a pedantic, linear progression of time is like trying to flatten an orange peel onto a flat surface; the mold does not fit the form. In this work, I will focus on the prophecy of the Seven-Sealed Book in particular and will make the case that the *mystery* of the book can be unraveled partly by referring to the imagery of a first-century book, partly by applying symbolism and patterns from Old Testament prophecy, and partly from the realization that the Seven-Sealed Book is a complete, stand-alone prophecy included in a collection of twelve such works that comprise the book of Revelation. In fact, I would say that with the realization that chapters 4-11 constitute a single, complete narrative or prophecy, comes the understanding of the true structure of the book, as outlined above. This reflects a qualitative view of prophecy as opposed to a strictly chronological interpretation. We could say that I view the Revelation as twelve cycles of events, as opposed to a single, linear story. Again, I will let the reader decide in the end if he agrees.[a] I will not quote extrabiblical sources such as the Apocrypha, Septuagint, the Books of Enoch, etc., in keeping with our thought experiment that if the Bible represents God's complete communication to mankind (that is to say, if we take it as God's Word*)*, then we should expect it to be thoroughly sufficient for the purpose of interpreting the Revelation of the Son, Jesus Christ, to His bondservant, John.[b]

Before we get started, it is important to lay out a few guidelines for interpretation. There are a few assumptions that I make to give us a starting point. Then we need to lay out a general methodology that will help us understand Scripture. First, the assumptions:

1. God does exist.
2. God is the God of the Bible.
3. The Bible represents God's message/communication to mankind.

---

[a] Most scholars try to cram the book of Revelation into a linear, chronological sequence. However, the Hebraic view of time emphasizes the *quality* of events over the chronology of events, which is to say that prophetic happenings are arranged in cycles that portray particular aspects of the future, and are not meant to be a predictive play-by-play. As such, we could think of the book of Revelation as twelve cycles of happenings that have been revealed in a specific order. More exposition on how the Hebrews viewed time is provided in Appendix D, *Qualitative Juxtaposition*.

[b] This is to simply say that the Bible is the only source to be quoted as inspired Scripture. I do use secular sources for explanatory purposes.

4. Jesus Christ is the second Person of the Trinity, and He is the One who showed the revelation to John.
5. Biblical Scripture, as presented in the original languages, has no errors.
6. Biblical Scripture, as presented in the original languages, is consistent.
7. Prophecy in Scripture, as presented in the original languages, perfectly predicts both ancient as well as modern events, many times with a double meaning implied in the same passage.
8. Sometimes Scripture is so precise that this leads to confusion, as it requires our knowledge of culture and history to be up to the same standard.
9. Apparent contradictions in Scripture imply a deeper meaning.
10. The central focal point of all prophecy is Jesus Christ.[a]
11. The rest of the Bible – as well as other parts of Revelation – can be used to interpret all of the signs and symbols that are presented in the book of Revelation.

This last point is perhaps the most important for the book you are about to read. It represents a unique approach, as far as I am aware, that has strengths and weaknesses. On the one hand it tends to be a bit formulaic, and straps our conclusions down to the mundane in many cases. However, if you travel this path for a while, fantastic avenues of understanding start to open up. For the record, I am a Christian, and I do believe in the Bible and Jesus Christ as a matter of faith, something of which the reader should be aware. However, for the atheist or agnostic, I would say that for any ancient document that proposes to be true or foretell the future, the first step for the critic should be to give it its due. That is, the first step in the critical thinking process is to understand that which you are critiquing. In order to do this for the Bible, the first step is to ask yourself the question: If we assume that this book is true, does it have enough internal consistency to be believable? This is, of course, a case that I will try to make as we go along.

In addition to making assumptions, we also need to establish a few guidelines for interpreting Scripture. Some of these are widely accepted, and some of these I have come up with on my own:

---

[a] Revelation 19:10

1. Scripture must first be understood in its original context before interpretation should be attempted.
2. We use Scripture that is clear and understandable to clarify Scripture that is more difficult to understand. The more scriptural references you can use to make a point, the better your interpretation; at least two references are required to establish sound doctrine.
3. Apocalyptic symbology is consistent, except in cases where the context indicates otherwise. (i.e., sometimes the word 'day' refers to a year of time, sometimes it refers to an age of time, and sometimes it refers to an actual 24-hour day; the context makes the difference.)[a]
4. Typology and the law of 'first use' figure prominently in my methodology. (Typology is simply a 'classification according to type' and the law of first use often informs typology. For instance, the first reference to sin or disobedience in the Bible is in the third chapter of Genesis, and it is immediately associated with nakedness. Therefore, everywhere you see the word 'naked' in the Bible, there is also a possible association with sin, according to type.[b])
5. The basic format of my approach is to first dig into a passage, examine the Greek or Hebrew, and formulate a possible interpretation based on the nuances of the passage. Then an attempt is made to apply that interpretation to the future.[c]
6. A distinction should be made between interpretation and application. As regards prophecy, interpretation is what the passage means, while the application is how that meaning applies to the future.
7. Context and type of literature matter. The Bible contains different types of literature: law, narrative, wisdom, poetry, gospel, parable, epistle, and apocalyptic. The biblical narrative contains figures of speech: metaphors, similes, hyperbole, idioms, proverbs, etc.

---

[a] A notable exception would be how many different symbols are used to designate judgment (such as brass, bronze, fire, brimstone, thunder, and the altar of God) which is a major *theme* in both the Old and New Testaments.

[b] This may not hold true in every case, as it depends on the nature of the text; however, I have found it to be very applicable to prophecy.

[c] In some instances, it applies to the past!

8. Biblical interpretation should be logical. The message the Bible represents is in the form of language, and therefore should appeal to human reason. (Don't confuse reason with unbelief!)

I would like to underscore the difference between interpretation and application with regard to prophecy, and how it is a two-part process. An interpretation is simply an unpacking of the meaning of a passage in its original context. In prophecy, the application is how we apply the meaning of that passage to future events. Many times the interpretation of a passage is fairly straightforward, such as the meaning of the star 'Wormwood' in Revelation chapter 8[a]; however, the application, that is, how this interpretation pertains to the future, is often much harder to figure out. The reader should be aware that the interpretation of Scripture in this book could be 100% correct, yet the proposed application could be 100% wrong. In reality, what you are about to read is likely not all correct (though not for lack of trying!) or all incorrect, but somewhere in between. I certainly am striving for 100% accuracy, but in the end Bible prophecy is very hard, and so inevitably any interpretation or application attempted by man is destined to fall short of predicting exactly what will eventually come true. At the end of the day, if we are able to achieve a greater understanding of the book of Revelation, this will prove invaluable for facing the troubling uncertainties of the future.

---

[a] According to Old Testament references, wormwood is symbolic of God's chastisement: See the 'First Four Trumpets' section.

The 70 Weeks of Daniel
&
The Church

Before diving into the mystery of the Seven-Sealed Book, we should first acquaint ourselves with some of the truly enlightening eschatological (end-times) work that already exists. I'm just going to summarize these several topics, noting that the scholarship is not my own; rather, we are standing on the shoulders of giants who came before us. There is certainly a lot more to be said concerning the 70 Weeks of Daniel and the church than what is presented here, so you should consider this as a primer for further study. I would like to ask the reader to bear with me for the moment; what may appear tangential at first will eventually prove to be a master outline which we can then use to inform our interpretation of the events of the Seven-Sealed Book.

Daniel was a prophet of the Old Testament who was taken captive by the Babylonians under Nebuchadnezzar. His prophecies stand today as some of the most accurate and detailed of all antiquity. In fact, his predictions have been proven to be so specific and so reliable that many critics argue by this very fact that the book must have been written centuries later than what is claimed. In addition to this, in my opinion, the book of Daniel represents the most comprehensive unveiling of end-times events outside of the book of Revelation. With this in mind, we pick up the story with Gabriel appearing to Daniel in Babylon and saying:

> "Seventy weeks have been decreed for your people and your holy city, to finish the transgression, to make an end of sin, to make atonement for iniquity, to bring in everlasting righteousness, to seal up vision and prophecy and to anoint the most holy place."[a]

Right off the bat, we observe that this prophecy is for Daniel's people (that is, Israel) and the holy city, Jerusalem. Christians are told in New Testament Scripture that we are grafted into the body of Jesus Christ,[b] or

---

[a] Daniel 9: 24

elsewhere, adopted into Christ's family[a] when we accept Him as our Savior. However, we cannot say that we are Daniel's people or that Jerusalem is our city. In my humble opinion, this excludes the church from the 70th week, which, as we will see, means that the rapture *must* occur before the coming seven years of judgment. As we move along, this point will become more clear, as the argument for a pre-judgment rapture event can be made from various angles.[b]

The 'sevens' to which Gabriel refers are generally regarded as weeks of years, or seven years for each week, totaling 70 'sevens' (70 X 7), or 490 years. This is the time required to put an end to sin, to atone for wickedness, to bring in everlasting righteousness, to seal up vision and prophecy, and to anoint the most holy place. To the casual reader, it seems as if this prophecy has already failed to come true; more than 490 years have passed since Israel was captive in Babylon, Jesus came and went, an end has not been put to sin, wickedness abounds, and everlasting righteousness has not materialized. The trick to understanding this passage is to realize that the 70 weeks represent a unique cycle of events that apply specifically to God's people, not all the peoples of the earth. As such, they are not contiguous; there is a gap. Gabriel continues:

> "So you are to know and discern that from the issuing of a decree to restore and rebuild Jerusalem until Messiah the Prince there will be seven weeks and sixty-two weeks; it will be built again, with plaza and moat, even in times of distress. Then after the sixty-two weeks the Messiah will be cut off and have nothing, and the people of the prince who is to come will destroy the city and the sanctuary. And its end will come with a flood; even to the end there will be war; desolations are determined."[c]

First there are seven 'sevens,' or 49 years, that many scholars believe designate the closing up of Old Testament prophecy, which in the Bible takes us through the book of Malachi. The next 62 'sevens' are 434 years until the coming of the Messiah, or some translations say 'Anointed One,' for a total of 7 + 62 = 69 weeks of seven years, or 69 x 7 = 483 years. Sir Robert Anderson, in his book *The Coming Prince*, did an exhaustive study of this timing way back

---

[b] Romans 11:11-31
[a] Ephesians 1:5; Galatians 4:4-5
[b] The timing of the rapture is a hotly debated topic in Christian circles.
[c] Daniel 9:25-26 (Unless otherwise stated, all Scripture quotes are from the New American Standard Bible, NASB)

in 1881.[a] Anderson converts years to days on the Hebrew Calendar (a 360-day year) to come up with 173,880 days and then figures forward to find which date in history that the prophecy was slated to come true. The interesting thing is that if you use the edict of Artaxerxes Longimanus on March 14th, 445 BC, to rebuild the city of Jerusalem, and figure forward by the same 173,880 days, it comes right up to 32 AD[b], the year Christ was crucified.[c] Anderson makes his case that the prophecy predicts the entrance of Christ into Jerusalem at the beginning of what we now know as Passion Week *to the very day*. The stunning accuracy of this prediction (even if it were only to the year) should wake up our minds as we consider the greater body of work that is biblical prophecy, especially when it is widely acknowledged that the entire Old Testament, including the book of Daniel, was translated into Greek for the Septuagint well over 150 years before the birth of Christ.[3]

Finishing verse 26, we've already stated that the Anointed One is Jesus Christ, and the imagery of His being cut off foretells His sacrifice on the cross. Finally:

> "And he will make a firm covenant with the many for one week, but in the middle of the week he will put a stop to sacrifice and grain offering; and on the wing of abominations will come one who makes desolate, even until a complete destruction, one that is decreed, is poured out on the one who makes desolate."[d]

In this single verse, a lot has changed. The 'Anointed One' mentioned in verse 26 is a prophecy about Jesus Christ. The 'he' mentioned in verse 27 refers to the 'ruler who will come' or the AntiChrist who, sometime in the future, during the 70th 'seven,' will set up a covenant with Israel for seven years. After three and a half years, he will commit the Abomination of Desolation in the temple, which is yet to be built. The 'he' in verse 27 refers back, contextually, to the 'ruler' mentioned in verse 26. 'The people of the

---

[a] I've included a summary of his derivation in Appendix A
[b] Anderson figures from the fifteenth year of Tiberius Caesar, the beginning of Jesus' ministry, as stated in Luke 3:1.
[c] This is figuring forward in the old BC method of reckoning from the reign of kings, etc. There is a fudge factor of 2-6 years or so when we convert to the AD method of reckoning from the birth of Christ, as at the time of the changeover, the exact birth date of Christ was misunderstood.
[d] Daniel 9:27

ruler,' sometimes translated 'the people of the coming prince', is widely accepted as signifying the Romans under Titus when they destroyed Jerusalem in 70 AD. However, as we can see, continuity in the verses above requires that the one who will commit the 'Abomination of Desolation' also be 'the ruler.' Many modern scholars interpret this passage as referring to a latter-days empire that is closely linked to the ancient Roman Empire. I personally think there is enough ambiguity here to also consider an interpretation that identifies the 'people of the coming prince' simply as 'earth dwellers,' or people of the world, or perhaps Babylon.[a]

In any event, we should note the significant amount of time that passes between verses 25 and 27: Enter the mystery of the church. The idea that the church is hidden in the Old Testament is key to understanding the prophecy in Daniel 9. The text skips over the epoch of the church almost entirely, with only a slight interruption between the 69th week and the 70th week, despite the fact that over two thousand years have elapsed.

There are other prophecies in Daniel where we find the church conspicuously absent. In the dream that Nebuchadnezzar has about the statue made of different metals, the image of the iron legs (Roman Empire) transitions directly into the feet of clay and the ten toes (Empire of the last days);[b] and again in Daniel's dream of four beasts, the fourth beast with teeth of iron (Rome) has ten horns (Empire of the last days).[c]

This gap in history is alluded to by Jesus Christ in Luke 4:18-19:

> "The Spirit of the Lord is upon Me, because He anointed Me to preach the good news to the poor. He has sent Me to proclaim release to the captives and recovery of sight to the blind, to set free those who are oppressed, to proclaim the favorable year of the Lord."

Jesus then rolls up the scroll and says: "Today this Scripture is fulfilled in your hearing." What is obvious to us today is that He is referring directly to Himself and His ministry on earth. What is not obvious from this passage is that Jesus is quoting from Isaiah, and He did not quote the entire passage:

---

[a] A study of Babylon in the Old Testament will reveal that it is more about a system of ritualized idol worship than it is about a specific city.

[b] Daniel chapter 2

[c] Daniel chapter 7. (Empire of the last days is how many scholars see these prophecies playing out in the future.)

> The Spirit of the Lord God is upon Me, because the Lord has anointed Me to bring good news to the afflicted; He has sent Me to bind up the brokenhearted, to proclaim liberty to captives and freedom to prisoners; to proclaim the favorable year of the Lord and the day of vengeance of our God; to comfort all who mourn, to grant those who mourn in Zion, giving them a garland instead of ashes, the oil of gladness instead of mourning, the mantle of praise instead of a spirit of fainting. So they will be called oaks of righteousness, the planting of the Lord, that He may be glorified. [a]

Jesus stops halfway through, between 'to proclaim the year of the Lord's favor' and 'the day of vengeance of our God.' What He is saying is that everything up until the point where He rolls up the scroll pertains to His first coming: His ministry on earth and death on the cross. What follows in Isaiah from 'the day of vengeance' onward was yet to come.

The conjunction 'and' that connects the first coming of Christ to the second in Isaiah 61 is that which was hidden in the Old Testament, which is the church. The Apostle Paul refers to the hidden church in Romans concerning the fullness of the Gentiles:

> I do not want you, brethren, to be uninformed of this mystery – so that you will not be wise in your own estimation – that a partial hardening has happened to Israel until the fullness of the Gentiles has come in;[b]

Paul speaks of the hardening (some translations use 'blindness') of Israel as a 'mystery;' God has put His plan for Israel on hold until the 'fullness of the Gentiles' is complete, that is, until a specific number of the elect who will be chosen to be part of the church are brought into the fold. Paul goes on to explain that after this comes to pass (that is, once the church is complete), 'all Israel will be saved.' This would indicate that, in time, God will fulfill every promise that He ever made in the Scriptures to the nation of Israel.

Paul specifically mentions the mystery of the hidden church in Ephesians:

> To me, the very least of all saints, this grace was given, to preach to the Gentiles the unfathomable riches of Christ, and to bring to light what is the

---

[a] Isaiah 61:1-3
[b] Romans 11:25

administration of the mystery which for ages has been hidden in God, who created all things; so that the manifold wisdom of God might now be known through the church to the rulers and the authorities in the heavenly places.[a]

It is very interesting here how Paul speaks of the 'manifold wisdom of God' being *now* known 'in the heavenly places;' that is, the church was a mystery not only to those on earth, but to the entities that inhabit the spiritual realm as well! One last interesting note concerning the church involves a unique promise:

> Simon Peter answered, "You are the Christ, the Son of the living God." And Jesus said to him, "Blessed are you, Simon Barjona, because flesh and blood did not reveal this to you, but My Father who is in heaven. I also say to you that you are Peter, and upon this rock I will build My church; and the gates of Hades will not overpower it."[b]

The Father, through the Holy Spirit, revealed to Simon Peter that Jesus was 'the Christ, the Son of the living God.' I take this to mean that Peter's confession of this truth represents the foundation upon which Christ would build His church. If you consider for a moment that this very same confession was also the confession of the martyrs of the 2nd and 3rd centuries, and that it was their testimony which toppled the Roman Empire, this interpretation makes sense. This was how Christ said He would build His church, and the promise that the gates of hell – or Rome, for that matter – would not be able to stand against it has been proven trustworthy. This promise is unique in all of Scripture and affirms the authority of every Christian, everywhere, to preach the gospel. Wherever the church increases, Satan must decrease. We've seen this play out over two millennia as faith in Jesus Christ has spread over the entire globe. This is the blessing of the Church Age; unprecedented power over the principalities of darkness, and the gates of hell will not prevail.

If we were to add in what has been left out of the prophecy of Daniel, we would insert parentheses between the 69th and 70th week and write the word 'church' inside. This basic construct forms the master outline which I use to interpret the book of Revelation. The giving of the Holy Spirit at Pentecost would be represented by the opening parenthesis and the fullness of the Gentiles can be interpreted as the ending parenthesis, signifying the end of the Church Age, and the

---

[a] Ephesians 3:8-10
[b] Matthew 16:16-18

resumption of the 70th week of Daniel – which, remember, is for the people of Israel and the holy city, Jerusalem.

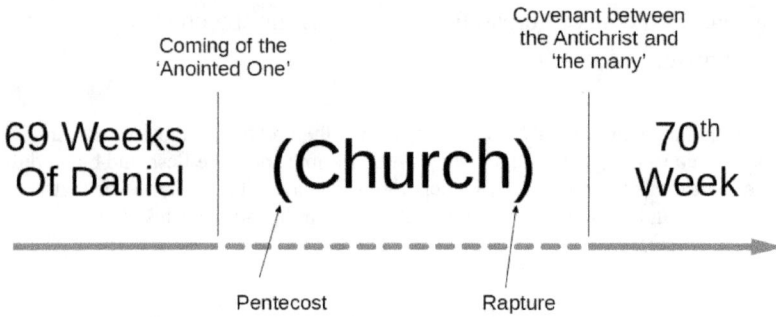

The Church Age constitutes, in my estimation, a separate prophetic cycle, with its own unique timing, and from its positioning as such, should not be expected to participate in the judgment that awaits the children of Jacob. Once that last member of the church is gathered in, the Holy Spirit will seal the 144,000 out of the 12 houses of Israel, preparing them for a worldwide, church-like ministry. Israel will rebuild the temple and reinstate the sacrifice (although the sacrifice in the temple has been replaced by the new covenant of Jesus Christ, the Jews will seek to revive Old Testament regulations for worship). I personally don't think the Holy Spirit will inhabit the next temple that will be built in Jerusalem – more on that later. The Church Age, which began with the gift of the Holy Ghost on the day of Pentecost, will end in rapture, when Christ will suddenly appear before His betrothed amidst the sounding of angelic trumpets and whisk her away to the wedding feast that He has prepared.

> The New Testament is *contained* in the Old Testament.
> The Old Testament is *explained* in the New Testament.
> The New Testament is *concealed* in the Old Testament.
> The Old Testament is *revealed* in the New Testament.
> The New Testament *authenticates* the Old Testament.

The Old Testament *anticipates* the New Testament.
The New Testament *lies hidden* in the Old Testament.
The Old Testament *lies open* in the New Testament.
The Old Testament *predicts* a Person.
The New Testament *presents* that Person.[4]

Prophecy of the
Seven-Sealed Book

As stated above, I view the book of Revelation as twelve stand-alone, independent, yet highly correlated prophecies. Each prophecy has a beginning, a middle, and an end. The prophecy of the Seven-Sealed Book or scroll, which is the subject of this book, is the second of the twelve, and is bracketed by two throne room scenes; one in chapters 4 & 5, and the other in chapter 11. In the following pages I will make the case that the breaking of the first six seals represents what Christ referred to in the Gospels as 'the birth pangs' of tribulation (that is, they occur during the process of opening the book), the breaking of the seventh seal represents that the book has finally been opened, and the seven trumpets constitute the book itself. Further, if we consider that once the seventh seal is broken, and the contents of the book are finally revealed, this means that God's judgment is about to be set in motion, which might well explain the thirty minutes of silence at the beginning of chapter 8 as the pause before the storm. The imagery of a sealed scroll supports this interpretation, as 'the scroll could not be opened until all the seals are broken.'[5] This view of the seals will make more sense once we take a step back and evaluate it from an Old Testament perspective, with respect to two of the night visions of Zechariah.

What is particularly compelling about this notion is that it puts the events of the seals in our time, and perhaps a bit surprisingly, we can already see them playing out in history over the past five hundred years! We'll find a wrinkle or two along the way, as I think I can provide biblical precedent that the fabled Four Horsemen of the Apocalypse embark on *two* patrols: the first prior to the 70th week of Daniel, and a second patrol later, in the midst of God's judgment. But I am getting a little ahead of myself; before we get into all of this, we must first visit the throne room of heaven.

The Throne Room of Heaven

> After these things I looked, and behold, a door standing open in heaven, and the first voice which I had heard, like the sound of a trumpet speaking with me, said, "Come up here, and I will show you what must take place after these things." Immediately I was in the spirit; and behold, a throne was standing in heaven, and One was sitting on the throne. And He who was sitting was like a jasper stone and a sardius in appearance; and there was a rainbow around the throne, like an emerald in appearance. Around the throne were twenty-four thrones; and upon the thrones I saw twenty-four elders sitting, clothed in white garments, and golden crowns on their heads.[a]

Here we find the phrase: 'behold, a door standing open in heaven.' I do not think this detail to be superfluous, as many believe that heaven exists on a higher plane of existence than the three-plus-one dimensions with which we are so familiar.[b] This door, then, would represent a passageway into those higher states of existence in which heaven resides, and what better place for John to witness the vast panorama of future history – well over three thousand years' worth – in its fullness?

John is told to 'come up here, and I will show you what must take place after these things.' This is the introduction to the whole rest of the Revelation, which deals mostly with the future. This leads many scholars to believe that the throne room scene that follows in chapters 4 & 5 is yet to happen from John's perspective. However, I would make the case that what is to follow here are eleven prophecies of the future.[c] Again, if you view the entire book as a collection of prophecies – 12 in total[d] – then it makes sense that we have 12 beginnings and 12 endings, one of each per prophecy. If we inspect the very next prophecy, which I maintain is chapter 12 in our modern Bibles, we have what I call the Prophecy of the Woman (which is Israel) as a stand-alone, yet related account of the future. In this subsequent prophecy, we have references to the formation of Israel,[e] the appearance of the dragon,[f] Satan's rebellion in

---

[a] Revelation 4:1-4
[b] Height, length, and width plus time.
[c] I count the Seven Letters to the Seven Churches as the first prophecy.
[d] See Introduction
[e] Revelation 12:1
[f] Revelation 12:3, cross reference 12:9

heaven,[a] and the birth of Christ.[b] All of these things occur *before* the revelation was given to John, and I think they represent the backstory that helps set up the Prophecy of the Woman. In much the same way, I consider chapters 4 & 5 to be the backstory for the Prophecy of the Seven-Sealed Book.

As part of the description of the throne room of heaven, which is full of sound and light, is a passage that mentions the seven lamps:

> Out from the throne come flashes of lightning and sounds and peals of thunder. And there were seven lamps of fire burning before the throne, which are the seven spirits of God;[c]

Many theologians position themselves with Clarence Larkin, a mechanical engineer turned Baptist minister whose seminal work in eschatology has stood for the better part of a century,[6] in proposing that the seven lamps of fire mentioned here represent the Holy Spirit, and by extension they assume that the church is present in heaven at this time as well. Larkin eloquently states:

> As confirmatory proof that the church is "caught out" at this time and place, we have in the description of the Throne, the statement that the Holy Spirit in the seven-fold plenitude of His power, is BACK IN HEAVEN. In none of the epistles is the Holy Spirit invoked along with the Father and the Son, except in II Corinthians 13:14, because He is viewed as abiding on the earth with the church, convicting of sin, comforting believers, and gathering out of the elect, but here He is no longer on the earth but back in Heaven, and before the Throne. This is the strongest kind of evidence that the church at this time has been "caught out" and is no longer on the earth, for when the Holy Spirit goes back to Heaven He will take the church WITH HIM. And the presence of the Holy Spirit in Heaven is conclusive evidence that the events which follow are to take place after the church has been caught out, and therefore the church is not to pass through the Tribulation.[7]

I agree that the seven lamps of fire indicate the Holy Spirit, as there is biblical precedent for this viewpoint – see Zechariah chapter 4. I also agree with Larkin's implied interpretation of II Thessalonians above that, where it is written: '...he who now restrains will do so until he is taken out of the way'[d],

---

[a] Revelation 12:4
[b] Revelation 12:5
[c] Revelation 4:5
[d] II Thessalonians 2:7

Paul is referring to the Holy Spirit. Larkin draws a key connection that the rapture will coincide with the time when the Restrainer is taken out of the way, or as he says, 'the Holy Spirit goes back to heaven.'[a] I disagree, however, with the notion that the presence of the Holy Spirit in heaven at this time confirms that the rapture has already taken place. If so large a crowd as millions of church saints were present at the presentation of the Seven-Sealed Book, I think John would have made mention of them as he certainly does in other places. I would suggest instead that the manifest presence of the Trinity at this event – the One sitting on the Throne (Father), the seven lamps of fire (Holy Spirit) and lastly the Lamb (the Son) – is significant in that it celebrates the moment when the Son begins the process of assuming kingship of the earth.

This perspective frees us up to place the throne room scene in its proper time. The Lamb is described as 'standing, as if slain.'[b] This phrase combines elements that would suggest both the resurrection and the crucifixion, respectively. The Lamb in the divine throne room sometime after the resurrection but before His final ascension might be an alternate assumption. The Holy Spirit is also present, as discussed earlier, so that potentially might place this event before Pentecost, when the Holy Spirit was sent to indwell, or come to live in, Christian believers. To recap: I think this scene in heaven occurs *before* the Holy Spirit is indwelt in Christian believers, not after those believers are raptured to heaven. Larkin places the throne room scene sometime in the future, earth-time, and I place this event in the distant past.[c]

The mention of the twenty-four elders provides further context:

> Around the throne were twenty-four thrones; and upon the thrones I saw twenty-four elders sitting, clothed in white garments, and golden crowns on their heads.[d]

Some scholars reason that the presence of the elders in heaven is further proof that the rapture has already happened at this point. That is, if the elders are men, and a good argument can be made that they are, then this could

---

[a] This deduction makes logical sense, but the timing of these events may not be exactly the same, see the discussion on the 5th seal, forthcoming.
[b] Revelation 5:6
[c] Most scholars would agree with Larkin, and place the throne room scene in the future.
[d] Revelation 4:4

possibly imply the participation of the church on the whole. However, there is another reason for the 24 elders to be present at this time:

> And they sang a new song, saying, "Worthy are You to take the book and to break its seals; for You were slain, and purchased for God with Your blood men from every tribe and tongue and people and nation. You have made them to be a kingdom and priests to our God; and they will reign upon the earth."[a]

The song the elders sing is one of praise and worship, but it also serves a function: they are *witnesses*,[b] and the song is their testimony. Central to the throne room scene of chapters 4 & 5 is the mystery of the Seven-Sealed Book, and I think the nature of this book gives us insight as to the witness of the 24 elders. There is writing on the outside of the scroll that represents the 'book,' and in ancient times this typically was done on land deeds, to designate the requirements for breaking the seal.[8] Reverend Larkin provides excellent commentary:

> ... something that was lost to mankind and the earth... is to be redeemed, and we do not have to go far to find out what it is. It is the inheritance of the earth and of immortal life given to Adam and Eve, and that was lost in the fall of Eden. When Adam sinned he lost his inheritance of the earth, and it passed out of his hands into the possession of Satan, to the disinheritance of all of Adam's seed. The forfeited title deed is now in God's hands and is awaiting redemption. Its redemption means the legal repossession of all that Adam lost by the Fall. Adam was impotent to redeem the lost possession, but the law provides (Leviticus 25:23-24) that a kinsman may redeem a lost possession. That KINSMAN has been provided in the person of JESUS CHRIST.[9]

John wept when no one was found worthy to open the book:

> And no one in heaven or on the earth or under the earth was able to open the book or to look upon it. Then I began to weep greatly because no one was found worthy to open the book or to look into it; and one of the elders said to me, "Stop weeping: behold the Lion that is from the tribe of Judah, the Root of David, has overcome so as to open the book and its seven seals."[c]

John weeps because it is the fate of the earth that is at stake. But not only this, the situation strikes home with him, because as a Jew, it is the *eternal*

---

[a] Revelation 5:9-10
[b] According to Old Testament Jewish Law.
[c] Revelation 5:3-5

disinheritance of his people that also hangs in the balance. Christians believe that Jesus is God and was able to live a perfect life, free of sin, and so meet the requirement of the Law. Christians also believe that Jesus was a man, and so qualifies as a kinsman to Adam and his seed. When the Lamb (Jesus Christ) took the book from the right hand (indicating power and authority) of the One who sits on the throne[a] he fulfilled the role of a Kinsman Redeemer,[b] and in that moment, reclaimed the earth from all illegal squatters, namely Satan and his servants.

The marriage of Ruth to Boaz in the Old Testament provides an illustration of the role of a kinsman redeemer.[c] Both Ruth and her mother-in-law, Naomi, were widowed while Naomi sojourned in Moab, and had returned to Judah, where Naomi's late husband, Elimelech, had once owned a field. The story does not go into the details, but it is likely the field had been sold years before. Naomi retains the right by law to buy it back into the family, but she does not have the money. Boaz was a kinsman of Naomi, so by law, he had the right, upon his discretion, to buy the land and redeem it for the family. This is in fact what he decides to do, with the addition of Ruth[d] as a part of the agreement. In order to make the purchase legitimate, Boaz 'took ten men of the *elders* of the city'[e] to bear witness to the transaction. The witnesses were a key part of the redeeming process for Boaz, and likewise, in the throne room of God Almighty, the 24 elders testify/sing to the fact that the Lamb is worthy to take the title deed for the earth from the One who sits on the throne, and that the price has been paid in full with His blood.

Ephesians provides further context:

> I pray that the eyes of your heart might be enlightened, so that you will know what is the hope of His calling, what are the riches of the glory of His inheritance in the saints, and what is the surpassing greatness of His power toward us who believe. These are in accordance with the working of the strength of His might

---

[a] Revelation 5:7

[b] The 'closest relative', also known as a kinsman-redeemer, was responsible for protecting the interests of needy members of the extended family – e.g., to provide an heir for a brother who had died (Deut 25:5-10), to redeem land that a poor relative had sold outside the family (Lev 25:25-28), to redeem a relative who had been sold into slavery (Lev 25:47-49) and to avenge the killing of a relative (Num 35:19-21)…' – NASB Study Bible note on Ruth 2:20

[c] Ruth 4:1-12

[d] As a Moabite (Gentile), Ruth was not technically a part of the family.

[e] Ruth 4:2 (Italics mine)

which He brought about in Christ, when He raised Him from the dead and seated Him at His right hand in the heavenly places, far above all rule and authority and power and dominion, and every name that is named, not only in this age but also in the one to come. And He put all things in subjection under His feet and gave Him as head over all things to the church, which is His body, the fullness of Him who fills all in all.[a]

When Christ assumed ownership of the earth, He also assumed the position 'far above all rule and authority and power and dominion,' and He also took as part of His inheritance *the saints*. This is something that, even at the time of writing of the book of Ephesians, had already taken place. It is Christ's role as a Kinsman-Redeemer that explains the presence of the 24 elders in heaven. Just as in the case with Boaz, the elders are unnamed. Their identity is not important; if it were, we would have been told who they are. All that matters for us in the present age is that Christ has redeemed or repossessed the earth, and mankind with it. Thus, Jesus reserves the right to commission His church:

> And Jesus came up and spoke to them, saying, "All authority has been given to me in heaven and on earth. Go therefore and make disciples of all nations, baptizing them in the name of the Father and the Son and the Holy Spirit, teaching them to observe all that I commanded you; and lo, I am with you always, even to the end of the age."[b]

Here we see Jesus telling His disciples that He has been given 'all authority… in heaven and on earth.' This could not be true unless He had *already* taken the Seven-Sealed Book – the title deed to the earth – from the right hand of the Almighty. In other words, I am saying that in a heavenly, legal sense, the throne room proceedings of chapters 4 & 5 would have to be completed before Christ could legitimately claim He had 'all authority' over the earth. As a result, the church has the unique right to 'make disciples of all nations;' Holy Spirit power that flows from Christ, the rightful owner of the earth, who now has the responsibility of harvesting the fruit of it. It is the assumption of Christ's ownership that has made possible the Church Age: a unique time in history where God's message has been preached to mankind so powerfully that some Christians literally mistake this epoch for the Millennium, when the Jewish Messiah will return to reign supreme over the earth. In short,

---

[a] Ephesians 1:18-23
[b] Matthew 28:18-20

Christ has all authority to redeem the inhabitants of the earth because He holds the Seven-Sealed book in His hand!

The Seals

And now we come to the seals. To properly understand the nature of the Seven-Sealed book, we must draw from the imagery of what constituted a book in the first century. They did not have spine-bound books as we know them today; they used scrolls made of papyrus or leather. An edict or bulletin or book would consist of multiple 'pages' that were stitched together, end to end, and rolled up in one long scroll that could reach a length of many tens of feet if unrolled upon the floor. The 'book' would then be sealed with a wax seal along the outside seam. In this way, information could be revealed only after the seal was broken.[10] As this relates to the construction of the Seven-Sealed book, we can view it as seven seals placed on seven different scrolls, all rolled up inside of each other. That is, after you break the first seal, this opens a scroll upon which is written the information we have about the riding of the white horse. Inside of this scroll we find another sealed document, upon which the second seal has been placed. The breaking of the second seal opens a second scroll which informs us of the red horse, and reveals yet a third scroll, and so on. As each successive seal is broken, it opens the next scroll only to reveal yet another inside of that one, until you reach the seventh and final seal. The opening of the seventh seal is the climax, which finally discloses the contents of the Seven-Sealed book.[a] The first six scrolls are short and have but a single point of focus, and as such, they function as a sort of preamble, and, I would argue, represent what Jesus referred to as 'birth pangs.'[b] The breaking of the seventh seal opens the seventh and innermost scroll, which is by far the longest of the set and

---

[a] An alternate construction of the Seven-Sealed Book would have all of the seven seals visible on the outside, as opposed to being rolled up inside of each other. Six seals on six outer scrolls (like sleeves), each 1/7th the width of a larger, inner scroll. The six outer scrolls would be wrapped around the seventh inner scroll so that the seals form a line along the crease, upon which the seventh seal is placed, with three outer scroll seals to one side and three to the other. The basic idea is the same: before the book of judgment can be opened, all seven seals have to be broken.

[b] Matthew 24:8

contains a complex progression of events, that on the whole can be summed up as the Seven Trumpet Judgments.

Birth Pangs

> And Jesus began to say to them, "See to it that no one misleads you. Many will come in My name, saying, 'I am He!' and will mislead many. When you hear of wars and rumors of wars, do not be frightened; these things must take place; but *that* is not yet the end. For nation will rise up against nation, and kingdom against kingdom; there will be earthquakes in various places; there will also be famines. These things are merely the beginning of birth pangs."[a]

This is an excerpt from the famous 'Olivet Discourse,' where Jesus describes the end of times to His disciples. As we get into the central message of the seven seals, we should reflect upon the fact that many scholars note the connection between the events of the first six seals and what Christ refers to as the 'birth pangs' in the passage above. The parallel passage in Luke adds 'plagues,' 'terrors,' and 'great signs from heaven' to the list.[b] This view fits into my general thesis, that is, the first six seals represent the preparation for the 70th week of Daniel, the birth pangs that lead up to the final seven years of judgment.

---

[a] Mark 13:5-8
[b] Luke 21:11

The Four Horsemen

Perhaps the most iconic figures in all of eschatology are the Four Horsemen of the Apocalypse. They have been portrayed as harbingers of evil, the purveyors of perdition, and a sure sign that the time of the tribulation is upon us. Following the general rule of using the greater work of Scripture for interpreting the signs of Revelation, I have stumbled upon a different approach to unraveling the mystery of the four horsemen; a notion that I have not encountered in any of my readings of some of the more popular sources on eschatology. The section that you are about to read should be considered in the category of 'not generally accepted' because of its novelty, the point being not to be new or different, but to try to follow the clues wherever they may lead.

The basic approach here is to correlate repeating patterns; specifically, references to groups of four that proceed to have worldwide effect, and that do so twice. Along the way, we'll also find that worldwide conditions during the running/reaping of these groups of four also correlate. The first instance is in the book of Zechariah.

> I saw at night, and behold, a man was riding on a red horse, and he was standing among the myrtle trees which were in the ravine, with red, sorrel and white horses behind him. Then I said, "My lord, what are these?" and the angel who was speaking with me said to me, "I will show you what these are." And the man who was standing among the myrtle trees answered and said, "These are those whom the Lord has sent to patrol the earth." So they answered the angel of the Lord who was standing among the myrtle trees and said, "We have patrolled the earth, and behold, all the earth is peaceful and quiet."[a]

Zechariah's visions pertain directly to the people of Israel as they are returning to Jerusalem after the Babylonian captivity, but I think there is a dual reference here that applies to end times as well, as that is a major theme of the book.[b] Four horses – two red, one sorrel and one white – are described as

---

[a] Zechariah 1:8-11

[b] The more I study the night visions of Zechariah, the more I am convinced that they all relate directly to the 70th week. Many passages of Scripture not only refer to events which might be considered as contemporaneous to the writer, but they also foretell the distant future. This has been labeled by some as the Law of Double, as there are two legitimate ways to interpret the passage.

patrolling the earth in the company of an angel of the Lord. (You could make the case that more than four total horses could be present, depending on grammar, but there are four 'mentions,' the horse being ridden and the other three.) The earth is found to be 'peaceful and quiet,' or literally translated, *sitting*. Myrtle trees, a symbol of tranquility, are mentioned three times.

There is a second patrol of horses in Zechariah that, it could be surmised, takes place under much different conditions. This second patrol also encompasses the whole earth and involves four chariots pulled by horses:

> Now I lifted up my eyes again and looked and behold, four chariots were coming forth from between two mountains; and the mountains were bronze mountains. With the first chariot were red horses, with the second chariot black horses, with the third chariot white horses, and with the fourth chariot strong dappled horses. Then I spoke and said to the angel who was speaking with me, "What are these, my lord?" The angel replied to me, "These are four spirits of heaven, going forth after standing before the Lord of all the earth, with one of which the black horses are going forth to the north country; and the white ones go forth after them, while the dappled ones go forth to the south country. When the strong ones went out, they were eager to go to patrol the earth." And he said, "Go, patrol the earth." So they patrolled the earth.[a]

This is the last in a total of eight visions that Zechariah has all in one night. As the images of horses patrolling the earth bracket the octet, many scholars recognize a connection between the first vision and the last vision. The first patrol of horses occurs while the earth is at rest, or sitting, but the second patrol emerges from between two mountains of bronze. Bronze and brass, both copper alloys, are associated with fire and judgment in Old Testament typology.[b] For instance, the altar in which the temple sacrifice was burned was made of brass. With the imagery of the chariots coming forth from between mountains of bronze, we can interpret this second patrol as occurring during a time of great judgment.

In my opinion, a portion of Revelation 14 parallels these two patrols of horses. There are seven angels mentioned in this chapter, and so the seven, taken as a whole, probably symbolize God's completed judgment of man, or the seven years of the tribulation, or something to that effect. The first angel is flying in midair and proclaiming the gospel, the second angel declares the fall

---

[a] Zechariah 6:1-7
[b] Both bronze and brass are formed though fire, so these might typify certain transforming or purifying aspects of judgment.

of Babylon, and the third angel warns against worshiping the mark of the beast. The last four angels, however, are acting in concert; they are tasked with the responsibility of harvesting the earth:

> Then I looked, and behold, a white cloud, and sitting on the cloud was one like a son of man, having a golden crown on His head and a sharp sickle in His hand. And another angel came out of the temple, crying out with a loud voice to Him who sat on the cloud, "Put in your sickle and reap, for the hour to reap has come, because the harvest of the earth is ripe." Then He who sat on the cloud swung His sickle over the earth, and the earth was reaped. And another angel came out of the temple which is in heaven, and he also had a sharp sickle. Then another angel, the one who has power over fire, came out from the altar; and he called out with a loud voice to him who had the sharp sickle, saying, "Put in your sharp sickle and gather the clusters from the vine of the earth, because her grapes are ripe." So the angel swung his sickle to the earth and gathered the clusters from the vine of the earth, and threw them into the great wine press of the wrath of God. And the wine press was trodden outside the city, and blood came out from the wine press, up to the horses' bridles, for a distance of two hundred miles.[a]

As you can see from the NASB excerpt above, the use of capitalized personal pronouns such as 'He' indicates that the translators have come to the conclusion that the first angel of the four, seated upon the cloud, is Jesus Christ, which represents a popular view among Bible scholars. I think the reason for this is the reference to 'one like a son of man' concerning the first angel. 'Son of Man' is a title Jesus gives to Himself in the Gospels. However, you could interpret this reference as a simile, and there are some clues here that give us reason to do so. First, the crown, mentioned in verse 14 is rendered in the Greek as *stephanos*,[11] which refers to a wreath given at an athletic competition.[12] If the individual seated on the cloud were the King of kings and Lord of lords, I would expect the Greek word *diadem*[13] to appear, which would refer to a royal, kingly crown.[14] Second, the next angel orders the 'one like a son of man' to get to work, swinging his sickle. I don't think there is an angel in heaven above or hell below that would dare give the true 'Son of Man' a direct order. Jesus is not just *like a* son of man, HE *is the* Son of man. I think the reference here indicates on whose behalf the angels are acting. Irrespective of your opinion on

---

[a] Revelation 14:14-20

the matter, we can still draw parallels between the four individuals mentioned here and the horse patrols of Zechariah.[a]

We find the first angel sitting on a cloud; that is, he is at peace, or rest. This mirrors the state of the world during the first patrol of horses in Zechariah, where they find the earth tranquil (literally *sitting*) and at rest. When the last two angels appear, references are made to fire and the altar, which can be taken as symbolizing judgment.[b] Also, the wine press of God's wrath is mentioned to further strengthen this imagery, and the final lines about blood running up to the horses' bridles calls to mind Armageddon. To summarize, we have four angels that are portrayed as reaping the earth. They reap the earth two distinct times; once when the world is at rest, and the second time when the world is being judged. As you may have already surmised, this is setting the stage for the four horsemen of the seals in Revelation 6 to have two patrols; once when the world is at rest, and a second time in the midst of God's judgment.

Before we get into the Horsemen of the Apocalypse, however, we need to take a step back and think about historical perspective. The story of the tower of Babel in the Old Testament is key to understanding the first patrol of the horsemen. Much of the book of Revelation is concerned with Babylon, which has its roots in Babel where mankind, instead of spreading out and populating the earth immediately after Noah's flood, banded together and built a tower or city with which they wanted 'to make (for themselves) a name.'[c]

> The Lord said, "Behold, they are one people, and they all have the same language. And this is what they began to do, and now nothing which they purpose to do will be impossible for them. Come, let Us go down and there confuse their language, so that they will not understand one another's speech." So the Lord scattered them abroad from there over the face of the whole earth; and they

---

[a] If you refer to the general outline of Revelation that was presented in the introduction, the Prophecy of the Reapers occurs as one of the four minor prophecies that are sandwiched in between the 6 prophecies that I categorize as the judgment prophecies. These four minor prophecies all seem to have a critical juncture at the midpoint of the 70th week; that is, when the man of sin commits the abomination of desolation in the temple. As such, the primary interpretation for the Prophecy of the Reapers should be that it predicts two harvests that occur during the 70th week: one harvest of souls for heaven during the first half of the week, and a second harvest for Armageddon at the end of the week. However, it is the mention of the angel as 'sitting' which gives good cause for a parallel interpretation that refers back to the first horse patrol of Zechariah, where the world is found literally 'sitting,' or at rest.

[b] Fire might represent purification and refinement, while the altar is a reference to blood sacrifice, which plays out in the rest of the passage.

[c] Genesis 11:4

> stopped building the city. Therefore its name was called Babel, because there the Lord confused the language of the whole earth; and from there the Lord scattered them abroad over the face of the whole earth.[a]

Essentially, all of mankind were one people, speaking the same language; they were one 'nation.' By the simple act of confusing language, God effectively compelled mankind to spread out and populate the earth. The reason for this dispersion was explicitly to reduce mankind's potential ('nothing they purpose to do will be impossible for them'). On the face of it, this seems like a mean thing for God to do; however, when you realize that man had fallen to a state where he was sinful and separated from God, this dispersion effectively decreased man's capability for evil. Reducing man's potential for/knowledge of evil allowed history to progress according to God's timetable; otherwise He may have had to bring judgment down upon humanity all over again not long after the flood.

Four millennia or so later, by the time we get to the first patrol of the four horsemen, I see things happening in reverse: instead of dispersing, I see God gathering mankind together into one nation again, which will increase evil, and in due time, will fill up the cup of God's wrath, the outpouring of which will culminate with judgment. The imagery of the gathering of grapes for the harvest is the general theme to keep in mind as we go through this next section.

---

[a] Genesis 11:6-9

The White Horse

> Then I saw when the Lamb broke one of the seven seals, and I heard one of the four living creatures saying as with a voice of thunder, "Come." I looked, and behold, a white horse, and he who sat on it had a bow; and a crown was given to him, and he went out conquering and to conquer.[a]

As the first four seals are opened they each reveal two characters: a horse and the spirit riding it. The horses are differentiated by their various colors, and the riders carry a tool or instrument, with the exception of the horseman of the fourth seal, who is identified as Death. As we try to identify these apocalyptic agents that go out to patrol the earth, we should state at the outset that our criteria for both horse and rider is that they have to bring wide and sweeping changes to the entire world in order to be considered an acceptable candidate.

The first horse, the white horse, is a bit of a curiosity. The Greek word used here is *leukos*,[15] which can mean white, bright, or brilliant.[16] It refers to something 'especially bright or brilliant from whiteness, (dazzling) white: spoken of the garments of angels, and of those exalted to the splendor of the heavenly state.'[17] Prominent examples are when Mary Magdalene and Mary the mother of James entered the tomb of Jesus and saw a young man wearing a white robe,[b] or how at the transfiguration the clothes of Christ became 'white and gleaming,'[c] or when the men in white clothing suddenly appeared to the disciples after the Ascension.[d] Six times in the book of Revelation the word *leukos* is used to describe the white robes which the saints are wearing in heaven,[e,f] and a seventh time it is also 'used of white garments as the sign of innocence and purity of soul.'[18,g] If we take our cue from these various

---

[a] Revelation 6:1-2
[b] Mark 16:5
[c] Luke 9:29
[d] Acts 1:10
[e] Revelation 3:5; 4:4; 6:11; 7:9, 13; 19:14
[f] One of these instances, Revelation 4:4, refers to the 24 elders (further evidence that they are men).
[g] Revelation 3:18

instances of the usage of *leukos* in Scripture, the white horse seems to represent something pure and blameless that passes out into the whole world; a heavenly truth that sweeps across the continents. More on this in a bit.

A great deal of attention has been given to the bow that the rider of the white horse carries. Usually, a case is made that the first time the word 'bow' occurs in Scripture is in Genesis 9:13, just after the flood, where the Hebrew word *qesheth,*[19] which primarily means 'bow,'[20] but can also mean 'rainbow,'[21] is used; *qesheth* can refer to either, depending on usage. Thus, many make a connection between the rainbow of God's covenant and the bow that this rider carries. In the New Testament, however, the original language has changed to Greek; and in Greek, a distinction is made between a 'rainbow, or halo'[22] (*iris*[23]), and a weapon[24] (*toxon*[25]). *Iris* is used in Revelation 4:3 and 10:1, and so is translated as rainbow/halo. In Revelation 6:2 the word *toxon* is used, and I think this clearly refers to a bow as a weapon. In the Old Testament, a bow was a symbol of military might[a], especially as of an invading army – hence, the white rider goes out 'conquering and to conquer'. It's a mundane interpretation compared to most, but it makes the most sense in the context of this passage. There is an obvious counterpoint between what the horse seems to represent, that is, something pure and holy, and its rider, the world conqueror. This paints a picture of, perhaps, two different world movements happening simultaneously.

As unconventional as it might sound, I think the brightness of this first horse represents the Gospel of Jesus Christ as a light that goes out into all the earth. Jesus sums up the essence of this powerful message in his interview with Simon Peter:

> Simon Peter answered, "You are the Christ, the Son of the living God." And Jesus said to him, "Blessed are you, Simon Barjona, because flesh and blood did not reveal this to you, but My Father who is in heaven. I also say to you that you are Peter, and upon this rock I will build My church; and the gates of Hades will not overpower it."[b]

The 'rock' to which Jesus refers in this passage is not Simon Peter the man, but rather the confession that Peter makes: 'You are the Christ, the Son of

---

[a] Job 29:20, Genesis 49:24, Psalm 18:34, 37:15 and others.
[b] Matthew 16:16-18

the living God.'[a] In the following centuries, it wouldn't be Simon Peter who carried Christians through intense persecution; it would be the confession that Jesus is the Son of God. During those tumultuous times Christians were faced with a simple choice: acknowledge that Caesar is God and escape persecution, or proclaim that Christ is God and die. It wasn't the power and authority of Peter which gave courage to the faithful; it was this simple confession, which percolated up through the sewers of Rome to topple an empire. Nearly fifteen hundred years later it would be this same world-changing confession, carried on the lips of visionary missionaries who were swept along in the tides of change during the 17th, 18th, and 19th centuries, that would inflame the remote parts of the globe with the news that Jesus Christ is the Son of God. This is the white horse which is revealed in the first opened seal; a bold prediction that the same confession that conquered an empire would go forth to change the world. The rider of this horse, however, is something quite different.

Some interpret the one who rides the white horse as Jesus Christ at the second coming, when He will return to rule over the nations of the earth. They cite the rider of the white horse in Revelation 19:11-16, as an archetype. Others maintain that this horseman represents the Antichrist, who will come in place of the true Christ. Many notable scholars hold to either of these two views. For my part, since the crown the horseman wears is described in Greek as a *stephanos* (wreath/award), not a *diadem*, I, in part, would say that the white horseman is not Jesus, but that he instead foreshadows the Antichrist. However, in my narrative, I have the man of sin showing up during a *second* patrol of the horsemen. For now, we have the first patrol, which, using Zechariah and Revelation 14 as a template, would lead us to believe that it occurs when the world is at rest, that is, prior to judgment or the beginning of the 70th week of Daniel.

If we consider for a moment that the four horsemen are essentially portrayed as spirits of God, referencing again in Zechariah how the chariots are described as 'four spirits of heaven, going forth after standing before the Lord of all the earth,'[b] I think we can agree with what secular philosophers have been observing for years: that the work of these spirits has been evident all along in the paradigm shifts of global thinking over the past few centuries. They call it

---

[a] There is also the interpretation that Jesus Christ Himself is the Rock.
[b] Zechariah 6:5

zeitgeist, or the spirit of the age. Only in this case, the spirits are real! If we interpret the first patrol of the white horseman effectively as a cosmic change agent, a spirit of the age, then we might agree with a popular interpretation of him as a spirit of conquest. Given my thesis of how this patrol happens before the time of judgment, I think we have already seen this rider in the form of what has been called the European Ages of Discovery, Colonialism, and Imperialism. My thesis being that all three of these periods, which historians tend to parse out into separate epochs, are actually all a part of the same movement, which I will refer to as the Age of Conquest. The major players were the kings and queens, military commanders, and even popes and priests and clergy of Europe who used the powerful, life changing message of the gospel for their own gain (hence, he rides a white/brilliantly shining horse). Such are the trappings of failing to separate church and state; when the church becomes institutionalized, all of the ambitious powermongers and manipulators and heretics end up in the choir. Once the rulers of Europe got a whiff of the vast, vulnerable world that lay before them, they couldn't resist indulging themselves.

It is beyond the scope of this work to provide an exhaustive explanation as to why the European powers became agents of change, a much debated subject about which a number of books have been written. However, if I were to hazard a guess from the perspective of Scripture, I think the answer might be Bibles. Granted, some explanation is required here, and again, I will summarize that which could be the topic of a rather extensive book. It was a confluence of events, which could be described as providential, that brought forth a movement that led to the proliferation of Bibles in the hands of Europeans in their native languages. To begin with, the capture of Constantinople in 1453 by the Ottoman Turks displaced learned Greeks from the Byzantine Empire. As these scholars fled west, they brought with them manuscripts of the old Greek literature and were soon teaching as professors from Italy to Oxford.[26] This development proved invaluable to Protestant Reformers in the 1500s, who were passionate about getting back to the original sources of the New Testament so that they could then translate the Bible into diverse languages, directly from the Greek. The invention of movable type in the early 1400s paved the way for large numbers of Bibles to proliferate across the European subcontinent, in spite of the best efforts of the institutionalized church to restrict public access. In fact, the church had made the possession of a Bible punishable by death, mainly because an individual so enlightened as to have read the good book for himself would find no reference to the sacraments as a means for salvation, no references to purgatory, no reason to pray to the virgin Mary or the saints, and no references to a long list of institutional heresies professed by the church for centuries. The newly distributed Bibles had life changing impact as the Bible addressed a massive readership starving for the inspired writings of the apostles.

The impacts of the Bible in the hands of the people were manifold; however, I would like to focus on two distinct implications. First, the ideals of the Bible were cast far and wide, with mainly the message that salvation comes by faith in Jesus Christ alone. This effected a profound unification of spirituality, and to a limited extent, culture. Second, and perhaps just as profound, was the effect that the Bible had on language. Before there was the widespread printing of journals, magazines, or newspapers, there was the printing of the Bible. Bibles, of necessity, were translated into one vernacular at a time. Many areas of Europe where different versions of the same base language were spoken became more unified by reading a book that they all studied and came to understand and about which they were able to converse. Bibles were often translated into the dominant vernacular of a particular region; where they were distributed, the dominance of that vernacular became extended. This is to say, that a secondary effect of the Bible was to enlarge the linguistic communities of Europe: communities which eventually resolved into nations… but we'll get to that a little later.

The psychology of language defines our world. It delineates *us* versus *them*; *us* being those who speak the same language, and *them* being those who speak a different language. When the rising tides of European expansion swept across the planet, in many regions they found greatly dispersed native tribes who spoke a myriad of diverse languages. Thus, when the Europeans suddenly came upon the scene, the indigenous tribes saw *us* versus *them*. That is to say, they saw tribal *us* versus tribal *them*, when they should have seen *Us* versus *Them*; American/African/Indian *Us* versus Spanish/English/French *Them*. Hence, a main tactic for the Europeans was to divide and conquer, and this they did in many parts of the globe.

Incidentally, the two regions of the world that proved highly resistant to European colonialism, the Ottoman Empire and China, each had unifying factors that resisted this tactic of divide and conquer. The Ottomans had the Quran, the holy book of Islam which, though it was not translated into the various languages of the empire, still was written in Arabic, which became the language of the religious intelligentsia and the culture of the people. China did not have a universal holy book, but instead was the benefactor of a 3000-year-old tradition of written language that was widely dispersed throughout eastern Asia.[a] It took World War I to topple the Ottoman Empire, and though China was never formally colonized by the West, they were coerced into unfavorable trade agreements, which impinged upon their sovereignty for over a hundred years.

Finally, if we assume that the God of the Bible does exist, and that He was sending His Spirit throughout the earth to begin the process of gathering mankind for the eventual, final harvest, it shouldn't be a surprise that He would pick a region where a book containing His explicit message to mankind would be found in excess. This might explain how, over just a few centuries, Christianity became the world's most widespread religion; not because a bunch of backward, arrogant, and morally corrupt Europeans had better technology or were descended from a superior race, but rather, simply because they were in possession of God's Word in a form that could be readily distributed to the masses.

This two-faced condition in which we find the church, that of being stewards of God's Word on the one hand and of being worldly and corrupted by power on the other, goes back deep into church history. The start of it all was the Roman emperor Constantine, who presents himself to history as a bit of an enigma. On the one hand, he did things that made it seem like he had made a true conversion to Christianity: he was very generous to the Christian faith, ending the 10 years of persecution by Diocletian from 303 – 313 AD; he funded the construction of many church buildings and in general supported a lot of public works that furthered the Christian cause. On the other hand, there were other things that he did that were in direct opposition to Christianity. He continued to participate in various pagan worship practices, and in particular, he did not end the Roman tradition of emperor worship; in fact, he seemed to encourage it on certain occasions.[27] This would have been in direct opposition

---

[a] Chinese has many dialects, meaning many different ways of pronouncing the same character, but two main written languages, Mandarin and Cantonese.

to the Christian belief that only Jesus Christ is God. Constantine, it appears, came up with a crafty compromise:

> This raises the question of how Constantine reconciled the tradition of imperial divinity with his monotheistic faith, which required him to believe that there was only one God in heaven… On the one hand, this threatened the authority of pagan emperors, but on the other hand it opened up a new possibility for the first Christian ruler: if Constantine was the earthly representative of the supreme solar deity, and if that deity could be assimilated to the Christian God, then it followed that Constantine was analogous to Christ and was therefore (at least according to Nicene orthodoxy) one with the Divinity.[28]

Here we find the genesis of the Vatican's heretical belief that the pope is the representative of Christ on earth, and thus imbued with His divine authority. Constantine, in assuming the role of Pontifex Maximus (head priest over the church) began the process of blurring the lines between the church's primary mission of salvation and governance. This collusion of church and state would only worsen over time. 'On February 27, 380 [AD], in Thessaloniki, the Eastern Roman Emperor Theodosius I signed a decree in the presence of the Western Roman Emperor Valentinian II that made Christianity the religion of the state and punished the practice of pagan rituals.'[29] This decree not only recognized Christianity as the official state religion of the Roman Empire, it essentially made church participation compulsory. 'Theodosius I was the first emperor to decree that all Roman citizens follow Christianity.'[30] If a member of the pagan aristocracy wanted to keep his land, his wealth, and his status, he would, of necessity, 'convert' to Christianity:

> But even before the closing of the temples in 391, the writing was on the wall. It was now the church people were flocking to, and if the nobility was going to maintain its position, they too had to join the church, where their wealth and connections enabled them to maintain their traditional ascendancy, if in rather different ways (and to continue to read the occasional classical text in the same villas). Last-ditch resistance would have led to political suicide, and there were no pagan martyrs.[31]

Constantine and Theodosius I, either wittingly or unwittingly, effected the institutionalization of the church to the detriment of all posterity. Pagans who joined the church brought their belief systems with them. The winter solstice festival of Saturnalia became Christmas, which borrowed traditions such as the yule log, Christmas tree, and gift giving from pagan practice.[32] The

Spring Equinox fertility celebration became Easter,[a, 33] giving rise to the Easter bunny and egg hunting traditions. Over time, other pagan traditions would seep into the church, such as Lent, celibacy for priests,[34] and many others. Today Christians celebrate these religious holidays largely in ignorance of pagan[b] influence, but what this history illustrates is how for a very long time, power seekers and manipulators have used the guise of Christian religiosity to achieve their own avaricious ends; and so we have our conqueror, the rider of the white horse.

Perhaps it seems trite to make such a sweeping assertion; perhaps it seems the symbology is overdone. However, I would maintain that one need look no farther than the Great Crusades to the Holy Land, the Inquisition, the burning of heretics, and the barbarous prisons of the papacy to see the true face of the institutional church:[c]

> It is a matter of incontrovertible historical record that many of the popes were as contemptible of human life as they were of freedom. Pope Gregory IX (1227-41) declared it the duty of every Catholic "to persecute heretics." A heretic was anyone who did not give complete allegiance to the Roman Catholic Church. Such persons were to be tortured, imprisoned and slain. Disloyalty to the pope was the same as treason, so close were the state and Church allied. "Of eighty popes in a line from the thirteenth century on," writes [Peter] de Rossa, "not one of them disapproved of the theology and apparatus of Inquisition. On the contrary, one after another added his own cruel touches to the working of this deadly machine."[35]

It was this unholy alliance between church and state that inspired the framers of the United States Constitution to painstakingly spell out that there should be a separation of these powers for proper governance of a truly representative republic. This duality between the church as an institution and its message appears not only a fitting description of the white horseman, but also we see him prancing about the fields of Europe centuries before he is set loose to trample upon the peoples of the earth. Church leaders had been abusing their

---

[a] The word Easter is a derivative of Ishtar, the ancient Babylonian goddess of fertility.
[b] Over the years, the word pagan as come to mean simply 'not Christian.' I use it here in specific reference to the priestly colleges of Rome, but which can be applied in a wider sense to worldwide practices of idol worship, which, I believe, had their genesis at Babel.
[c] I use the term 'institutional church' to refer to the condition where the goverenance of man has replaced Christ as the head of the church. It can apply to the Roman Catholic Church, Eastern Orthodox, and a number of protestant denominations as well.

power and violently trying to stamp out all opposition to their authority for centuries. Untold millions were either tortured or put to death for the heresy of possessing a Bible in their local vernacular, or slaughtered in Crusades all across Europe for refusing to recognize the primacy of the pope. Viewed from the luxurious vantage point of the freedoms that we have in the twenty-first century, it is easy to forget how oppressive the institutional church had become during the Middle Ages.[a, b]

This brings us around to a second far-reaching consequence related to the end of that last bastion of the Roman Empire. The fall of Constantinople not only sent learned Greek scholars west; it also cut off Europe from many of the prized goods and spices of the Far East which flowed west over trade routes that would be later referred to as the Silk Road.

> 'Despite repeatedly surviving many geopolitical changes and disruptions, the Ottoman Empire and other gunpowder empires expanded efforts to gain greater control of it [the Silk Road] from 1453 onwards. This prompted European efforts to seek alternative routes to trading with the gunpowder empires, as well as other nations and communities, while also gaining leverage over them in turn after the Ottomans increased their usage of land-based trade, thereby ushering in the Age of Discovery, European colonialism, and a more intensified process of globalization, which had arguably begun with the Silk Road.'[36]

And so the stage was set for an Age of Conquest like no other. Of the great empires of the past (the Mongols, Romans, Greeks, etc.), none were nearly so comprehensive and world-changing as the Age of Conquest, whereby 1914, Europeans had at one time or another directly controlled about 84% of the globe,[37] and as stated above, the only significant exceptions were the Ottoman Empire and China. After World War I, the Ottoman Empire was divided between France, Russia, and Britain. Though China was never formally

---

[a] See Appendix F, *The Church Clock*, (the Church of Thyatira, in particular), for further exposition.

[b] It would be naive to assume the elaborate infrastructure of political power established by the Vatican during the Middle Ages simply vanished with the advent of Nationalism. The Vatican is a power broker with roots that go all the way back to Constantine and Theodosius I. Some would argue that what was once accomplished through outright despotism is in the present day effected through clandestine chicanery. One has only to think of American presidents and political figures who in recent times have traveled to the Vatican to kiss the ring of the pope to formulate a guess as to who – if there is one – might be a top candidate for what is referred to in whispers as 'the deep state.'

colonized, it did not escape European dominance. 'In 1839, China went to war with Britain over the latter's desire to trade opium on Chinese soil. China lost, and in 1842 had to sign the first of the 'unequal treaties' that forced the country to open up its territory and trade on terms defined by Western imperial powers.'[38] 'For almost exactly a century, between 1842 and 1943, China was subjected to an internationally sanctioned regime that prevented it from being fully sovereign on its own territory.'[39] So, in effect, there was almost no place on earth that did not feel the brunt of European conquest. Even Antarctica, when you consider the whaling and seal harvesting industries, did not escape its influence. This was truly a worldwide phenomenon.

The far-reaching impact of the Age of Conquest cannot be understated. '...[T]he states of Portugal, Spain, the Netherlands, France and England start[ed] the process of Colonization by discovering, settling and annexing areas throughout the world; a process which so begun *became a global order.*[a,] [40] 'What occurred in the course of Europe's expansion had a profound impact on the modern history of all continents.'[41] It was a system of rule where ruling was a means to an end – exploitation; hence, the prize/award (*stephanos*).

We can look at a few regions around the world to illustrate how the Age of Conquest radically consolidated the peoples and lands living therein. We shall do so starting with India.

India

'Only after the arrival of the Portuguese navigator Vasco Da Gama in 1498 and the subsequent establishment of European maritime supremacy in the region did India become exposed to major external influences arriving by sea, a process that culminated in the decline of the ruling Muslim elite and absorption of the subcontinent within the British Empire. Direct administration by the British, which began in 1858, effected a political and economic unification of the subcontinent.'[42] When the British unified India into one colony, they were organizing a vast, eclectic array of people groups that even today consists of '...innumerable castes and tribes, as well as... more than a dozen major and hundreds of minor linguistic groups from several language families unrelated to

---

[a] Italics mine.

one another.'[43] *Figure 1* provides a visual overview of the ethnic diversity of India, circa 2012, represented by language. This is present day, after hundreds of years of existing first as a colony and then as a nation; initially diversity must have been much greater. It is important to remember that what we are tracking is the *effect* of conquest, that is, the gathering of the nations, not to suppose the primacy of one culture over another.

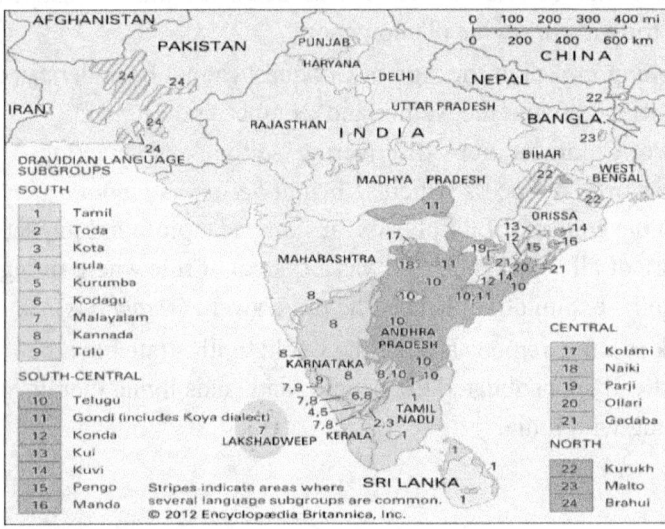

Figure 1

Africa

Until 1880, the continent of Africa was still largely unaffected by European influence. With the convening of the Berlin Conference in 1884, all of that changed.

> Convened in late 1884 and concluded in February of the following year, the Berlin Conference, which had been summoned by Germany's Prince Bismarck, sought to color in the map of what was commonly known as the "dark continent." According to the General Act of the Berlin Conference, Africa was to be partitioned among five primary European national contestants – Britain, France, Germany, Portugal and Italy – and King Leopold II of Belgium. The project to partition the continent and portion it out nonetheless did little more than sanction the ongoing "scramble for Africa."[44]

The 'scramble for Africa' was a race between the colonial powers to claim their piece of the pie before it was all gone. The subsequent effect on the political map of the 'dark continent' was historic. (*Figure 2*)[45]

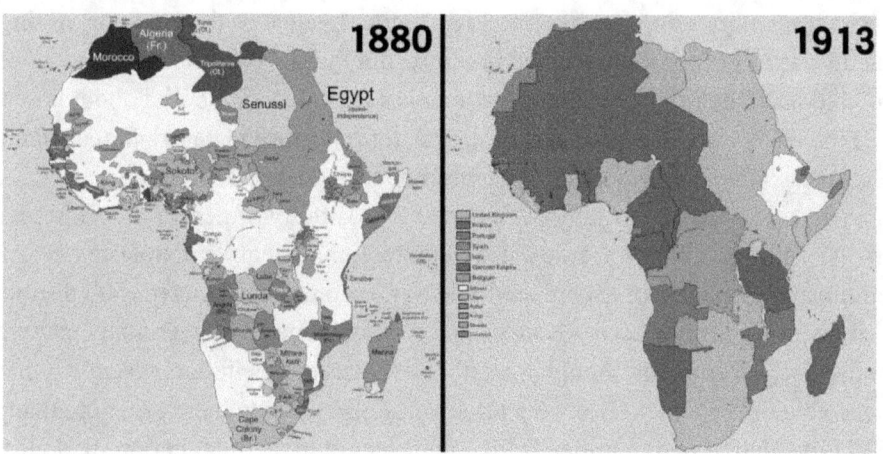

Figure 2

From the map above, one can readily see how many indigenous African nations, depicted on the left, were brought under the relatively few jurisdictions of the European powers in a little over thirty years. In particular, we notice the consolidation of people and lands. Though many Africans maintain their tribal identity even to the present day, we cannot deny the profound effect of European Imperialism in shaping the history of the continent.

North & South America

In the Americas, the spread of diseases like smallpox and measles, introduced by the Europeans, sharply reduced native populations. 'In the century following the [Spanish] Conquest, the population of Central Mexico was reduced to one-tenth of its previous size; in Peru, it shrank by 40 percent.'[46] If such sharp declines in population are evinced in the scant pages of recorded history, one can only imagine the untold millions who perished with no written record to commemorate their existence. This unfortunate circumstance, plus systemic animosity between native peoples which made them naturally divisive and prone to turn upon each other, made the Americas easy pickings for the European powers. Confederations of Native Americans did form at times to resist foreign invasion, such as the Five Nation League of the Iroquois, or the plains nations of the Comanche and Sioux, but these were too limited in scope to hold back the tides of change. Differences in philosophy/belief about how to use the land, with the American reverence for undisturbed nature pitted against European values of changing the environment (industry/farming/mining) to suit the needs of society, virtually excluded any possibility of peaceful coexistence.

As a result of this epic clash of culture, many native peoples were eliminated/displaced or assimilated into new colonies/states. Over 500 distinct people groups in the lower 48 states and Alaska alone were eventually gathered under one government, though a number of reservations in the present day have been able to claw back their own jurisdiction. 'In Canada there are more than 630 First Nation communities, which represent more than 50 nations and 50 Indigenous languages.'[47] 'There are 68 different Indigenous Peoples that inhabit Mexican territory, each of which speaks a native language of their own.'[48] 'Latin America (which includes Mexico) is home to over 800 different Indigenous Peoples.'[49] The political and cultural assimilation/elimination of the native peoples of the South Pacific and Australia took place within this time frame as well.

Conclusion

All of the peoples of the world were eventually brought into the 'new world order' introduced by the Age of Conquest.[a] One could say that, for most indigenous cultures, this time was truly apocalyptic, as in, the end of the world as they knew it. Europeans brought with them the monstrosity of undivided church and state, as well as the message that Jesus Christ is the Son of God; a duality that becomes apparent when viewed from the perspective of history. The point here is to illustrate how the spirits that go out from standing before God are prompting the gathering of the nations; these are not only agents of change, but also agents of God's judgment. In order for us to recognize the four horsemen for what they are, the results caused by these cosmic change agents have to be noteworthy: The two main criteria are that the event has to be worldwide in scope, and also have the effect of gathering the peoples of the earth into a more tightly-knit global community. The culmination of this process will be a one-world government, a reversion back to Babel. Global conquest was but the first step of consolidation.

All of these ruminations leave us with a rather perturbing question: Could the fall of Constantinople possibly represent the opening of the first seal of the apocalypse? Did this event set in motion both the message and the conqueror; the white horse and its rider? Perhaps. It was indeed a signal event that marked a major turning point for all modern history, and so provides a provocative correlation. Many modern scholars go so far as to point to the exodus of Greek intellectuals to Italy as marking the end of the Middle Ages and the beginning of the Renaissance.[50] But does the application fit the interpretation? One could make the case that we have not seen the white horse yet; perhaps there will be some future movement of people and happenings that will occur before the start of the 70th week of Daniel which will prove to be even more world-changing and thus be a better fit to our predictions. My interpretation of the seals is noteworthy, for it is biblically derived; however, the application (how these seals actually play out in time) is somewhat a matter of my opinion, and I should leave room, at least, for other ideas about how these things may come to pass. But I will say that, as for me, it is hard to imagine another historical development that could prove to be so significant in

---

[a] With a few far-flung exceptions, such as the bushmen of New Guinea and other very remote tribes.

terms of its effect on the course of humanity. Perhaps exposition on the seals that follow will further my case. I will let the reader decide for himself.

The Red Horse

> When He broke the second seal, I heard the second living creature saying, "Come!" And another, a red horse, went out; and to him who sat on it, it was granted to take peace from the earth, and that men would slay one another; and a great sword was given to him.[a]

Most scholars interpret the second horseman as a personification of war. This makes sense; he rides a red horse, carries a large sword, takes peace from the earth, and makes men slay each other. Every way in which John describes him seems to be symbolic of war, yet he stops short of bestowing that appellation upon this spirit. He names the fourth horseman, yet to be discussed, Death, so there is little left to guess about *his* identity, yet the individual on the red horse is left nameless. I do think that during the 70th week this red horseman will perform a second patrol in which he will play the part of bringing war to the earth, but for this first patrol, during the birth pangs of judgment, I believe that there is more to this apocalyptic rider.

One of the first things we notice about the horse is its color: red. The Greek word for red is *eruthros*,[51] but that is not the word used in this instance. The word used to describe the red horse is *purrhos*,[52] which means 'fire colored'[53] or 'fiery.'[54] This same word is used to describe the red dragon in chapter 12 of Revelation, which has 'seven heads and ten horns.'[b] The Dragon also is described as seeking to 'devour,'[c] 'waging war'[d] (against God and the woman), persecuting 'the woman who had given birth to the male child,'[e] and as being 'enraged,'[f] among other things. His 'fiery' color seems to describe his temperament as much as anything, and we can apply this to our red horse by identifying him as the spread of discontent and rebellion among all the peoples of the earth.

---

[a] Revelation 6: 3-4
[b] Revelation 12:3
[c] Revelation 12:4
[d] Revelation 12:7, 17
[e] Revelation 12:13
[f] Revelation 12:17

The one who rides this fiery horse carries a sword. In Greek, the word translated 'sword' here is *machaira*,[55] which refers to a slaughter-knife: 'a short sword or dagger mainly used for stabbing; (figuratively) an instrument for exacting retribution,'[56] or 'a large knife, used for 'killing animals and cutting up flesh.''[57] The Greek word for 'great' is *megale*,[58] which means 'great,' 'large,' or 'in the widest sense.'[59] This creates an interesting nuance which seems to be hinting at a deeper meaning, that is, slaughter to the widest extent, or on a worldwide scale.

If we accept that the white horseman might represent the zeitgeist of conquest, then following right on his heels would be the red horseman, the spirit of nationalism, or according to secular philosophers, Volksgeist – the spirit of a nation. Where Colonialism drew dashes all over the map, nationalism came along and painted solid lines in bold in many and various colors. As colonies languished due to the waning influence of their metropoles, nations were forged out of the remainder, further binding people together in a tighter unification of societies.

As we entertain ideas about nationalism, it is important first to acknowledge the complexity of the subject. Nationalism, on the face of it, is something that does not seem to need explanation, as we currently live in a world populated by nation-states. Nation-states exist, and therefore they seem to be easily definable by simply observing them. However, when we take a closer look, we begin to discover that all over the world, nation-states came into being through radically different histories, and so the word 'nationalism' becomes rather difficult to nail down to just one process or definition. For instance, in the European theater, ideas about revolution inspired many indigenous people groups to rise up against the existing feudal system to overthrow monarchies and empires, where in other parts of the world it was colonialism that shaped the history of future nation-states. So for a start, we will define nationalism simply as the process by which nation-states arise.

It will also prove helpful to clarify the word 'nation' as denoting something quite different from a nation-state; that is, as a cultural community as opposed to political. We often find multiple nations grouped together into a single nation-state, each different from the other in both ethnicity and history, and often these qualities are shared, making distinctions difficult. For the purpose of this discussion, I will adopt a reductionist viewpoint, and leave the finely detailed definitions to the volumes of books and encyclopedias that have been written on the subject. As our current thesis involves interpreting the book of Revelation and how the rest of the Bible can be used to decode its secrets, it might be worth our time to consult Scripture and see what it has to say about the nations of the earth. It is interesting to note that when Jesus speaks of 'birth pangs' and 'nation rising up against nation' in Mark 13:5-8, referenced earlier, the Greek word that the writer uses for nation is *ethnos*,[60] which means 'a race, people, nation; the nations, heathen world, Gentiles.'[61] 'In the Greco-Roman world, 'ethnos' was commonly used to describe a group of people bound by common culture, language, and heritage'[62] and has 'a very strong emphasis on the language that is spoken. A 'nation' is a language basin; a non-centralized collective of people who speak the same language and exchange the same stories.'[63] This emphasis on language has historical, biblical significance.

At the tower of Babel in Genesis 11:6-9 when God says: 'behold, they are one people, and they all have the same language,' He is speaking of all of mankind as one nation. God's judgment at Babel was to confuse man's language; that is, He bestowed upon each of the different families of man a unique language. These families then spread out across the face of the earth, to such an extent that different regions became synonymous with the patriarchs of these families. Canaan settled in the area that would eventually become modern-day Israel. Elam went to Iran, Cush to the southern Nile region, and Tubal to Anatolia, and so forth.[64] All of these lands in ancient times bore the names of the patriarchs. The Apostle Paul referenced this history when he spoke to the Greeks on the Areopagus in Athens:

> The God who made the world and all things in it, since He is the Lord of heaven and earth, does not dwell in temples made with hands; nor is He served by human hands, as though He needed anything, since He Himself gives to all people life and breath and all things; and He made from *one man*[a] every nation of mankind to live on all the face of the earth, having determined their appointed times, and the boundaries of their habitation, that they would seek God, if perhaps they might grope for Him and find Him, though He is not far from each one of us; for in Him we live and move and exist, even as some of your own poets have said, 'For we also are His children.'[b]

It is important to recognize that at Babel, before all the confusion, the race of man was one people, as Paul says, descended from 'one man,' or

---

[a] Italics mine
[b] Acts 17:24-28

sometimes translated as 'one blood.'[65] According to tradition, the Caucasoid race descended from Japheth, Negroid from Ham, and the Jews from Shem. This might lead one to believe that such differences were evident even in the sons of Noah, and perhaps they might in appearance look like an interracial family. As I study Scripture, however, I am led to believe that Noah's offspring were not racially distinct; if you saw the three of them walk out of a tent and stand next to each other, they would appear as brothers, not as men from three different races.[a] To say this another way, I would propose that – per the biblical record – linguistic diversity *preceded* ethnic and racial differentiation. As people went their separate ways from Babel in small family groups, genetic diversity declined, recessive traits emerged, and the many and various 'races' of man emerged through what we might call inbreeding: and so the nations were born[b]. It should not be a surprise, then, when God sends out His horseman to judge the earth, to find that the reverse process (that is, a reduction in the diversity of language) might be one of the mechanisms that brings men back together into one nation or government.

    According to secular sources, the differentiating features usually specified as the basis for nationhood are namely: ethnicity, culture, language, and religion[66]. As we have seen above, if we overlay this secular viewpoint with biblical history, ethnicity and culture would have precipitated out the various family groups as they left Babel. In its most basic form, religion is the communication of complex spiritual ideas, which relies heavily on language; hence it is possible to simplify the definition of the word 'nation' as a community of people that speak the same language – *ethnos*. What becomes really interesting is how many and various nations, so defined, rose up in modern times against each other to form present-day nation-states. This brings up another thing to keep in mind: the formation of the modern nation-state, in most corners of the world, was a violent and bloody affair that was usually the result of some kind of revolution or uprising. We might say that nationalism is the product of the 'fiery' rage of the nations.

---

[a] The significant implication here is that for the generations from Adam down through the sons of Noah, the peoples of the earth were essentially one race; a people that we would refer to today as a 'brown' race. It would have been this 'brown' race from which all the peoples of the earth are descended.

[b] It is interesting to note that longevity fell off precipitously a generation or two after Babel.

After the French Revolution, the spirit of nationalism took hold in Europe: '...it has been argued that national consciousness was essentially a nineteenth-century phenomenon – indeed, that it was unthinkable before the French and Industrial Revolutions.'[67] '...the twin ideals of national consciousness and uniformity of language depended for their realization on new developments in communications, from the railways to the daily newspaper...'[68] Granted, the change did not happen all at once, everywhere, but rather, swept across Europe as an irresistible, swelling tide. Also, the revolution in communication associated with the invention of Gutenberg's printing press back in the early 1400s did not change the face of the continent overnight. As such, we might think of the nineteenth-century as the tipping point, when things really got going as opposed to the beginning of it all.

'The spread of literacy encouraged what [Benedict] Anderson calls "the convergence of capitalism and print technology on the fatal diversity of human language"[a], permitting and indeed encouraging the process of standardization...'[69]. As national consciousness spread across Europe, 'The transformation of 'dialects' into a common literary standard was employed to unify dispersed populations into communities and differentiate them from neighboring 'others.''[70] In other words, the wide circulation of printed material, which of necessity was restricted to a specific vernacular or dialect, encouraged everyone to speak the same version of the regional language. As our working definition of a nation is a community that speaks the same language, this standardization expanded regional communities in France, for example, to include all speakers of French-like language; and so because everyone began to speak the same version of French, a nation-state called France is eventually born. (This is not a one-step process. Most nations took a while to find their way, as in the case of France, which first endured a bloody revolution to become a republic before falling back into imperialism under Napoleon, and waging a devastating war across the whole of Europe. France eventually re-formed as a republic in 1848.) There are many variations on the theme of nationalism, but language always plays a foundational role.

In British North America, it was Thomas Paine's *Common Sense* that cast the vision of 'America as a nation in the making.'[71] 'To Paine goes the credit for being the first to set forth publicly a vision of a new American nation

---

[a] This 'fatal diversity of human language' is what Christians believe is a consequence of Babel.

and for turning much of his American audience from loyal British subjects into rebel nationalists.'[72] Of course, the colonies in America all spoke the same language, so one could argue for *that* reason they already were a nation-state in the making; all they needed was a spark to settle their differences and bring them together. And what a spark it was!

> The first shot of the American Revolution at the Battle of Lexington and Concord is referred to as the "shot heard 'round the world" due to its historical and global significance. The Revolutionary War victory not only established the United States as the first modern constitutional republic, but marked the transition from an age of monarchy to a new age of freedom by inspiring similar movements worldwide. The American Revolution was the first of the "Atlantic Revolutions:" followed most notably by the French Revolution, the Haitian Revolution, and the Latin American wars of independence. Aftershocks contributed to rebellions in Ireland, the Polish–Lithuanian Commonwealth, and the Netherlands.[73]

The transformation of the original 13 British colonies into a fledgling nation sent shock waves around the world. Similar to the fall of Constantinople, it was a turning point in history that directly or indirectly affected all the peoples of the earth. Many nations took inspiration from the example set by the United States and their newly crafted constitution, which set up a uniquely democratic form of government:

> The U.S. Constitution, drafted shortly after independence, remains the world's oldest written constitution, and has been emulated by other countries, in some cases verbatim. Some historians and scholars argue that the subsequent wave of independence and revolutionary movements has contributed to the continued expansion of democratic government; 144 countries, representing two-thirds of the world's population, are full or partially democracies of the same form.[74]

Not all nations forged democracies, but the spirit unleashed by the American Revolution would not rest until all the world's monarchies bowed to the new political regime of the nation-state. On the heels of the Age of Conquest, nationalism was born, often in the throes of bloody uprisings; an unstoppable movement that continued well into the 20th century. As stated above, the path to nationhood was different everywhere you look; however, if we follow the demographics of language around the world, this proves to be a guide.

In South America, papal arbitration in the 'Treaty of Tordesillas in 1494 established Portuguese and Spanish spheres of dominance.'[75] This demarcation was not only a line of separation between Spanish and Portuguese rule, it divided according to language as well. Thus, as the spirit of nationalism swept over the continent, it formed nation-states along two key linguistic pathways: Portuguese-speaking Brazil, and the rest of Central and South America, which spoke Spanish. The Spanish-speaking states ended up being 'legally divided along racial lines, into modern republics based on concepts of individual liberty and popular sovereignty.'[76]

When the English first encountered India, it was a subcontinent divided: 'With fourteen major languages and more than two hundred dialects, India had no single culture based on language that could be deployed to create a sense of national identity.'[77] For all intents and purposes, the English intended to keep them that way. 'The British in India were not in the business of promoting nationhood amongst their subjects: indeed, when challenged by critics claiming to speak for an Indian nation, their line was to declare that India was nothing more than a 'geographic expression'.'[78] However, in spite of their best efforts, the British, through administrative reforms following the revolt of 1857, inadvertently handed India the key ingredient to nationhood. 'In 1858, the Crown in Parliament replaced the rule of the East India Company.'[79] Over the next thirty years Indians began to serve in local governments. 'The growing intervention of the state gave Indians... an incentive to take part in these fledgling institutions ... [where] they had to learn new modes, forms and languages of politics.'[80] And, of course, the language of these new politics was English. 'From its very beginning, Indian nationalism relied on English to overcome parochialism and to counter the communicative advantages of the British Raj.'[81] Many and varied factors contributed to the building of a nation-state in India, but on its most fundamental level we find the common denominator of language figuring in most prominently.

In Africa, the colonial era left behind a linguistic footprint into which the arcane elements of nationalism could pool. The French colonies gave rise to Tunisia (1956), Algeria (1962), Mauritania (1960), Senegal (1960), Gambia (1965), Guinea (1958), Ivory Coast (1960), Niger (1960), Chad (1960), the Central African Republic (1960), and Madagascar (1960). The British colonies became Ghana (1957), Nigeria (1960), Sudan (1956), Uganda (1962), Kenya (1963), Zambia (1964), Rhodesia (1965), Botswana (1966), and South Africa

(1934). The Italian colonies became Libya (1951) and Ethiopia (1962), and it was the Congo (1960) that rose from the ashes of the Belgian colonial fiasco.[82] This is simply to show the obvious: that nation-states in Africa formed along the old colonial era lines, in which case we can attribute a common language as the foundation upon which they were built. It is important to note that in Africa, tribal communities served as a reservoir for communication, and so the 'post-colonial history produced... sub-national regionalisms as much as states.'[83] Ethnic or tribal differences on the local level were highly divisive factors during the transition from colonial rule to statehood, but in spite of this, African nation-states '...have proven remarkably durable during the first half-century of independence, and especially during more than a quarter-century of escalating violence.'[84] Over time, administrations and governments have changed wholesale, yet these nation-states endure much the same.

Language builds communities, and communities are the basis for nation building; however, Africa is a prime example of how linguistic identities often cut both ways. While the language of administration left behind by the various metropoles has served to be largely a unifying force, preserving much of the original colonial borders over time, diverse tribal tongues have led to many civil wars that have often spilled over said boundaries and have been a constant source of disunity. This is all to say that what we have in the modern day is a political patchwork, where the boundaries of nation-states run contrary to tribal boundaries, each existing within and across one another as defined by the complex geographic dispersion of languages.

Southeast Asia is a great case study of how language influences history. Upon independence, French Indochina split into three nation-states (Vietnam, Cambodia, and Laos), while the Dutch East Indies unified to become one (Indonesia).[85] Why the difference? Of course, there are many reasons. One significant reason, per the present conversation, is the difference in how language was taught and administered in the two colonies:

> In Indochina... the colonial government decided to concentrate upon promoting mass literacy in the main vernacular languages – Vietnamese, Khmer, and Lao – rather than in French, which consequently could not become a language of national unity. Instead, Vietnam, Cambodia and Laos each acquired a separate reading public. Dutch educational policy in Indonesia also favored indigenous languages, but here one particular language, Malay, was taught even in areas where it was not the local vernacular. Although already widely spoken in trade and diplomacy in pre-colonial times, Malay became the national language of

Indonesia essentially because of its systematic promotion by the colonial state, and its consequent emergence as the medium of the nationalist press and literature.[86]

Again, we see how the colonial period facilitated linguistic pathways through which the spirit of nationalism could channel and take hold.

There is much, much more that could be said about nationalism; the topic is quite literally as big as the world in which we live. As it is not the main focus of this book, I aim to only provide a smattering of examples to make a point: language, per the biblical context, played a foundational role. Let me illustrate: In any given neighborhood, you might find houses of brick, wood, stone, or perhaps some new synthetic material. You might find each house to be laid out and built very differently, and by various processes. You might find small, medium, and large houses, each with its own unique history as to how it came into existence. The one thing that all of these houses would have in common is that they all have a foundation. Houses are built with foundations because without this key element, houses soon fall. In the building of a nation-state – even though each is very different from any other – language forms the foundation.

Another way to consider this is to think about language as a basin. Just as a basin might collect water, language collects people. How the water gets into the basin depends on how much rain falls, if there has been a flood, and the lay of the land. Some basins pool together to form large lakes, while others only form small ponds. Each basin realizes a different history concerning how it collects water, with variations mostly in size and shape, but each with a unique ecosystem. My thesis is that language can be thought of as a basin in which nation-states form. Thus, nationalism is the story of how 'nation [*ethnos*] shall rise up against nation [*ethnos*]'[a] to forge the world we know today.

Directly related to this, I would say, per the biblical account of Babel, that language is foundational to *ethnicity*. As we noted earlier, when mankind departed from Babel in a myriad of families/languages, this caused cultural and eventually racial differences to develop between the peoples of the earth. The difference in language occurred first; then people of the same language developed cultural and racial uniqueness. The basic lesson we learn from Babel is that differentiation in language led to differentiation in culture and race, not

---

[a] Mark 13:5-8

the other way around. We see the same principle at work in the world today, only in the modern case, the mode is convergence; that is, as the world eliminates linguistic variation (the inverse of Babel), the various cultures and races of man tend to converge. For example, in the United States, we are largely a people of one language but of many cultures and races. As cultures clash, communication takes place and eventually understanding, which has the effect of breaking down barriers, ultimately reducing differentiation. As diverse cultures converge, so will race. A few hundred years from now, I would expect the US to become a much more culturally and therefore racially homogeneous nation comprised mostly of what we would call 'brown' people. Perhaps in a few thousand years, the entire world would converge into a single people again, all espousing a common language, culture, and racial makeup, with minor variations from region to region. This would be our future if the wheels of history are permitted to grind on unabated; I do not think, however, that we have that much time.

A Great Sword

...and a great sword was given to him.[a]

To repeat several sources quoted above, the age of nationalism would have been 'unthinkable before the French and Industrial Revolutions.'[87] '... the twin ideals of national consciousness and uniformity of language depended for their realization on new developments in communications, from the railways to the daily newspaper, together with other social, political, and cultural changes.'[88] '... industrial society strengthens the boundaries between nations rather than those between classes'.[89] As it is our thesis that the essence of a nation of people is language, that is, community based on language or communication, you could argue that the nations of the earth, so described, were simply waiting throughout the balance of history for the technology of industrialization to provide the spark to nationalize. It is not a coincidence that these two phenomena grew in tandem: industrialization needs the labor and capital that nationalism can provide. With industrialization comes the mass production of food and armament that a nation-state requires to grow and effectively defend its sovereignty.

The advent of industrialization was just as momentous an event as the American Revolution:

> The Industrial Revolution marked a major turning point in history, comparable only to humanity's adoption of agriculture with respect to material advancement. The Industrial Revolution influenced in some way almost every aspect of daily life.[90]

> Economic historians agree that the onset of the Industrial Revolution is the most important event in human history since the domestication of animals and plants.[91]

The American Industrial Revolution, sometimes called the Second Industrial Revolution, was notable in particular for machining technology and the utilization of a system of manufacture referred to as 'interchangeable parts.'

---

[a] Revelation 6:4

Important American technological contributions during the period of the Industrial Revolution were the cotton gin and the development of a system for making interchangeable parts, which was aided by the development of the milling machine in the United States. The development of machine tools and the system of interchangeable parts was the basis for the rise of the US as the world's leading industrial nation in the late 19th century.[92]

This new manufacturing capability, referred to as 'the American system' in the early days, was quickly turned to the making of weapons.

> The [American] system was also known as armory practice because it was first fully developed in armories, namely, the United States Armories at Springfield in Massachusetts and Harpers Ferry in Virginia (later West Virginia), inside contractors to supply the United States Armed Forces, and various private armories.[93]

> It was not long before the military started harnessing some of these inventions. Mass production in factories churned out not only large numbers of standardised guns and bullets, but also boots, uniforms and tents. The guns were more reliable and hence more accurate. A bullet was 30 times more likely to strike its target. Developments in transport were also utilised, with steel becoming standard in battleships and trains starting to be used to quickly ferry large numbers of troops to war zones. Advances in chemistry led to new high explosives. The first wars in which these new military technologies were used on a large scale included the Crimean War (1854-56) and the American Civil War (1861-65). Both of these provided a taster for the carnage of WWI, being characterised by trench warfare in which frontal assaults against well-defended positions led to massacres of infantry soldiers.[94]

> Industrialisation played a major role in World War One. New military machinery could be produced at a much larger scale and at a much faster rate than before. Along with innovative technology, this led to one of the most devastating wars in human history.[95]

World War I saw the introduction into warfare on a large scale of artillery, machine guns, rifles, tanks, warships, planes, submarines, and chemical weapons.[96] The two world wars are testaments to the scale on which industrialized nations are capable of waging war. 'Never has nationalism's destructive potential been more fully revealed than during the period encompassing the two World Wars.'[97] 'Nationalism[,] not Imperialism, set off Armageddon.'[98]

The two world wars in particular gave rise to a form of American industrialization centered around the manufacture of weapons, a juggernaut of manufacturing prowess which was to become known as the Military Industrial

Complex, first named such by President Dwight D. Eisenhower in his farewell address on January 17, 1961:

> This conjunction of an immense military establishment and a large arms industry is new in the American experience. The total influence—economic, political, even spiritual—is felt in every city, every statehouse, every office of the federal government. We recognize the imperative need for this development. Yet we must not fail to comprehend its grave implications. Our toil, resources and livelihood are all involved; so is the very structure of our society. In the councils of government, we must guard against the acquisition of unwarranted influence, whether sought or unsought, by the military–industrial complex. The potential for the disastrous rise of misplaced power exists, and will persist.[99]

Combined with American ingenuity and seemingly endless financial resources, the Military Industrial Complex of the United States has set the standard worldwide for cutting-edge weapons technology, doling out old, outdated equipment to various fledgling nations along the way, to help them arm and protect themselves, as well as to further American interests. As violence carried on from the 1940s into the '50s, '60s, and '70s in many parts of the world, nationalism continued to spread to places like Africa and Southeast Asia: '… more than 180 million people … died from conflicts and atrocities during the twentieth century…'[100] In the wake of two devastating world wars, weapons produced by more advanced nations flowed into the hands of those reeling in the throes of civil unrest, resulting in slaughter on the widest scale.

Could the American Revolution, 'the shot heard around the world,' represent the opening of the second seal of Revelation? Does the fiery unrest of nationalism over the past two hundred years or so echo the temperament of the red horse? Do the Industrial Revolution and the Military Industrial Complex that it birthed represent the slaughter knife of the red horseman? It is an intriguing proposition. In my opinion, what Revelation says about this second apparition of the apocalypse, '… a red horse, went out; and to him who sat on it, it was granted to take peace from the earth, and that men would slay one another'[a], correlates quite well to the phenomenon of nationalism.

---

[a] Revelation 6:4

The Black Horse

If you accept my thesis up to this point, then you may have already realized that we are up to the present day on our apocalyptic timeline. The Age of Conquest is all but over, and it seems that we are currently living in the twilight years of nationalism. The desovereignization of major Western nations has already begun with the formation of international representative assemblies such as the United Nations, the World Health Organization, the World Economic Forum, etc. The '...universalism of generally accepted international norms'[101] creates the '...new and immensely powerful force of 'world opinion'.'[102] Many can see the writing on the wall for the existing nation-states of the world to become globalized[a] into a single community under the jurisdiction of a central world government. Biblically speaking, that is indeed what is prophesied to happen during the rule of the Antichrist, so I consider it the end game of the whole gathering process.

For now we have the present, which is much harder to understand than the past. As such, we will set aside our role as amateur historians and assume the mantle of neophyte prophets. In short, we are making a transition in our journey through prophecy into an epoch of time that is rather uncertain. It should be acknowledged that from this point forward, as it pertains to the future, our discussion will take a rather sobering turn. According to my thinking, the black horse may have frightening implications for the near future:

> When he broke the third seal, I heard the third living creature saying, "Come!" I looked, and behold, a black horse; and he who sat on it had a pair of scales in his hand. And I heard something like a voice in the center of the four living creatures saying, "A quart of wheat for a denarius, and three quarts of barley for a denarius; and do not damage the oil and the wine."[b]

Food sold by weight has long been understood to represent famine in Jewish society, and this is the most common association for the black horse.

---

[a] Globalization in academic circles is a hotly debated topic. It is hard to analyze history *before* it happens, and so how the present/next spirit of the age presents itself is anybody's guess. I adopt a viewpoint derived from the biblical account of history, where I reference the Towel of Babel narrative in the Old Testament as a blueprint of a world government to which mankind will return, full circle.

[b] Revelation 6: 5-6

The problem that I have with this particular interpretation is that the code word in the Bible for famine is... well, famine. It is specifically mentioned in reference to the pale horse where it says 'to kill with the sword and *famine*[a] and pestilence....'[b] My point is, if famine is expressly mentioned in the very next seal, why adopt a complex symbology for it here? If the black horse brings in famine, why not just say so? If we accept what the book of Revelation says about itself, that is, Jesus Christ Himself rendered it into signs, then we should expect the code to be consistent. In my humble opinion, this is a clue that something else is intended.

The Greek word for black that describes the color of the horse of the third seal is *melas,*[103] which means, as one might expect, 'black.'[104] The Hebrew word *shachor,*[105] which also means black,[106] is used in the Old Testament, and seems to simply refer to the color of something, in particular, hair,[c] skin,[d] and horses.[e] No significant typology readily emerges from these specific instances that reveals what the color black might symbolize. Job refers once to his skin as *shachar,*[107, f] which means 'make black'[108] or we might say 'blacken,' to describe physical affliction: slightly different word, similar concept.

From a scientific perspective, we know that the color black is not really a color, but actually the absence of color or light in the visible spectrum. This is why a very dark night appears black to human eyes. This same connection was made in biblical times, and so – as even the casual observer can see[g] – there is an association in Scripture (and other ancient sources) between the color black and darkness. The Hebrew word for darkness is *chosheck,*[109] which means 'darkness'[110] or 'obscurity.'[111] It is used in a number of places as a metaphor for distress,[h] dread, or terror,[i] mourning,[j] perplexity,[k] and confusion.[l] We can sum

---

[a] Italics mine
[b] Revelation 6:8
[c] Leviticus 13:31, Leviticus 13:37, Song of Solomon 5:11
[d] Song of Solomon 1:5
[e] Zechariah 6:2, Zechariah 6:6
[f] Shachar appears in Job 30:30
[g] Pun intended.
[h] Isaiah 5:30; Isaiah 8:22
[i] Amos 5:18-20; Zephaniah 1:15; Nahum 1:8; Ezekiel 32:8
[j] Isaiah 47:5
[k] Job 5:14; 12:25; 19:8

up this general usage as code for 'oppression' or perhaps 'affliction,' and it is a combination of these two concepts which informs my idea of what the black horse represents; the future will tell as to what extent either may be applied. *Melas* is used again in Revelation 6:12 to describe the sun as 'black as sackcloth'; surely in this case the sun could be considered afflicted and/or oppressive.[a]

The rider of the black horse is portrayed as carrying a pair of scales in his hand. The word used here is *zugos*,[112] which literally means 'a yoke.'[113] It is most often used in the context of 'a yoke;... (a Jewish idea) of a heavy burden, comparable to the heavy yokes resting on the bullocks' necks; a balance, pair of scales.'[114] The connection to a balance or a pair of scales is explained as: '*unites* two elements to work as *one unit*, like when two pans (weights) operate together on a balance-scale – or a *pair* of oxen pulling a *single* plough.'[115] A pair of scales has a mechanism that acts as a yoke, called the beam, which ties together the action of the two pans so that they work in unison. As I have stated above, the popular interpretation for the black horse is famine, and it is the *zugos* that the rider carries in his hand that tips the scales – so to speak – for most scholars. Measuring food by weight is thought to be implied as that is what typically would happen during a famine in ancient times. I disagree with this interpretation. This is not to say that scarcity, which we might think of as a precursor to famine, will not be an issue during the time of the black horse; in fact, in the rest of the passage, scarcity seems to be playing a significant role. Of course, if scarcity of food stores were to obtain worldwide, outright famine would occur in many places.

However, I maintain that if this third horseman is destined to bring famine it would be specifically called out, just as it is specifically called out as one of the four sore[b] judgments that the fourth horse brings, which we will get to momentarily. Also, if there were a worldwide famine, I would expect there to be some mention in the third seal of some significant percentage of the

---

[1] Psalm 35:6

[a] Revelation 6:12 speaks directly to the biblical association between the color black and darkness. In Joel 3:15 we find a similar end times description of a darkened sun and moon, which associates the concept of darkness with the color black. Also see I Kings 18:45 for similar usage of the Hebrew word for darkness, which the NASB interprets as 'black' clouds.

[b] severe

population of the earth dying or affected, such as we see in the fourth seal; you might figure that perhaps a tenth of all people might die in such a widespread famine. Instead, the Scripture is silent on this point.

    If we focus on the more common usage of *zugos*, as a yoke or a burden, 'such as is put on draught-cattle,'[116] I think that this makes more sense in the larger context. This yoke is 'metaphorically, used of any burden or bondage: [such] as that of slavery,'[117] and so would mesh better with the overall theme that we are building, which is affliction or oppression. We see in Matthew 11:30, where Jesus says, 'My yoke is easy and My burden is light,' the same Greek word *zugos* is used to refer to serving Christ; that is, accepting Christ as your Master is easy or pleasant, compared to accepting the world or sin as your master which is the implied opposite, or harsh. At the end of the day, Jesus does have a yoke: we are described as His bondservants or slaves. Not our will, but His be done.

    It is interesting that the voice that is heard in heaven is quoting prices for wheat and barley, such as might be heard in a market somewhere on Earth. The price is a *denarius*,[118] which was 'a small Roman silver coin, weighing in Nero's time, 53 grams. Its value and purchasing power varied from time to time.'[119] During biblical times the denarius 'was equivalent to a day's wages.'[120] The word translated as 'quart' in the passage above is *choenix*,[121] which is 'a dry measure, almost equal to a quart.'[122] The note on Revelation 6:6 in the New American Standard Bible says: 'One quart of wheat would be enough for only one person. Three quarts of the less nutritious barley would be barely enough for a small family. Famine had inflated prices to at least ten times their normal level.' Again, the assumption is famine, but food shortages are not the only conditions that lead to runaway inflation. A steep devaluation of fiat currency over a relatively short period of time can have the same effect, such as we have only seen in a handful of hyperinflation events in modern history. In fact, I think the mimicry of an earthly market speaks to economic conditions as the cause of the inflation, not the result. Again, if we apply our rule of consistency, that is, we expect the 'code' of Revelation to be consistent with itself, that would mean that if the word famine is used in one place to mean famine, then it should be used everywhere the conditions of famine are to be expected; where it is *not* used then gives us a clue that something else is meant.

Hyperinflation, which is described as 'cases in which monthly inflation has reached in at least one month 50 percent or more,'[123] is a strictly modern phenomenon. 'All hyperinflations in history have occurred during the 20th century, that is in the presence of discretionary paper money regimes, with the exception of the hyperinflation during the French Revolution, when the French monetary regime, too, was based on a paper money standard.'[124] In fact, '…no hyperinflation has ever occurred without a huge budget deficit financed by money creation…,'[125] something you can do to a limited extent with gold or silver by reducing precious metal content in your coins, but which can be done to the extreme with paper money. 'In [a paper] monetary regime no 'natural' limit for the expansion of the money supply like a scarcity of monetary gold or silver exists.'[126]

If we accept the above definition for hyperinflation, that is, the price of goods growing as much as half again each month, or by a factor of 1.5, it would only take six months for prices to rise to over 10 times their original value, and thus bring about the conditions spoken of in the third seal. Throughout history, there have been 56 episodes of hyperinflation,[127] and each one has been currency-specific.[128] This goes without saying, as inflation always involves a currency that is being devalued by definition, but the point that I am making is that hyperinflation events have always been contained within specific regions of the world, with effects to other economies being relatively limited. The hyperinflation that the black horse brings will be worldwide, something we've never seen before.

> Inflation is always a monetary phenomenon, quite in contrast to a one-time rise in the price level because of bad harvests in former times or an increase in the price of oil by the Organization of Oil Exporting Countries (OPEC) since the 1970s.[129]

Inflation brought about by scarcity is recoverable; when the supply shock is alleviated (as after a famine when food becomes widely available again, or when the availability of a widely-used commodity like oil reverts back to normal levels), deflation sets in, and prices normalize. However, inflation brought about by currency devaluation of paper money is much more devastating. Those who hold all their savings in paper are rendered destitute in a matter of months, while the wage earners are able to scrape by, but only as much as wages keep up with inflation. I think that the oppression brought about by the black horse is inflationary in nature, rather than a famine, which would be transitory. Episodes of very high inflation can turn into a powerful form of economic oppression through impoverishment.

> Unemployed men took one or two rusacks [during the Austrian hyperinflation] and went from peasant to peasant. They even took the train to favorable locations to get foodstuffs illegally which they sold soon afterwards in the town at three or fourfold the price they had paid themselves. First the peasants were happy about the great amount of paper money which rained into their houses for their eggs and butter.... However, when they came to town with their full briefcases to buy goods, they discovered to their chagrin that, whereas they had only asked for fivefold price for their produce, the prices for scythe, hammer and cauldron, which they had wanted to buy, had risen by a factor of 50.[130]

The sharp devaluation of fiat currency eventually renders paper money useless and markets resort to bartering.

> From this time they [the Austrian peasants] tried to get only industrial products and asked for real goods for their own produce. Goods for goods; after humans had already... returned with the trenches [during World War I] to the times of cave-dwelling, they now abolished the thousands of years old convention of money and returned to primitive exchange by barter. A grotesque exchange began throughout the country. The people from the cities carried out to the peasants everything they could spare: Chinese vases and carpets, sabres and shotguns, photographic equipment and books, lamps and decorations.[131]

Worldwide hyperinflation in the modern era would be particularly debilitating, as resorting to a barter system only works if you have something to trade that other people actually need. A sharp revaluation of goods and services ensues between that which is necessary and that which is not. Luxury items become superfluous; people will always need foodstuffs. Therefore, during hyperinflation, if you have food, you have money – especially if a quart of wheat is worth a day's wages! In the early 1920s, inflation in the Weimar Republic was just as bad in many respects.

> There were stories of shoppers who found that thieves had stolen the baskets and suitcases in which they carried their money, leaving the money itself on the ground; and of life supported by selling every day or so a single tiny link from a long gold crucifix chain. There were stories (many of them, as the summer wore on and as exchange rates altered several times a day) of restaurant meals which

cost more when the bills came than when they were ordered. A 5,000 mark cup of coffee would cost 8,000 marks by the time it was drunk.[132]

Granted, some of these stories invoke hyperbole, but they capture the spirit of a time that was very difficult to navigate; when people had to live day by day, and meal to meal. The great irony here is that hyperinflation caused such extreme supply disruptions that famine plagued Germany in spite of an abundance of food.

> The fact was that although the farmers' barns all over the country were bursting with unsold food, Germany was suffering from widespread famine. Every Zurich provision shop has a placard saying: 'Send food parcels to your friends in Germany.' As ever, and worse than ever, the conditions and prospects of the middle and professional classes were fearsome. Only two remedies seemed possible, the one preposterous, the other elusive to the point of absence: food from abroad, or a stable medium which would persuade Germany's farmers to release food in exchange for paper.[133]

The farmers had food in great excess, but were unwilling to part with it for worthless paper! Play that forward to the current generation: the vast majority of the population depends on large corporations for their produce; the 'peasants' of the twenty-first century have no farming skills. Hyperinflation today would quickly turn into a form of economic slavery for the masses.

The Global Economy

World economics is best understood in the context of history. From about 1875 to World War I, most trading countries operated on a gold standard.

> ...the currencies of all the major countries in the world were fixed at a certain price to a certain quantity of gold. This thereby resulted in fixed exchange rates between the currencies of those countries. Gold coins circulated in daily use as the medium of exchange. Commercial banks accepted gold as deposits which they, in turn, re-lent. Those banks were able to create credit by lending out more than the original amount of gold deposited; however, they were compelled always to maintain sufficient gold reserves on hand in order to meet the demand of their depositors for withdrawals. Banks dared not lend out too great a multiple of their reserves for fear of insolvency should they be unable to repay deposits on demand.[134]

When banks lend, they create money. If you borrow $20,000 from the bank to buy a car, that action increases the amount of money in the economy by as much again: There is the $20,000 in cash that you got from the bank that you give to the car dealer, and there is also a $20,000 IOU that the bank writes to its depositors until you pay the money back, which is what we call credit. The money created in the banking system through lending dwarfs what the Federal Reserve contributes, because base money[a] gets lent out multiple times. That is, the car dealer takes the $20,000 that you paid him and deposits that money in his banking account, upwards of 90% of which *his* bank then subsequently lends out, depending on how much they are required to hold in reserve. This cycle gets repeated over and over again, as people borrow money which gets re-deposited into other banks, and then re-lent to others who hold that money in deposits at still other banks. 'Since bank deposits are considered to be a kind of money, by extending credit, the banking system can create an amount of money that is a multiple of the initial deposit.'[135] This multiple can be calculated by dividing the number 1 by the reserve ratio.[136] 'If the required reserve ratio is 10%, ... the banking system can create an amount of money 10 times the size of the initial deposit.'[137, b] Because most people wish to keep their money in the bank, it is able to lend out more money than it has in deposits, and as long as

---

[a] Base money is the money that a central bank creates.
[b] This is not a straightforward calculation, as not all banks have the same reserve ratio.

everyone doesn't withdraw all of their funds at the same time, this model works. (Just don't think about that too much.)

On the gold standard, the amount of gold that a bank had in its reserves limited the amount of money it could lend. Gold reserves acted as a sort of natural governor to bank lending, and thus limited the overall money supply. This same standard also acted as a check on a macro scale to regulate trade surpluses and deficits between nations.

> The gold standard prevented imbalances in countries' trade accounts through a process that acted as an automatic adjustment mechanism. A country experiencing trade surpluses would accumulate more gold, since gold receipts from exports would exceed gold payments for imports. The banking system of the surplus country would create more credit, as more gold was deposited into that country's commercial banks. Expanding credit would fuel an economic boom, which in turn, would provoke inflation. Rising prices would reduce that country's trade competitiveness, exports would decline and imports rise, and gold would begin to flow back out again. Conversely, countries with trade deficits would experience an outflow of gold. As gold left the banking system, credit would contract. Credit contraction would cause a recession, and prices would adjust downward. Falling prices would enhance the trade competitiveness of the deficit country and gold would begin to flow back in, until eventually, equilibrium on the balance of trade would be re-established.[138]

Because gold was a physical commodity of limited supply and had to be traded back and forth as payment for goods, the amount of money in the economy was always limited to some multiple of the amount of gold that was available. When gold reserves increased, credit increased, and when gold reserves fell, credit fell. Countries went through economic booms and busts periodically as a part of the natural business cycle of settling payments in gold. The gold standard was not a magical, trouble-free system, but at least it kept the excesses of government spending in check. World War I and World War II disrupted this economic balance between nations.

> As it did in World War I, the U.S. entered World War II well after combat began. Before it entered the war, the United States served as the Allies' main supplier of weapons and other goods. Most countries paid in gold making the U.S. the owner of the majority of the world's gold by the end of the war. This made a return to the gold standard impossible by the countries that depleted their reserves.[139]

The war in Europe exacted a heavy toll: many countries found themselves frightfully short on manpower, their infrastructure destroyed, and in addition, they had spent their gold to maintain their armies. So before the war was over, with some participants standing on the brink of economic collapse, 44 delegates from the allied countries met in Bretton Woods, New Hampshire, in 1944 to take a first step in departing from the gold standard. 'The delegation decided that the world's currencies would no longer be linked to gold but could be pegged to the US [dollar]. That's because the greenback was, itself, linked to gold.'[140] 'The arrangement came to be known as the Bretton Woods Agreement. It established the authority of central banks, which would maintain fixed exchange rates between their currencies and the dollar. In turn, the United States would redeem US dollars for gold on demand.'[141]

Bretton Woods birthed a novel international monetary system.

> The 730 delegates at Bretton Woods agreed to establish two new institutions. The International Monetary Fund (IMF) would monitor exchange rates and lend reserve currencies to nations with balance-of-payments deficits. The International Bank for Reconstruction and Development, now known as the World Bank Group, was responsible for providing financial assistance for the reconstruction after World War II and the economic development of less developed countries.[142]

Both the IMF and the World Bank Group are located in Washington, D.C., which was perhaps symbolic of a new era of dollar hegemony. The new monetary system forged by the Bretton Woods Agreement would end up linking together all of the world's economies by pegging other fiat currencies to the US dollar.

> The dollar's rise to global hegemony started early in the 20th century and was formalized at Bretton Woods, the conference that established the postwar monetary order in 1944. Over the following 25 years, the dollar came to dominate global finance, trade, and banking, and nearly all foreign currency reserves were held in dollars.[143]

Redemption of dollars for gold lasted less than 30 years. In just a few decades, the US printed far more dollars than it had gold to convert, and government spending ballooned in the 1960s because of the space race and the Vietnam War, among other things. Nations holding US dollars took notice.

When US gold reserves began to dwindle during the 1960s, the governments of other countries became concerned that the United States would soon not have enough gold left to allow them to convert the dollars they had accumulated into US gold. The more these concerns grew, the faster those countries converted their dollars into gold.[144]

The situation finally came to a head during the third year of Richard Nixon's first term as president.

On August 15, 1971, President Nixon unilaterally declared the United States would no longer abide by its commitment to allow other governments to convert dollars into gold. By that time, the US simply did not have enough gold left to allow dollar convertibility to continue.

Nixon's announcement was the death knell of the Bretton Woods system. The regime in which all currencies were directly or indirectly pegged at a fixed exchange rate to gold disintegrated. Fixed exchange rates gave way to a new system of floating exchange rates. Soon thereafter international trade ceased to balance and cross-border capital flows ballooned. Credit growth exploded. This Money Revolution fundamentally changed the nature of the global economic system that had emerged under the gold standard. A new era, financed merely with fiat money, got underway. This new monetary regime quickly transformed the global economy.[145]

This new monetary regime is sometimes referred to as Bretton Woods II,[146] in part because dollar hegemony survived it.

The US dollar continues to underpin the world economy and is the key currency for medium of international exchange, unit of account (e.g., pricing of oil), and unit of storage (e.g., treasury bills and bonds) and, despite arguments to the contrary, is not in a state of hegemonic decline.[147]

We are living in a new era of global economic transformation where, for the first time in history, countries all over the world buy and sell goods not with precious metals/materials, or certificates or currencies backed by the same, but with fiat currency, which is essentially just paper. This fiat money does not have intrinsic value nor does it have use value; it is just declared by the government to be worth something. 'When the Fed stopped backing dollars with gold certificates in 1968,[a] dollars ceased to be money (as money had been defined in the past) and became simply another credit instrument issued by the

---

[a] Public Law 90-269, which was put into effect on March 19, 1968, freed the Fed from its obligation to hold gold certificates to back the money it created. [Duncan (2022) p.110]

government, a kind of non-interest-bearing small denomination government bond.'[148] In the modern computer age, central banks don't even exchange paper; accounting is done in a digital ledger system.

'The evidence is clear, after money ceased to be backed by gold, credit broke free of the bindings that had constrained its expansion until the 1970s. Afterwards, credit grew so markedly that it became the most important driver of economic growth by directly financing more consumption and investment, while at the same time pushing up asset prices and creating unprecedented amounts of wealth that allowed the American public to spend freely.'[149] In other words, it created the biggest credit bubble the world has ever seen. 'It is important to understand that credit creation, not savings, financed the surge in lending and borrowing that has driven economic growth since the early 1970s'[150]; that is to say, when credit creation began to greatly exceed bank reserves.

'Total credit is equal to total debt.'[151] '... for every dollar of credit extended there is a dollar borrowed.'[152] It has been said that the United States is the Saudi Arabia of money; it would be more accurate to say that the United States is the Saudi Arabia of debt. Unhinging the world economy from the natural limitations of directly-exchanged physical assets has led to excessive imbalances in 'cross-border capital flows'.[a] The gigantic trade deficit that the US runs with the rest of the world would have been impossible on a gold standard; as noted above, we ran out of gold 50 years ago. Being the holder of the reserve currency allows the US to export its debt to the rest of the world to an extent that is unprecedented. How does this work? Well, let me tell you a little something about 'American Exceptionalism.'

When the US buys goods from Europe, for instance, the balance of payments is settled in dollars. The companies that receive these dollars can't use them in Europe, so they sell them to the European Central Bank in exchange for euros. The bank 'prints' the euros with which to buy the dollars, which has the effect of expanding the credit system in Europe.[b] Then the European Central Bank, in order to earn a positive rate of return, invests the dollars it bought from its constituents into US dollar-denominated assets –

---

[a] i.e. trade

[b] This is because those companies then deposit their newly minted euros into the bank. This increases the bank reserve notes that can be extended as credit.

largely US treasuries. And what are US treasuries? US government debt. US government debt expands the US economy; however, debt must always be increasing in order to have this effect, due to the interest that is owed on previous debt. As more debt is serviced in the US, this in turn increases the money available to flow to Europe to buy more goods. As more dollars are used to pay for European exports, the European Central Bank has to 'print' more euros with which to buy those dollars, and thus has more dollars with which to buy US government debt. The end result is that the gargantuan trade deficit that the US runs with the rest of the world acts as a key source of foreign financing which the US government then uses to service more debt.

It is important to note that the money that returns from abroad in this way does not increase the money supply; other countries simply return to us the dollars we gave to them in the first place. Hence, though this process resembles something of a global ponzi scheme, it is not generally inflationary. When the Federal Reserve creates money out of pixie dust in order to service the interest on the debt, that *is* inflationary, especially as said base money filters into the banking system and then banks multiply it many times over through lending. 'Today, credit creation and consumption have replaced savings and investment as the dynamic that makes the economy grow.'[153] Our economic system is driven by credit growth.[154] In a way, we are caught in a credit trap; we are so far over our skis that in order for the government to pay its past debt plus interest, it has to keep printing money and taking on increasing amounts of new debt.

If government debt doesn't continue to grow, the economy doesn't grow; and if the economy contracts, deflation will take hold. The Federal Reserve fears deflation much more than it does inflation. Deflation makes servicing our oversized debt much more expensive; it decreases the money supply, which makes both dollars and credit much harder to obtain. To understand deflation, consider the example above where you had borrowed $20,000 from the bank to buy a car. As we said before, the bank gives you the money to pay the car dealer and *also* writes an IOU to its depositors for the $20,000 until you pay it back. If you total your car, have no insurance, and then flee to Mexico to avoid your obligations, the bank is now on the hook to pay back that IOU for 20 grand. As far as the bank is concerned, $20,000 has just vanished into thin air; what was initially considered an asset has become a liability in the blink of an eye.

This is what makes deflation a much scarier scenario than inflation, as usually during periods of economic contraction people start defaulting on their debt, which causes money to vaporize from the system. Debt unwinds very quickly and in a chaotic and uncontrolled manner; banks and financial institutions can fold over a weekend. Lightning-fast, scorched-earth consequences make deflation terrifying to central banks, so they avoid it at all costs. The higher the debt, the greater the danger of default. Our economy has become dependent on credit to such an extent that in order to avoid deflation: 'The government is going to have to continue to borrow and spend to make total credit grow and to make the economy expand.'[155]

'Globalization, in its modern form, got underway in the early 1980s when the United States began running very large trade deficits.'[156] Before long, the United States began financing its extraordinarily large trade deficits by borrowing money from abroad, primarily money created by foreign central banks.'[157] This is the period when deep-rooted inflation should have taken hold because of the increases in the money supply. A big reason that this did not happen in the 1980s was the phenomenon of offshoring, where 'the US began buying more and more goods from low-wage countries that drove down wages and prices in the United States.'[158] This provided a powerful deflationary ballast that worked to offset the increases in the money supply.[a] 'After the US began running large trade deficits, US capacity constraints no longer mattered – only global capacity constraints mattered.'[159] That is, local demand was supplied by global capacity. This trend of globalization continued throughout the 1990s, buying the US time against the inflationary pressures of large increases in the money supply.

In the mid to late 1990s, foreign capital flows created by the US current account deficit began to supercharge credit creation as foreign central banks diversified their investments in US dollar-denominated assets.[160] '… the rest of the world took its current account surplus and bought increasing amounts of US stocks, corporate bonds, and agency debt [such as Fannie Mae and Freddie Mac]… '[161] These inflows were not only a significant contributor to the dot-com bubble of the early 2000s, but they continued to inflate the US economy into the Great Financial Crisis (GFC) of 2008-2009. The Federal Reserve's

---

[a] There are often simultaneously inflationary and deflationary trends that originate from different sectors of a very complex world economy.

response to the GFC was to crank up the printing presses and flood the market with dollars. 'During its near century of existence up to mid-2008, the Fed had created less than $1 trillion altogether. In the second half of 2008 alone, it created $1.3 trillion more.'[162] This historic infusion of money was not enough.

> ... the Fed extended $3.4 trillion of Federal Reserve credit between the end of 2007 and the end of 2014. Consequently, the monetary base of the United States leapt by 370% in only seven years.[163] Conventional wisdom suggests that such an extraordinary surge in the money supply over such a short period of time should have resulted in very high rates of inflation. It did not.[164]

The massive amount of money printing that occurred in response to the GFC should have led to hyperinflation, in line with Milton Friedman's monetary theory, which states that 'inflation is always and everywhere a monetary phenomenon.'[165] This implies a direct relationship between the amount of money in the system and inflation. That is, if the amount of money goes up by 370% over a short period of time, inflation should follow suit. Officially, it did not, which has led some economists to propose that Friedman's axiom no longer applies in the modern monetary regime of credit-fueled growth. 'The monetary base grew by a mind-boggling 109% in 2009 and then by a further 34% in 2011 and by 39% more in 2013. And yet the peak rate of inflation following the financial crisis was 3.9%.'[166]

While this is technically true, government figures of inflation have significantly lowballed the actual cost of goods for years.[167, 168] More recently, certain estimates place inflation rates following the 2020 pandemic as high as 16% in 2022 as opposed to the 9% that was officially reported.[169] One reason for this is because the government has moved to a cost-of-living calculation as opposed to a cost-of-goods calculation.[170] This is due in part to something called a chain-weighted Consumer Price Index (CPI). Chain-weighted CPI purportedly accounts for 'changes in consumer preference and product substitutions due to changes in relative prices of goods made by consumers.'[171] What this means is if you have been buying prime rib for the past few years and you decide to switch to hot dogs because prices have increased so much that you can no longer afford better, and you spend the same amount of money on hot dogs as you used to spend on prime rib, as far as the government is concerned, your living expenses haven't gone up because you are still choosing to spend the same amount of money on meat. The substitution of hot dogs for prime rib is viewed simply as 'consumer preference.' I will leave it up to the reader to decide if this calculation actually has anything to do with the cost of goods or not, but it gives Washington an excuse to keep cost-of-living increases for programs like Social Security lower for longer, as well as to report a lower rate of inflation to the world, as CPI[a] figures into both of these.

Even so, we haven't had hyperinflation. If Milton Friedman's monetary philosophy still applied, all of that money had to go somewhere. Somehow, much of the money that was printed in response to the GFC did not make it into the economy. I'm no economist, but if I had to guess as to what happened, it probably had something to do with how big of a hole the failure of large financial institutions created in the money supply. Remember, as we discussed earlier, when debt unwinds, it has the effect of vaporizing money (credit). I would speculate that if the GFC was actually worse than admitted, then much of the money that was printed would have gone to the shoring up of financial institutions simply to replace money that no longer existed. In other words, the reason that much of that money didn't spill over into the economy is because, behind the scenes, bankers were frantically using it to fill in the gigantic sinkhole created by the GFC.

In contrast, much of the money printing in response to the pandemic of 2020 went straight to the public in the form of financial stimulus. This funneled money directly into the economy, resulting in an official year-over-year CPI rise of 9% in June of 2022, in spite of all the cheats and tricks that the government uses to understate that metric. So yes, Milton Friedman is still correct: inflation is always and everywhere a monetary phenomenon.

Money creation with no limits, possible only with fiat currency not pegged to gold or anything of intrinsic value, always has consequences. The upside is that the government will never run out of paper with which to pay its soaring debt. The downside is that, as it pays back that debt by printing more and more, the dollars with which that debt is repaid become worth less and less. The little guys, like you and me, get carried along for the ride whether we like it or not. As dollars get doled out, the lower class gets those dollars last, long after they have already lost most of their value. In this way, the middle class is impoverished while the upper class becomes uber-elite: 'Don't damage the oil and the wine!'

---

[a] Percentage change in CPI over time is the inflation rate.

The dollar underpins everything: there is no other fiat currency on the face of the earth that has the clout to replace the dollar.

> 'The international monetary system that evolved after the breakdown of the Bretton Woods system in the early 1970s is badly flawed. It lacks a mechanism to prevent persistent trade imbalances. That has made it possible for the United States to incur enormous current account deficits[a] totaling a cumulative US$3 trillion since 1980 [circa 2005]. Those deficits have acted as an economic subsidy to the rest of the world, but they have also flooded the world with dollars, which have replaced gold as the new reserve asset.'[172] 'When that deficit corrects, as it inevitably must, the global economy will suffer an extraordinary shock.'[173] [b]

The US current account deficit (trade deficit) has been piling up higher and higher for the past 50 years. The system almost broke when the Great Financial Crisis hit, but the world's central banks responded by quickly printing astronomical amounts of money. When the next shock comes, and we probably have room for one more big one like the GFC, the central banks of the world will turn on the printing presses again and prove once and for all that there is no limit to how much money they can print. The amount of money needed for the next bailout of the financial system will probably run into the tens of trillions of dollars in light of the current leverage in the global system. It is in the wake of the next global monetary crisis, whenever that happens, that I expect to see hyperinflation take off worldwide. During this time we will see the dollar precipitously lose value, and perhaps, the first $1,000 cup of coffee! The illness is bad enough, but it is the cure that will kill you.

The point of this discussion is not to make economics experts out of us, but to underscore two points. First, that worldwide hyperinflation would have been impossible before the emergence of the global fiat system of the twentieth century, unhinged as it is from any hard asset like gold. We are living in a time when not only is global hyperinflation plausible given the current economic landscape, but some would go so far as to say it is inevitable. Written some 2000 years ago, it is strange to think that the book of Revelation might actually

---

[a] Current Account deficit is how trade deficits are measured.

[b] It should be noted that, although I am quoting heavily from Richard Duncan's work, *The Money Revolution*, our viewpoints concerning the future differ. Because of the low reported inflation rates during recent periods of Quantitative Easing, he sees inflation as disconnected from the money supply, and therefore the future is bright because there are no traditional limits on the creation of money. I maintain that inflation is still a monetary phenomenon, as asserted by Milton Freedman.

be predicting such a thing. The second reason for this discourse on economics is to continue building perspective on a process of globalization that started with the European Age of Conquest over 500 years ago, then subsequently grew into the worldwide consciousness of nationalism, and finally matured into a global trade system where the fate of all economies on the earth are intricately tied together.

As if all of this were not enough, the new economic world order ushered in by Bretton Woods created a fertile environment for the rise of transnational Non-Governmental Organizations such as the World Economic Forum (WEF), founded in 1971 as a nonprofit organization. Since then, the WEF has grown into a global cabal composed of the most influential leaders from around the world, mainly from finance, business, and government. Perhaps a critic might refer to them as 'elitist.' The mission statement of this group includes something called the Great Reset.

> In June 2020, Klaus Schwab, who founded the World Economic Forum (WEF) in 1971 and is currently its CEO, described the three core components of the Great Reset. The first includes creating conditions for a "stakeholder economy;" improving policies and agreements on taxes, regulations, fiscal policies and trade to result in "fairer outcomes." The second component addresses how the large-scale pandemic spending programs with private investments and pension funds could improve on the old system by building one that is more "resilient, equitable and sustainable" over the long term by "building green urban infrastructure and creating incentives for industries to improve their track record on environmental, social and governance (ESG) metrics." The third component of a Great Reset agenda is to "harness the innovations of the Fourth Industrial Revolution" for the public good.[174]

This all sounds fine and dandy until you start asking questions. Who are the 'stakeholders,' and how do they get chosen? Are they elected or privately appointed? This seems to be a rather important inquiry, as these stakeholders hold considerable sway over the rest of the world. Who determines what constitutes a 'fair outcome'? Why, the stakeholders, of course. Who determines what metrics are to be met on environmental, social, and governance issues? You guessed it: the stakeholders. And finally, who can be called upon to determine for the rest of us how technology can best be used 'for the public good'? Again, the stakeholders. This puts all the power in the hands of a very few people who, especially if they aren't elected, would seem to be accountable to no one.

> According to the Transnational Institute (TNI), the WEF is planning to replace a recognised democratic model with a model where a self-selected group of "stakeholders" make decisions on behalf of the people. The think tank summarises that we are increasingly entering a world where gatherings such as Davos[a] are "a silent global coup d'état" to capture governance.[175]

> According to the European Parliament's think tank, critics see the WEF as an instrument for political and business leaders to "take decisions without having to account to their electorate or shareholders."[176]

Critics perceive the goals of the WEF as a ruthless power grab through economic domination. The WEF labels naysayers as conspiracy theorists. I would say we should always be suspicious of people who want to corral authority for themselves, especially when their plan puts the rest of us in such a disadvantaged position.

So then: does Bretton Woods, when all the world's economies became inextricably bound together into a single, economic framework, represent the opening of the third seal of Revelation? Perhaps. Honestly, it is too early to tell. We have the International Monetary Fund and the World Bank Group as a legacy of this landmark agreement, though they are yet to manifest overtly as instruments of oppression. Also, we have the World Economic Forum sprouting up from the same fertile soil, so to speak. As my thesis is that the rider of the black horse represents economic slavery, you can almost hear his approaching hoofbeats in WEF rhetoric. Perhaps he has already begun his first patrol; time will tell if this is true or not. The wheels of history turn slowly, so for now we watch and wait, eyes wide open.

As bad as it sounds, the third seal does not put an end to the birth pangs of judgment; there is one more rider scheduled to make the rounds before that fateful final week begins.

---

[a] The WEF holds annual meetings in Davos, Switzerland.

The Pale Horse

> When the Lamb broke the fourth seal, I heard the voice of the fourth living creature saying "Come!" I looked, and behold, an ashen[a] horse; and he who sat upon it had the name Death; and Hades was following him. Authority was given to them over a fourth of the earth, to kill with sword and with famine and with pestilence and by the wild beasts of the earth.[b]

I must admit that upon first inspection of this fourth and final rider, I looked at the war and suffering and death of the preceding horseman and came to the premature conclusion that he would be destined to conduct his patrol concurrently with his comrades. However, as I have taken the time to give Death his due, so to speak, I am persuaded that this fourth apocalyptic rider constitutes a fourth and separate judgment from the other three. In fact, not only does he represent a distinctly separate judgment, but the fourth horseman also is far worse than the first three as he effectively represents four judgments in one. (This next section is rather sobering in light of the possibility that these events may be appearing on the horizon in the near future.)

It is a bit of a curiosity that the pale horseman seems to be largely overlooked in eschatological literature; that is, he is listed as *one* of the four, as opposed to – perhaps as he should be – the *worst* of the four. His name is Death, so right off the bat that sounds ominous. What is more ominous is that a personification of Hades follows or attends him. Hades, or Sheol as it is referred to in Jewish culture, is the abode of the dead. Death and Hades are given authority over a fourth of the earth. The Greek word for authority in this passage is *exousia*,[177] which refers to 'authority, *conferred* power; *delegated empowerment* ("authorization"), operating in a *designated jurisdiction*.'[178] The jurisdiction in which Death is given to operate is a fourth of the earth, *ge*,[179] which typically indicates arable or dry land.[180, c] He is given four tools with which to kill: sword, famine, pestilence, and wild beasts.[d] Hades is in

---

[a] Lit. sickly, pale
[b] Revelation 6:7-8
[c] Matthew 13:5, 8, 23; Mark 4:8, 20, 26, 28, 31; Luke 13:7; Luke 14:35 (34); John 12:24; Hebrews 6:7

attendance, giving the impression that the land of the living has been usurped by that of the dead; this might indicate that the dead outnumber the living. If such were the case, we can imagine that corpses would be left to rot where they lie, as there would not be enough manpower, nor enough space, to bury them all.

The word that describes the color of the horse is *chloros*,[181] which means 'green' or 'pale green'.[182] It appears that this word can be used in reference to 'green grass,'[183] or more generally can mean pale green and take on a meaning more like the English word 'pallid.'[184] Given the master who rides him, 'pale green' or 'pallid' is more apropos, and as such, might indicate flesh in a sickly state, or perhaps more directly, pale or dead flesh. This would give us the uniquely atrocious case of the rider and his steed as literally being presented as Death on death.

The sword with which he kills is a *rhomphaia*,[185] which is 'a long Thracian sword... 'a *large*, broad sword' that both *cuts and pierces* – an *imposing* sword, synonymous with *finality (dominance)*.'[186] Also: 'A large sword; properly, a long Thracian javelin,'[187] which means this term could also apply to something thrown through the air to strike from a distance. It figuratively refers to 'war' or 'piercing grief.'[188] Given that our antagonist is Death, it seems reasonable that both meanings might apply. It is important to note that this sword is different from the slaughter knife that was given to the red horseman; the use of a *rhomphaia* signifies finality. Famine and pestilence usually follow the devastation of war, so in this instance we might presume that these take a historically tragic toll. The mention of predatory wild beasts speaks to the total collapse of civic order, which would leave survivors weak and exposed.

We have seen these conditions mentioned before in the four sore/severe judgments of Ezekiel.

> For thus says the Lord God, "How much more when I send My four severe judgments against Jerusalem: sword, famine, wild beasts and plague to cut off man and beast from it"[a]

---

[d] Since the killing of men is implied here, it is reasonable to assume a quarter of the livable space on the earth, or a quarter of all dry land.

[a] Ezekiel 14:21

These severe judgments of God seem to typically be reserved for a country[a] or a city (Jerusalem); that is, they are levied against a specific region. Taking all of this into consideration, this passage seems to foretell of a war so destructive that it marks the end of civilization as we know it for a quarter of the earth. As countries and cities are geographically defined regions (i.e., they can be measured in square miles), I make the assumption that this fraction refers to a percentage of dry land, as opposed to population or total surface area of the earth.

If we make the assumption that the presence of Hades means that the dead will outnumber the living, this would indicate a greater than 50 percent casualty rate, *including* civilians. There has never been a war in history where the devastation was so complete as to consume half of all people from each of the combatant states. Killing people in large numbers actually presents a difficult logistical problem. The Nazis found this out in World War II. They first tried executing Jewish prisoners by gunning them down. The sheer quantity of bullets needed to murder tens of thousands turned out to be too expensive and actually took resources – men and ammunition – away from the war effort. They invented the gas chambers out of necessity; the exhaust from a captured T-34 tank proved to be cheaper and more efficient than the firing squads. These process improvements enabled them to exterminate millions. The fact of the matter is it took meticulous planning and innovation to carry out Hitler's hellish final solution. In modern times, it doesn't matter which quarter of the earth gets hit with these four severe judgments, the result could be hundreds of millions if not billions dead. This puts potential loss of life at two to three orders of magnitude greater than the Holocaust. If we did not live in an atomic age, where mankind possesses weapons of mass destruction capable of annihilating entire cities, the very prospect of these judgments would seem far-fetched. Instead, the very thought of it is chilling.[b]

The future is impossible to predict. This final apocalyptic rider may not conduct his patrol for a hundred years or more, in which case the geopolitical climate may be so entirely different as to make the particulars impossible to

---

[a] Ezekiel 14:12-20

[b] Actually, famine and pestilence have killed many more people throughout history than war, so there are other possible scenarios. However, in the case of nuclear war, radioactive fallout could be considered a form of pestilence, and would kill far more people than the initial blast.

imagine. However, if we see him in our lifetime, especially within the next twenty or thirty years, I think I can provide an educated guess as to where he might ride. Asia, excluding the Middle East, comprises approximately 25% of the earth's dry land. (We should keep in mind that God probably doesn't pay much attention to how mankind divides the land.) If we consider how China, a nuclear power, has been enriched and technologically empowered by foolish Western business tycoons, and how the Chinese Communist Party seems ready – almost eager – to use that relatively newfound power to subdue Taiwan, then perhaps we have a recipe for disaster.

    I suspect that, much like Hitler in the 1930s, China will not be satisfied with just a single acquisition. If they are successful in Taiwan, they might then turn their eyes southward to India – another nuclear power – with a mind toward settling the world's longest border dispute. If China and India engage in a conventional war, neighboring Pakistan – another nuclear power – is likely to get dragged into the conflict, though at this point the fighting might resemble a free-for-all, as Pakistan and India harbor intense animosity toward each other. In fact, China, India, and Pakistan each have disputed borders with the other two in the regions of Jammu and Kashmir. I don't expect North Korea – yet another nuclear power – to sit idly by and leave all the warmongering to the Chinese. An incursion into South Korea would draw in the United States – yet another nuclear power – and Japan. Russia – yet a sixth nuclear power – has vested interests in the region in the form of territory and natural resources that it would feel compelled to protect against potential threats. Six of the eight countries in the world that are known to possess nuclear arms could be drawn into a continent-wide conflict; given that five of them are historically bad actors and the United States has already used nuclear weapons in an act of war, it may be only a matter of time before somebody starts lobbing 'tactical nukes.'

    Another possible scenario that could play out is that after the worldwide hyperinflation the black horse brings, fiat currency becomes greatly devalued, if not obsolete, and the world economy enters an unprecedented commodity super cycle. This kind of commodity boom would fuel the exploration for and acquisition of metals like lithium, cobalt, nickel, copper, and other rare earth minerals. The mountainous regions of Jammu and Kashmir have high potential for deposits of all of these. Given the lack of border stability between global powers there, this could be a recipe for disaster.

Numerous border areas fall within rivers or on top of glaciers, meaning the physical geography actually changes year to year. This presents all three countries with opportunities to change the state-of-play by moving troops and development into border areas. In the past, these battles have led to war. Jammu and Kashmir has been called the "most militarized region in the world" and the likely site of a future state-to-state conflict.[189]

The bottom line is, if China decides to flex its military might in the region for whatever reason, it will upset the balance of power in all of Asia and actively engage four other nuclear powers. It is also likely to involve the United States on some level. Asia is home to some four billion people, roughly half of the world's population. Even a very limited nuclear exchange between China and India could result in tens of millions of civilian casualties, death, and destruction so extensive it is hard to imagine. Sheol, the abode of the dead, might be an apt description for such a horror-scape.[a]

Given the possibility that Scripture may be prophesying a catastrophe of this magnitude, we might ask ourselves what we can do to possibly avert it. Ezekiel seems to be speaking down through the ages directly to us.

> "Son of man, if a country sins against me by committing unfaithfulness, and I stretch out My hand against it, destroy its supply of bread, send famine against it and cut it off from both man and beast, even though these three men, Noah, Daniel and Job were in its midst, by their *own* righteousness they could only deliver themselves," declares the Lord God.[b]

Noah was saved from the flood. Daniel was saved first from the conquering Babylonians who razed Jerusalem to the ground, and later from the lion's den. Job, a rich man, was reduced to abject poverty, losing most of his family in the process, but was then fully restored, through faith, to his former station in life. Yet these three men, renowned for their faith, could only save themselves. We learned from our study of Abraham that righteousness is attributed to those who believe that God will do what He says He will do, in other words, provide a way, which eventually was revealed as Jesus Christ and His completed work on the cross. As righteousness is an individually conferred attribute, it is not transferable to those who choose not to participate. The only

---

[a] This is the place I arrive following a strictly logical flow from what Scripture says and how it might relate to current events; I candidly admit – hope even – that this prophecy may come true in a different way.
[b] Ezekiel 14:13-14

way to save mankind from God's severe judgments is to make an appeal to the people to turn to God in faith.

Of all the ramifications associated with my interpretation of Zechariah's horse patrol visions, the appearance of this fourth horseman of the apocalypse before the 70th week of Daniel gives me pause. It seems too intense, too severe, to be described as part of the birth pangs of judgment. In spite of how many other things seem to simply fall into place, the patrol of the pale horseman is so truly apocalyptic it feels out of order, the one piece of the puzzle that does not seem to fit. Perhaps the casualty rate will only be 20 percent or so, which would still lead to horrific conditions that would seem as if Hades had materialized upon the earth, but would not be quite so catastrophic. Regardless, at the end of the day, it fits into the overall formula that I am using for interpretation. As it is only the severity of the judgment that tends to dissuade me from this viewpoint, and as this is the only source of dissension in my internal logic, I present this to the reader as a possible outcome.

I am reminded of the story of Jonah in the Old Testament. God sent Jonah to the Assyrian capitol of Nineveh to preach that in 40 days the city would be overthrown. The king and the people of Nineveh repented and called upon the mercy of the Lord, and 'God relented concerning the calamity which He declared He would bring upon them.'[a] God did not have to relent; He would have been perfectly just and right to have destroyed the city after giving fair warning, given their bad behavior. It seems, even in the Old Testament, during times when God had to deal most severely with mankind, that He was always willing to give people a second chance. Several generations later the prophecy eventually did come true: Jonah was most likely written somewhere between 722 – 721 BC,[190] around a hundred years before Nineveh's eventual destruction, at the hands of the Babylonians.[191] Perhaps this episode can be instructive for what may await us in the future.

Ultimately, the prophecy of the fourth apocalyptic rider is fatalistic; one way or another, it will come true. (The prophecy that is, not necessarily my interpretation.) However, the *How* and the *When* and even the *WHO* seem to be much less deterministic.[b] As God told Solomon so many years ago, He always listens to those who cry out to Him.

---

[a] Jonah 3:10
[b] See Appendix F, *The Church Clock*. Once judgment begins, events progress on a very specific timeline. Seven years till Christ returns, the Antichrist reigns for 1,260 days, etc. It is the

> If I shut up the heavens so that there is no rain, or if I command the locust to devour the land, or if I send pestilence among My people, and My people who are called by My name humble themselves and pray and seek My face and turn from their wicked ways, then I will hear from heaven, will forgive their sin and will heal their land.[a]

God is a just God; wickedness must not go unpunished. But He is also a patient and merciful God. Those who cry out to Him for forgiveness, He promises to hear and forgive, Jew or Gentile, just as He did in Jonah's and Solomon's day. In the case of the fourth horseman of the apocalypse, I do believe that this judgment could come quickly, that is, within the next 40 years, given the current state of the world. However, if people humble themselves and turn to God for forgiveness, I also believe He will hear them and cleanse them from all unrighteousness. In such case, the death rider may perhaps delay his patrol to some later generation.[b]

---

starting point of this time of judgment that seems to be somewhat negotiable; it depends upon the apostasy, which could be said to be a measure of the beliefs of the church. As long as the church still calls on the name of Jesus Christ, this delays the time of the apostasy.

[a] II Chronicles 7: 13-14

[b] Many people would say that God was more severe in the Old Testament and more kind in the New Testament. I would say that God has not changed how He deals with sin. The difference is simply this: with the resurrection of Jesus Christ comes the baptism, or filling of the Holy Spirit, which acts as a significant restraint on demonic influences. When man is allowed to commune with fell spirits, this greatly increases his capacity for evil. If man's access to these entities is restricted, then so is his capacity for evil. With substantially less evil in the world comes less of a need for corrective action. The difference is not in God's methods, but in man's behavior. When the restrainer is removed just before the last week of Daniel, and dark powers and principalities proliferate, God will again be moved to respond severely.

The Fifth Seal

> When the Lamb broke the fifth seal, I saw underneath the altar the souls of those who had been slain because of the word of God, and because of the testimony which they had maintained; and they cried out with a loud voice, saying, "How long, O Lord, holy and true, will You refrain from judging and avenging our blood on those who dwell on the earth?" And there was given to each of them a white robe; and they were told they should rest a little while longer, until the number of their fellow servants and their brethren who were to be killed even as they had been, would be completed also.[a]

The word for altar here is *thusiastérion*,[192] which refers to 'an altar (for sacrifice),'[193] so there is a direct association between the altar and those standing under it; the altar in heaven is where those who were sacrificed will gather. The word for soul used in this passage is *psuché*,[194] which can be used in a number of different ways to describe: '(a) the vital breath, breath of life, (b) the human soul, (c) the soul as the seat of affections and will, (d) the self, (e) a human person, an individual.'[195] The phrase 'cry out' is rendered in the Greek as *krazó*,[196] which means 'to scream, cry out;'[197] essentially 'an onomatopoetic term for a raven's piercing cry ('caw'); (figuratively) cry out *loudly* with an *urgent scream* or shriek, using 'inarticulate shouts that express *deep emotion*.'[198] This presents the lamentations of the saints before God as visceral, almost animal-like in intensity. It conjures to my mind the idea that perhaps they are arriving in heaven with the memory of their dying breaths still fresh in their minds.

The fifth seal is unique if only for its apparent lack of consequence. All the other seals bring sweeping changes to the earth, dire outcomes and death. The first question here is: where are the earth-shattering changes? The saints stand before the throne and complain about how long God is taking to bring judgment, and God responds by saying, 'rest a little while longer.' How does this compare with the mayhem and destruction the four horsemen bring? The answer to this question is that the fifth seal does indeed change the world as we know it, and that it does represent God's judgment, but in order to get to that conclusion we have to read between the lines.

---

[a] Revelation 6:9-11

Many scholars interpret the souls standing underneath the altar as tribulation saints who have recently been killed. Revelation 20:4, however, clearly lays out that those who did not receive the mark of the beast, i.e., tribulation saints, 'came to life and reigned with Christ for a thousand years,' subsequent to the Antichrist being vanquished and Satan being thrown into the abyss. That is, the tribulation saints are resurrected at the 'first resurrection,' which occurs *after* the 70th week has reached its conclusion, and all of the seal breaking and the trumpet blowing is over and done with; having them show up at the fifth seal is completely out of place, time-wise.

Further, if these tribulation saints were just recently slain, why are they asking God, 'How long will You refrain from judging and avenging our blood?' The term 'tribulation saint' would imply that these people became Christians during the 70th week. This period of time being one of the few places in Scripture where we are given such a precise timeline, tribulation saints would be keenly aware of the start of the Week – that is, the signing of the seven-year covenant between the Antichrist and Israel – and would also be waiting with bated breath for its scheduled end, that is, exactly seven years later. As such, why would they be asking God how long it will be before He brings judgment when they already know when it started and exactly how long they will have to wait? I think it much more likely that the saints are pleading with God to *begin* judgment week, which implies that it has not started yet. Judgment implies a process of separating out the good from the bad; thus, I interpret the whole 7 years of the 70th week as judgment. God seems to affirm this viewpoint when He says, 'rest a little while longer' (for their brothers in martyrdom to join them). It should be noted that the time to which God is responding per the request of the saints is until God judges *and* avenges; judgment is a process that will take place over the whole seven years;[a] the avenging part happens when Christ touches down upon the earth as King of kings and Lord of lords and dispatches the Antichrist at Armageddon.

For these reasons, I interpret the souls mentioned here as saints of the church (instead of the popular view that they are tribulation saints), a multitude of martyrs who have been waiting for up to two millennia for their blood to be avenged. Also, as these saints are portrayed as arriving in heaven with the memory of their unjust deaths seemingly so fresh in their minds, we cannot rule

---

[a] I will expand on this when we get to the eagle flying in midheaven, in Chapter 11 of revelation.

out a day of persecution for Christians in the not-so-distant future; perhaps as a result of the great falling away (apostasy) mentioned in Scripture.[a] They are given white robes, which, according to Revelation 3:18, are for the purpose of covering their nakedness. This would imply they are not spirits only, but have physical bodies; otherwise, they wouldn't be naked.[b] If the church is in heaven standing before God in their physical, incorruptible bodies, this means that the astounding answer to all of these questions is that the fifth seal judgment indicates that the rapture has already occurred by this point.

What I believe will happen at the moment of the rapture is implied by Paul in a letter to the Thessalonians regarding end times:

> Now we request you, brethren, with regard to the coming of our Lord Jesus Christ and our gathering together to Him, that you be not quickly shaken from your composure or be disturbed either by a spirit or a message or a letter as if from us, to the effect that the day of the Lord has come. Let no one in any way deceive you, for it will not come to pass unless the apostasy comes first, and the man of lawlessness is revealed, the son of destruction, who opposes and exalts himself above every so-called god or object of worship, so that he takes his seat in the temple of God, displaying himself as being God. Do you not remember that while I was still with you, I was telling you these things? And you know what restrains him now, so that in his time he will be revealed. For the mystery of lawlessness is already at work; only he who now restrains will do so until he is taken out of the way.[c]

Paul reveals so much that it is difficult to focus on just one topic. I interpret the Restrainer as the Holy Spirit, who has dwelt in every believer since Pentecost, as outlined previously, who is here revealed to be involved in a role of suppressing the 'mystery of lawlessness.' We are given a specific order of events here: First comes the apostasy, then the Restrainer is removed, and then the man of lawlessness is revealed. Believers of the church are sealed with the Holy Spirit, and are also temples of the Holy Spirit, so when the Holy Spirit is 'taken out of the way,' I think it makes sense that Christians would be 'taken' at

---

[a] See Appendix G, *The Great Falling Away*.

[b] You could spiritualize the term 'nakedness' here, but there is precedent starting from Genesis 3:7 and on throughout Scripture that it is the physical condition of nakedness that is associated with sin. In other words, if they did not have physical bodies, they would not need robes to cover them, as nakedness is a physical condition.

[c] II Thessalonians 2:1-7

about the same time.[a] It also means that the Holy Spirit is no longer preventing evil from achieving its full measure. The fifth prophecy in Zechariah's night visions addresses this.

> Then the angel who was speaking with me went out and said to me, "Lift up now your eyes and see what this is going forth." And I said, "What is it?" And he said, "This is the ephah going forth." Again he said, "This is their appearance in all the land (and behold, a lead cover was lifted up): and this is a woman sitting inside the ephah." Then he said, "This is wickedness!" And he threw her down into the middle of the ephah and cast the lead weight on its opening.[b] Then I lifted up my eyes and looked, and there were two women coming out of the ephah with the wind in their wings; and they had wings like the wings of a stork, and they lifted up the ephah between the earth and the heavens. I said to the angel who was speaking with me, "Where are they taking the ephah?" Then he said to me, "To build a temple for her in the land of Shinar; and when it is prepared, she will be set there on her own pedestal."[c]

An ephah is a unit of measure that equates to a little over a bushel. This imagery symbolizes that the full measure of wickedness is capped with a lead weight, literally over the 'mouth' of evil, and a time will come when this evil will be taken to the land of Shinar, the ancient site of Babylon, and a temple will be built for it. If we infer from Thessalonians and Zechariah that when the Restrainer (the Holy Spirit) is removed, a shrine will be built for wickedness/evil in Babylon, then it becomes evident how the rapture might be a very significant pronouncement of worldwide judgment.

If this assessment is correct, then the breaking of the fifth seal would usher in an era of demonic activity of biblical proportions. Things would be seen that have not been witnessed for over two millennia; basically, all hell breaks loose! This could also be the catalyst that releases the locusts of the fifth trumpet from the abyss and the four chained angels of the sixth trumpet from the river Euphrates, which is the river that flowed through the ancient city of Babylon.[d] Zechariah does seem to indicate there may be a short period of time between when the lid is taken off and when the house for evil is built – that is, when wickedness reaches its full potential.

---

[a] There could be a lag between when the rapture happens and when the restrainer is removed.
[b] Literally: mouth
[c] Zechariah 5:5-11
[d] The Euphrates literally flowed right though the city of Babylon; its walls spanned the river.

One aspect of the rapture upon which many scholars comment is how it appears to have no effect on the people who are left upon the earth. They continue to rebel against God and commit murders and thievery, etc. and generally seem to act like God does not exist. There is a popular opinion that the rapture will occur right under the noses of the people of the earth, and that somehow, nobody will notice the sudden disappearance of such a large number of people. As I read the Scripture, I find myself coming to the opposite conclusion. I think that the rapture will be a very public event, and that there will be a very public reaction to this event.

One clue we will find in the sixth seal, shortly to be discussed. We can find another clue provided by none other than the Antichrist himself:

> And he opened his mouth in blasphemies against God, to blaspheme His name and His tabernacle, that is, those who dwell in heaven.[a]

Who are 'those who dwell in heaven' at this time? I'm of the opinion that the Antichrist is blaspheming those humans who have already been caught up into heaven in the rapture. The Antichrist would have no reason to rage against the angels in heaven; his audience of unbelievers would be largely unaware of them. However, millions of suddenly vanished people would present a tactical problem; a cause for disbelief in him and belief in God. Satan, the accuser, has never missed an opportunity to point out the scandal of God's grace, and his minion will not miss the opportunity to mimic him. I'm sure there will be mass confusion about the meaning of the rapture and many will not understand what happened, but the earth dwellers will be keenly aware of the missing.

Before we move on to the sixth seal, we need to address one issue. Whenever you place the rapture on a timeline of prophecy, essentially identifying things that have to happen before it can take place, this introduces an apparent contradiction to the doctrine of Christ's imminent return. We are exhorted in Scripture to be ready for the return of Christ at any time, which implies that Christ could indeed return at any moment throughout history. On the surface, imminence negates any notions of placing the rapture on the timeline of prophecy; as soon as you claim that an event has to happen before the rapture, then you introduce the condition that the rapture can't happen until

---

[a] Revelation 13: 6

said event takes place, and therefore Christ could not come back until those preconditions are met.[a]

My claim that the breaking of the fifth seal signals that the rapture has already occurred is not at odds with the conventional interpretation of the doctrine of Christ's imminent return, as it merely records the saints in heaven gathering under the altar; it does not necessarily designate the moment of their arrival. I would propose that the order of the seals tells us when, from a heavenly perspective, the Holy Spirit is removed and evil is no longer restrained (as implied by the rapture). The significance of the *timing* of the fifth seal gives us an indication of when this removal occurs, not necessarily when the rapture happens.[b] The subsequent unleashing of demonic forces that will result represents the dire judgment associated with the fifth seal.

---

[a] See Appendix F, *the Church Clock*, for a more thorough treatment.

[b] The rapture could happen at any time, so there is the possibility that Christians will be taken out from the earth sometime *before* the Holy Spirit ceases to restrain evil. Christians are indwelt with the Holy Spirit, that is, our bodies are a temple in which He dwells. As Christ promises that He will never leave us or forsake us through the ministry of the Holy Spirit, it would be impossible for Christians to remain after the Holy Spirit leaves.

The Sixth Seal

> I looked when He broke the sixth seal, and there was a great earthquake; and the sun became black as sackcloth made of hair, and the whole moon became like blood; and the stars of the sky fell to the earth, as a fig tree casts its unripe figs when shaken by a great wind. The sky was split apart like a scroll when it is rolled up, and every mountain and island were moved out of their places. Then the kings of the earth and the great men and the commanders and the rich and the strong and every slave and free man hid themselves in the caves and among the rocks of the mountains; and they said to the mountains and to the rocks, 'Fall on us and hide us from the presence of Him who sits on the throne, and from the wrath of the Lamb; for the great day of their wrath has come, and who is able to stand'?[a]

One thing that really stands out in this passage is the phrase: 'the sky was split apart like a scroll.' Many have surmised this to be a nuclear warhead detonation, and it may well be, but when an asteroid or comet enters the atmosphere, the visual effect is the same. A nuclear warhead, however, does not pack enough punch to move every mountain and island – except on a scale undetectable to humans – so I rule out a nuclear exchange for this seal in favor of a cosmic impact event. An asteroid strike, simply due to the relative speeds involved, might be something physically felt all around the globe. The second thing about this passage that stands out is that the translation seems to be pretty straightforward; that is, as I peruse the original Greek for clues as to nuances of meaning, very little seems to come to the surface to hint at something deeper; so I guess the translators did an especially good job.

The phrase 'moved out of their places,' referring to every mountain and every island, could possibly be interpreted to mean anything from a relatively small displacement to a total upheaval of the earth's crust. The Greek word for move is *kineo*,[199] which means to set in motion or move.[200] The word for place is *topos*,[201] which refers to a locality or region.[202] Finally, *ek*[203] is the word used for 'out of,' which means 'from out' or 'out from among.'[204] The Greek word '(*ek*) has a two-layered meaning ("*out from* and *to*") which makes it *outcome* oriented (out of the depths of the source and extending to its impact on the object).'[205] This last definition gives the impression of movement coming from within the earth and might imply that the tectonic plates of the earth's crust have destabilized, causing the continents to drift to new positions. This would

---
[a] Revelation 6:12-17

seem to indicate an earth-shaking event, though widespread death and destruction are not described. In fact, it is the lack of damage caused by this seal that is the third thing that stands out in this passage. We aren't told how much of the earth is injured or how many people are killed, something that is specifically mentioned in other seals and trumpets. If the continents were to change positions after a celestial object hit the earth, this would no doubt cause earthquakes of historic proportion, but perhaps not result in deaths on a truly biblical scale; that is, the fraction of casualties might be only a thousandth of those on the earth, as opposed to a quarter or a third, as listed in the other seals/trumpet. This would still represent quite a catastrophic event to mankind, however.

For this reason, the purpose of the sixth seal appears to be more about a wake-up call than the actual commencement of the 70th week of Daniel. I see it as God sending a shot across the bow, to get mankind's attention before starting in with the real deal.[a] It is the reference to the figs falling from the tree that gives me the impression that this seal is meant to be a sign.

> "Now learn the parable from the fig tree: when its branch has already become tender and puts forth its leaves, you know that summer is near. Even so, you too, when you see these things happening, recognize that He is near, right at the door."[b]

The fig tree is used by Christ to represent a sign of the times; the reference to a fig tree in this passage makes me think it is about God giving fair warning to all who are left on the earth that everything is about to change.[c] Many appear to get the message and realize that the wrath of God will soon be upon them. A similar message is found in the Gospel of Luke.

> "There will be signs in sun, and moon and stars, and on the earth dismay among nations, in perplexity at the roaring of the sea and waves, men fainting with fear

---

[a] For those who think the seven seals happen during Judgment, the response given by the men of earth is telling: 'for the great day of their wrath has come, and who is able to stand?' If, as many scholars propose, the wrath of God has already begun at this point, why are they saying as late as the sixth seal that this event marks the coming of God's wrath?

[b] Mark 13:29

[c] The reference to unripe figs may also indicate that this event is a precursor to the first four trumpet judgments, vis-a-vis the reference to the 'stars of the sky' falling to earth.

and the expectation of the things which are coming upon the world; for the powers of heavens will be shaken."[a]

The signs of the sixth seal are mentioned here: the sun, the moon, and the stars. The roaring of the sea and the waves could implicate gargantuan tsunami waves generated by the changing of the positions of the continents, which would be terrifying in many respects. The mention of 'men fainting with fear and the expectation of the things which are coming upon the world' echoes how in the time of the sixth seal, men call upon the mountains and rocks to fall on them.

This brings us to a fourth thing that stands out about the sixth seal: 'Him who sits on the throne' and the 'Lamb' are acknowledged by all of mankind as the cause of this cataclysmic event. Not 'god' in general, but the *Lamb*, or Jesus Christ will be on the tongues of men, spoken in vain, as they run and hide in fear. Curious that they should be giving 'Him who sits on the throne' – the God of Israel – credit, after denying His very existence just a few years before in the great falling away. However, if you think about it, this fits right on our timeline. With the fifth seal, Christians have suddenly gone missing with no explanation other than maybe it was the rapture and perhaps all this 'Jesus mumbo jumbo' about the end of the world was true after all. Then a heavenly body strikes the earth, and everybody freaks out because they suddenly realize that world events are about to go biblical. Fair warning: there is no easy way out at this point.[b]

---

[a] Luke 21:25-26

[b] This would be another consequence that the fifth seal brings as the rapture: everyone left behind has to go through the judgment of the 70th week.

Interlude

Revelation chapter 7 represents an interlude; a period of time that describes events happening as the sixth seal is unfolding yet still prior to the opening of the seventh seal. While all mankind is trembling with fear and running to hide in caves, God will be gathering His elect from the four corners of the earth. This interlude is comprised of two main parts: the sealing of the 144,000 and a scene of the tribulation saints in heaven around God's throne, which happens sometime after judgment, and shows the effect of their ministry.

> After this, I saw four angels standing at the four corners of the earth, holding back the four winds of the earth, so that no wind would blow on the earth, or the sea, or on any tree. And I saw another angel ascending from the rising sun, having the seal of the living God; and he cried out with a loud voice to the four angels to whom it was granted to harm the earth and the sea, saying, "Do not harm the earth or the sea or the trees until we have sealed the bond-servants of our God on their foreheads." And I heard the number of those who were sealed, one hundred and forty-four thousand sealed from every tribe of the sons of Israel.[a]

The sealing of the 144,000 denotes the setting apart of a mysterious group of people that have inspired a false religion and endless speculation. It tends to make modern Christians feel somehow left out, or not quite as special, to think about a group of people who have been singled out in this way for a unique relationship with Jesus Christ. However, in light of the 70th week of Daniel, we should remember how the church itself was a mystery in the Old Testament, much like the 144,000 are a mystery to us in the present age. In due time, the ministry of the church will have run its course, and the most likely explanation is that these representatives from the tribes of Israel will be raised up to replace God's witness to mankind after the church has been taken out in the rapture. Throughout history, God has never left mankind alone on the earth without a witness to Him and His word. On our timeline, if the rapture has just occurred, and every Christian has been whisked away to

---

[a] Revelation 7:1-4

be with Jesus in heaven, then it seems fitting to say that the sealing of the sons of Israel is simply God bringing in the replacements.

Referring to the 144,000 as the 'replacements' is my way of using a popular phrase to communicate that God will set up His witness during the 70th week of Daniel in a similar manner to how He raised up the church in the present age. However, these guys are more than just replacements.

> These are the ones who have not been defiled with women, for they have kept themselves chaste. These are the ones who follow the Lamb wherever He goes. These have been purchased from among men as first fruits to God and to the Lamb.[a]

Paul also refers to Christ as the first fruits.

> But now Christ has been raised from the dead, the first fruits of those who are asleep.[b]

The 144,000, although they show up rather late in history, also represent the first fruits of the millennial kingdom. So, they are indeed much more than just replacements.

Another point bears mentioning: Paul refers to Christ as the first fruits of the *resurrection*. We could make a direct connection here to the 144,000 as being the first fruits of the resurrection of Israel. The first time they appear, in chapter 7 of Revelation, they are referred to as 'bond-servants.' The second time they appear, in chapter 14, they are referred to as 'first fruits' to the Lamb and to God. In my mind, this very well might imply that the 144,000 are the first to be resurrected at the end of the tribulation. This would also imply that the 144,000 will be martyred at some point, unless they are suddenly taken up to heaven in a rapture event like Enoch and the church. The fact that they have a seal placed on their foreheads, and that this seal protects them from the demon-locusts of the fifth trumpet (more on that later), makes me think

---

[a] Revelation 14:4
[b] I Corinthians 15:20

that they possess mortal bodies at the outset of the tribulation and then are subsequently killed/raptured during the 70th week.[a]

Also, drawing from the teaching of Paul the apostle that Christian believers are the temple of the Holy Spirit, I think it plausible that these newly-sealed witnesses would represent God's temple on earth during the tribulation,[b] not the physical temple to be rebuilt in Jerusalem. This represents a supposition on my part, certainly not a point elaborated in Scripture, but it seems to me that God would never inhabit a sanctuary built by a people that reject the perfect sacrifice of His Son. I see the sealing of the 144,000 as an event much like Pentecost, where the first indwelling of the Holy Spirit in Christian believers occurred. Many scholars infer that there may be an actual mark on the forehead which would signify this seal of the Holy Spirit.

To sum up, just before the earth is harmed (which we will see in the first four trumpets), the 144,000 are sealed. They represent newly commissioned witnesses as the ministry of the church is now complete, and God is resuming His plan for Israel. The second part of chapter 7 bears testament to the effectiveness of their ministry, as can be seen by the 'great multitude which no one can count,'[c] which 'has come out of the tribulation.'[d]

---

[a] If the 144,000 were to initially possess their incorruptible bodies in which they will spend eternity, I don't think they would require a seal from the Holy Spirit to protect them. A lot of scholars believe that the 144,000 will not die during the tribulation. I include this here as an alternate theory.

[b] I use the term 'tribulation' colloquially here to refer to the whole seven years of the 70th week.

[c] Revelation 7:9

[d] Revelation 7:14

The Seventh Seal:
Silence in Heaven

> When the Lamb broke the seventh seal, there was silence in heaven for about half an hour.[a]

Much has been made about these thirty minutes of silence. Obviously, something of moment has just happened or is about to happen. A turning point, perhaps? Many scholars say that the seventh seal unleashes the next set of judgments, the seven trumpets, which I think is true. Continuing with our imagery of how a first-century book was constructed, the breaking of the seventh seal finally unlocks the contents of the Seven-Sealed book: The book of God's judgment is now open!

In my opinion, this heavenly pause signifies the beginning of the 70th week of Daniel. The nation of Israel will have just signed a covenant with the Antichrist. Such an event, where God's chosen people sign a covenant with the Man of Sin, signifying the commencement of God's wrath upon mankind, would be worthy of a moment of silence in heaven. What is really telling in the first few verses of chapter 8 is that after this moment of silence, mention is made of the prayers of the saints – remember the prayers of the saints in the fifth seal? 'How long, O Lord... will you refrain from judging and avenging our blood on those who dwell on the earth?'[b] Incense is added to these prayers, and the smoke of it goes up before God.

> Then the angel took the censer and filled it with the fire of the altar, and threw it to the earth; and there followed peals of thunder and sounds and flashes of lightning and an earthquake.[c]

Fire is taken from the altar: this speaks of judgment. What does the angel do with the fire from the altar of God? He throws it to the earth. If we had

---

[a] Revelation 8:1
[b] Revelation 6:10
[c] Revelation 8:5

any doubts about the opening of the seventh seal before, we don't now; verse 5 clearly illustrates that the judgment of the earth has officially begun.

Something else very interesting changes after the breaking of the seventh seal. The Lamb opens the seven seals, but it is the angels that blow the seven trumpets and pour out the seven bowls of wrath. This change from the Lamb to the angels taking over the duties and carrying out God's judgment denotes a key transition. As we learn from the parable of the tares in Matthew 13, the angels are the reapers. We also learned that the reapers do their reaping 'at the end of the age'[a] when the 'tares are gathered together and burned with fire,'[b] which represents judgment. One possible interpretation is that after the Lamb opens the seals during the birth pangs, the seventh seal marks the commencement of the seven years of judgment with silent observance, and then the angels begin the duties of reaping, that is, blowing the trumpets and pouring out the bowls of God's wrath.

As at this point, as we have reached an important inflection point, it might be apropos to take stock of where we are so far. We have now finished with the elaborate process of opening the book of God's judgment, that is, all of the seals have been removed and the contents of the book itself are ready to spill over into reality. Let me summarize a few talking points in favor of my theory of the end times so far:

- First and foremost, I would suggest that a more complete understanding of the Seven-Sealed Book comes to the forefront.
- A chronological flow can be recognized as we move from the seals to the trumpets, where Revelation chapters 4-11 are seen to happen sequentially.
- Revelation chapters 4-11 can now be understood as one continuous prophecy, that is, as one of twelve, shedding light on the rest of the book.
- A consistency emerges with the imagery/idea of a sealed book: that is, the book cannot be opened until all the seals are broken.

---

[a] Matthew 13:39
[b] Matthew 13:40

- The view that the four horsemen conduct two patrols can be supported by patterns observed in two instances in Scripture: the first and the eighth of the night visions of Zechariah, and the angelic reapers of Revelation 14.
- World changing movements such as the European Age of Conquest, nationalism, and economic globalization, developments which have radically changed the course of humanity, can be accounted for in biblical prophecy.[a]
- The process of globalization, a modern phenomenon that started in the 1500s and is headed in a direction which the secular world does not understand, can be explained as the reversal of a process begun at Babel in the Bible.
- The questions of the saints after the breaking of the fifth seal are explained, i.e., why are they asking God to judge mankind if judgment week has already started? Answer: it hasn't!
- The sixth seal is explained as a warning to all mankind about coming judgment – hence the lack of destruction associated with this seal.
- Men proclaiming the great day of the wrath of the Lamb in the sixth seal is explained as an event that follows the rapture, along with the suggestion that judgment hasn't begun up until this point.
- The mention of the earth as having not been harmed in Revelation 7 is explained as being immediately prior to the opening of the Seven-Sealed Book and the beginning of judgment.
- The meaning of the 30 minutes of silence in heaven after the breaking of the seventh seal is explained as a dramatic pause before the start of the 70th week of Daniel (judgment week).
- The meaning of the prayers of the saints (for God to judge mankind) and the angel throwing the fire of the altar of heaven down to the earth in Revelation 8:4-5 is explained as the commencement of judgment.

---

[a] You could make the case that, whereas a good argument has been made from Scripture for the four horsemen to conduct two patrols, one before judgment and one during judgment, this does not necessarily correspond to the European Age of Conquest, nationalism and economic globalization. Though the interpretation is sound biblically, the application is assumptive. I leave it to the reader to decide if the last five hundred years qualify for the kind of global upheaval and disruption that these horsemen are slated to bring. If not, then we wait for events even more momentous and world changing than we have yet seen.

- The observation that the Lamb opens the seals but that the angels blow the trumpets and pour out the bowls of wrath can be explained as the transition from the birth pangs of judgment to judgment itself. (see Matthew 13)
- The prophecy of the Seven-Sealed Book can be understood as being bookended by the throne room scenes of Revelation chapters 4-5 and chapter 11.

And the cons:

- This interpretation is unorthodox.
- The fourth seal judgment is so severe that it seems counterintuitive to place it before judgment begins.

    Perhaps the observant reader/theologian may find a few more cons, but I personally find the list of pros compelling. The sense of clarity and flow that emerges when you free your mind from strictly chronological interpretations is striking. In and of itself, this is not conclusive, but it seems like a step in the right direction. Time will tell. My hope is that maybe I have stumbled onto a few truths that will speak to others who are more adept and scholarly than I am and that they will be inspired to branch off in new directions and eventually correct some of my mistakes. In any event, I believe we are all better off for having the discussion.

The First Four Trumpets

'On March 25, 1993, a previously unknown comet positioned close to Jupiter was discovered by Eugene and Carolyn Shoemaker and David Levy in photographs taken by using the 18-inch (46-cm) Schmidt telescope at Palomar Observatory in California. Its appearance was very unusual—it comprised at least a dozen active cometary nuclei lined up like glowing pearls on a string. As the nuclei spread farther apart, a total of 21 fragments were seen. An analysis of their common orbit revealed that the original comet had been revolving about the Sun and had been captured into orbit around Jupiter, most probably around 1929.'[206] 'Tidal forces from the giant planet's gravity broke the original nucleus (estimated to be 1.6 km [1 mile] in diameter) into many pieces. The resulting 21 nuclei followed a highly eccentric two-year orbit around Jupiter.' [207] 'The train of fragments from Shoemaker-Levy 9 smashed into Jupiter's atmosphere with a velocity of 221,000 km (137,300 miles) per hour beginning on July 16, 1994.'[208] 'The cataclysmic event, the first collision between two solar system bodies ever predicted and observed, was monitored from Earth-based telescopes worldwide, the Hubble Space Telescope and other Earth-orbiting instruments, and the Galileo spacecraft, which was en route to Jupiter.'[209] 'Its impact delivered energy equivalent to at least 48 billion tons of TNT – many times the yield of the world's supply of nuclear weapons.'[210] The cosmic encounter between comet Shoemaker-Levy 9 and Jupiter inspired several blockbuster movies and spurred significant investment in detecting other celestial objects that might pose a threat to Earth. And for good reason; there is evidence on the moons of Jupiter that multiple impact events have occurred before: 'Prominent crater chains[a] on Ganymede and Callisto[b] are most likely the impact scars of comets tidally disrupted by Jupiter...'[211]

If we pull together the prophecies of the sixth seal and the first four trumpets, we can begin to stitch together a plausible narrative that connects these events to a cosmological sequence, and in doing so, some of the details come into better focus. If a comet were to become 'tidally disrupted' as it passes through the inner solar system, with the sun playing Jupiter to Earth's

---

[a] A crater chain is a line of craters along the surface of an astronomical body, presumably caused by 'tidally disrupted' comets or asteroids.
[b] Moons of Jupiter

Ganymede or Callisto, this could possibly result in a 'crater chain' across the surface of the Earth. In this case, the collision that the sixth seal represents would be the first fragment of a chain or line of objects hurtling toward the Earth at over a hundred thousand miles an hour. If the disrupted comet were to approach from the direction of the Sun, scientists may not be aware of it until the first chunk plows into the atmosphere and splits the sky wide open; 'and the stars of the sky fell to the earth, as a fig tree casts its unripe figs when shaken by a great wind.'[a] Once the full magnitude of the coming apocalypse becomes clear, 'the kings of the earth and the great men and the commanders and the rich and the strong and every slave and free man… [will hide] themselves in the caves and among the rocks of the mountains.'[b]

On the one hand, God does not need an asteroid or a comet to accomplish His purpose. On the other hand, perhaps the spectacle of Shoemaker-Levy 9 is meant to serve as a sign of things to come: the first fig to fall from the tree, or one of the 'signs in sun and moon and stars,'[c] so to speak. As such, the commencement of judgment and the blowing of the first four trumpets can be read, perhaps, in a new light:

> The first angel sounded his trumpet, and there came hail and fire mixed with blood, and it was hurled down upon the earth. A third of the earth was burned, a third of the trees were burned up, and all of the green grass was burned up. The second angel sounded his trumpet, and something like a huge mountain, all ablaze, was thrown into the sea. A third of the sea turned into blood, a third of the living creatures in the sea died, and a third of the ships were destroyed. The third angel sounded his trumpet, and a great star, blazing like a torch, fell from the sky on a third of the rivers and on the springs of water – the name of the star is wormwood. A third of the waters turned bitter, and many people died from the waters that had turned bitter. The fourth angel sounded his trumpet, and a third of the sun was struck, a third of the moon, and a third of the stars, so that a third of them turned dark. A third of the day was without light, and also a third of the night.[d]

Upon first inspection, it seems that it is actually the second trumpet that does by far the worst of the damage, with the third and fourth trumpets accounting for the aftereffects of the 'huge mountain, all ablaze… thrown into

---

[a] Revelation 6:13
[b] Revelation 6:15
[c] Luke 21:25
[d] Revelation 8:7-12

the sea.'ᵃ The first trumpet sounds like a mixture of dust and small debris – by cosmological standards – hitting the earth. The text says that a third of the earth is burned, and a third of the trees are burned up, so one particular third of the earth would have it worse than others, though everywhere is affected by the heat, as evidenced by the mention of 'all the green grass' being burned up. If the comet were to approach from the sunward side, our planet would encounter it tail first,ᵇ and the gravity well of the Earth would act like a funnel, sucking in a wide swath of particles big and small to fall in a constant barrage on all points around the globe. The friction of so much cosmic debris entering our atmosphere as flaming missiles would cause the air to heat up, potentially to several hundred degrees, such that it very well could scorch green vegetation on a worldwide scale.[212, c]

The second trumpet sounds like the main body of the comet hitting the Earth, and landing in the ocean. Though it is not described as causing harm to more than sea creatures and ships, this is potentially the most devastating impact of the series, as it sounds like a gargantuan piece of space rock and ice actually making contact with the earth. When celestial objects collide, the material at the impact site, both incoming and resident, would be vaporized. At the relative speeds involved, it doesn't matter whether the impact occurs on land or in water. This vaporized rock, heated to temperatures hotter than the surface of the sun, would be ejected into the upper atmosphere where it would condense into super-heated particles which would rain down all over the world.[213] Essentially, the third of the earth that receives this direct hit would experience the worst of it.

'Astronomers using Hubble [to inspect the damage on Jupiter from Shoemaker-Levy 9] were surprised to see "sulfur-bearing compounds" such as hydrogen sulfide, as well as ammonia, as a result of the collision.'[214] An extraterrestrial traveler such as a comet might bring with it a sizable dose of acidic or poisonous compounds in situ or could vaporize a cloud of chemical

---

ᵃ Revelation 6:8
ᵇ A comet's tail always points away from the sun, like a sail billowing in the solar wind.
ᶜ Computer simulations of asteroid collisions with the Earth predict that high speed ejecta thrown up into space by the impact would rain back down all over the world in the form of an extensive cloud of small particles. It is theorized that the friction from all these particles entering the atmosphere could temporarily raise the global temperature to 600 – 700° F. I think that it is plausible to presume that an encounter with a comet's dust cloud might produce a similar effect.

compounds from the earth's crust, propelling them into the upper atmosphere. So, perhaps a secondary effect of this mountain that falls into the sea is an acidic rain that falls over a large area causing heavy metals to leach out of the soil and contaminate the water supply,[215] thus bringing about the conditions of the third trumpet.

The impact would also pump a vast amount of dust and ash high into the atmosphere, similar to a volcanic eruption, but on a much larger scale. Soot and ash would blanket the earth for many months, if not years, causing light from the sun to be diminished.[216] The effect might not be a total solar blackout; layers of dust in the atmosphere might be thick enough to filter out only a portion of the sun's light. When the sun is directly overhead, it might penetrate through the haze, but when it is down near the horizon it would be totally obscured, effectively shortening daylight hours. The same would apply to the moon and stars at night – hence, after some time, rendering the conditions described by the fourth trumpet. And so, from a purely materialist perspective, the aftereffects of the second trumpet could account for the conditions of the third and fourth trumpets, that is, a poisoned water supply and a shortened day.

The third trumpet, however, is rather interesting in its own right, as it speaks of a star that is given a name: Wormwood. It is described as blazing like a torch. It appears smaller in the mind's eye than the 'mountain' described in the second trumpet, but perhaps wreathed in smoke and dust. It is not described as falling into the sea, or making direct contact with the earth, so maybe it burns up or explodes in the upper atmosphere. Much has been made of the name of this falling star, '*apsinthos*'[217] in Greek, defined as: 'a bitter plant known as "wormwood"; (figuratively) what is intensely bitter (grievous), bringing on very sad results…'[218] There is a much-touted theory that this is a cryptic reference to nuclear contamination through a vague association with the Chernobyl accident in 1986, but I have not found any reliable information to substantiate this claim. If we turn to the Bible, however, we do find references to wormwood in the Old Testament:

> … therefore thus says the Lord of hosts, the God of Israel, "Behold, I will feed them, this people, with wormwood and give them poisoned water to drink."[a]

---

[a] Jeremiah 9:15

> Therefore thus says the Lord of hosts concerning the prophets, "Behold, I am going to feed them wormwood and make them drink poisonous water, for from the prophets of Jerusalem pollution has gone forth into all the land."[a]

In both passages, there is a close association between wormwood and poisoned water, and in both places the Hebrew word *laanah*[219] is used, which means: 'only figurative of bitter things: of ...*chastisement.*'[b, 220] In Revelation there is also a close association between wormwood and poisoned water. The use of this bitter plant in Jeremiah represented God's chastisement of wayward prophets who had been prophesying lies (pollution) about Him, and I think that in Revelation 8:11, 'wormwood' is used as code for God's 'chastisement.' Thus, where it says that this star fell on the rivers and spring of waters, it means that God's chastisement will fall on the water supply, poisoning it and making it undrinkable. The fact that the text states that the star will be called wormwood signifies that mankind will widely recognize this event as an act of God.[c]

I suspect that there will be something about the nature of the falling star of the third trumpet that will make it clear to people left on the earth that it is no random event. Perhaps it will be very similar in appearance or fall in the same locality as the object of the sixth seal, which was heralded as the beginning of God's judgment, and so bookend the series of impacts. Or perhaps it will just be the fact that all these impacts/falling stars affect the same third of the earth, while the other two-thirds remain relatively unscathed except for the burning up of all the green grass.

Impact site

If you are ready to buy into the theory that the first four trumpets are describing a cosmic impact event, or if at least you are open to the idea, then the sixty-four-thousand-dollar question becomes: *Where will it hit?* I believe that this will be no random occurrence. One area that we can definitely rule out,

---

[a] Jeremiah 23:15

[b] Italics mine

[c] Strangely enough, this 'star' may actually come to be named 'wormwood,' as the biblical account of it has been greatly sensationalized (in effect, a self-fulfilling prophecy).

as it is central to the rest of the story, is in the vicinity of the nation-state of Israel. There is clear indication that the impact site would be a body of water ('something like a mountain, all ablaze, was thrown into the sea'), so this rules out the Mediterranean, Caspian, and Black Seas.

In fact, the remainder of Revelation reads as if no calamity has taken place, outside of the mysterious omission of any reference to the United States. Not only is such an impact event definitely not going to happen in the vicinity of Israel, but we can also rule out, I would propose, eastern Europe, Africa, and western Asia (Iran), as they are identified in prophecy as being significant players in the end times. This rules out the Atlantic, Arctic, and Indian Oceans, and leaves only the Pacific Ocean and the Antarctic Ocean.

If you consider the location of Jerusalem on a globe, and trace the lines of longitude up through the north pole, and then down again to the exact opposite side of the world, you come to an obscure point in the eastern Pacific that is as far away as you can get from the land of Israel. Add the fact that the land masses of North and South America represent about a *third* of dry land on the face of the earth measured in square miles, and you have a reasonably acceptable candidate for the address of the first major stanza of the apocalypse. This is not the only possible scenario, mind you, but somewhere in the eastern Pacific off the western coasts of the Americas would meet all of the particulars listed above in Revelation 8, could possibly leave the Middle East all but unscathed – except for such effects as would present worldwide, that is, all of the grass being burned up and the dimming of the sun, moon, and stars – and would also offer a plausible explanation as to why the United States doesn't so much as qualify for an honorable mention in the book of Revelation.

In retrospect, if the Americas do indeed take the brunt of the impact, the reference to wormwood becomes especially poignant in consideration of the fact that the peoples left in those regions after the rapture would have lived their whole lives in the shadow of the church. The ones who are left behind would be those who had rejected God's grace and also those who had engaged in false teachings. Wormwood represents God's punishment against people who misrepresented His character and His name by telling lies about Him. God's chastisement is to pollute the drinking water of those who pollute His name.

Electromagnetic Pulse

Another theoretical effect of an asteroid/comet strike involves the production of an electromagnetic pulse, or EMP, that would result from the immense release of energy. Vast amounts of electrons become energized and supercharge the Earth's magnetic field. Anything conductive, especially sensitive electronics, experiences an inductive surge of current which destroys the circuit. Power grids worldwide would be fried, and any modern device which employs computer circuits would be rendered useless, from aircraft to automobiles, to cell phones, etc., unless hidden underground or otherwise shielded.

In Figure 3, I have drawn a circle[a] where the EMP would be the weakest if a comet struck the antipode[b] of Israel. Everywhere outside the circle, the clock of technology would be practically turned back in time, changing world order overnight. Those nations able to preserve their relatively advanced weaponry would possess the ability to overwhelm those shocked back to the stone age. The destructive effects of the EMP would diminish exponentially the farther you get from the impact site so, depending on the size of the comet, and if it struck the globe opposite Israel, you could imagine a world tragically incapacitated everywhere except for the Middle East, which would give rise to those nations listed in Psalms 83:

> They have said, "Come, and let us wipe them out as a nation, that the name of Israel be remembered no more." For they have conspired together with one mind; Against you they make a covenant: The tents of Edom and the Ismaelites, Moab and the Hagrites, Gebal and Ammon and Amalek, Philistia with the inhabitants of Tyre; Assyria also has joined with them; They have become a help to the children of Lot.[c]

---

[a] This is a theoretical suggestion: the size of the unaffected area could vary greatly. To produce this effect would require a rather specific impactor, in size, relative speed and composition.
[b] The point on the globe diametrically opposite (i.e., Australia is roughly the antipode of the United States).
[c] Psalm 83: 4-8

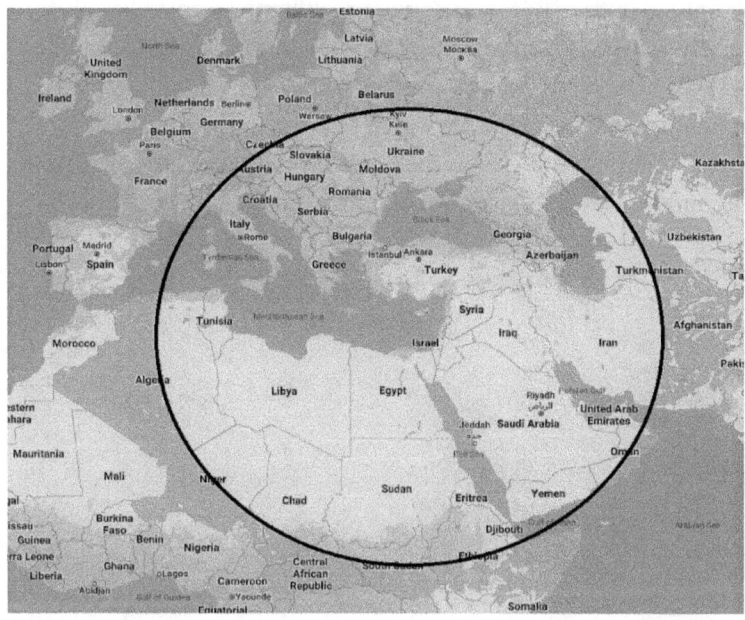

Figure 3: Circle of nations potentially unaffected by the EMP (credit google maps)

All the nations mentioned in the above text were Old Testament tribes/cities that bordered Israel, with the exception of Assyria, whose power would have been extended from as far away as modern-day Iraq. They were often in conflict with Israel throughout history but have never formed a single alliance against God's people. When this invasion finally does occur, it will likely lead to the final battle known as Armageddon.

If an EMP from an impact event destroyed modern technology everywhere on Earth except the Middle East, this would leave predominantly Muslim nations in the catbird seat as regards world power.[a] Under the circumstances, we might not be surprised to see Israel sign a peace agreement

---

[a] Alternatively, if such an EMP were strong enough to wipe all electronic devices and render the advanced weaponry of all nations useless, the Middle East might suffer the least physical damage from a comet strike all the way on the other side of the globe. In some way or form, I expect these nations to emerge from calamity with civilization intact, and thus be in a position to press their advantage against those less fortunate.

with her neighbors at this juncture. A standoff might ensue as Israel and her neighbors are the only countries left with a modern equipped army.[a] Israel agrees not to interfere as Muslim nations use their newfound power to subdue Europe, Asia, and Africa.[b] This would be a mixed-technology campaign not seen since the beginning of World War II, which saw the transition from horse-drawn to mechanized equipment. Perhaps the repeated references to horses for use in warfare throughout Revelation are much more literal than symbolic.

---

[a] Perhaps also because Israel is the last nation standing with viable nuclear weapons.
[b] Technically, this peace accord should happen before the first four trumpets, but I expect world politics to be rather fluid during this time.

White Horse: Second Patrol

As we mention this peace accord in reference to prophecy, we should also take note of with WHOM this agreement is made: the Antichrist. Daniel's prophecy of the 70th week begins with this momentous event. If you will recall, I have the four horsemen of the Apocalypse participating in two worldwide patrols each, once during peacetime and once during judgment. With the first patrols of each already completed, and the commencement of judgment, this peace agreement would signify the beginning of the rise to power of the Antichrist, the white horseman on his second patrol.

In light of our conversation, it is rather interesting to note the characteristics of the Muslim messiah at this point, whom they refer to as the *al-Mahdi*, or the guided one. 'Among the Major Signs, the most anticipated and central sign that Muslims await is the coming of a man know as 'the Mahdi'.[221] His calling card reads like a laundry list lifted from the verses of Scripture that speak about the Antichrist. Here are a few that seem to directly apply:

- He will emerge after a period of great turmoil and suffering.
- He will establish a new world order.
- He will invade many countries.
- He will make a seven-year peace treaty with a Jew of priestly lineage.
- He will conquer Israel for Islam and lead the 'Faithful Muslims' in a final slaughter/battle against Jews.
- He will establish a new Islamic headquarters from Jerusalem.
- He will rule for seven years.
- *He will appear riding a white horse.*[a]
- He will have supernatural power from Allah over the wind and the rain and crops.
- He will possess and distribute enormous amounts of wealth.
- He will be loved by all the peoples of the earth.[222]

---

[a] Italics mine.

Whether the scenario I present above of an EMP causing a technological blackout plays out or not, Muslim nations are waiting with bated breath for the coming of the Antichrist; they are his ready-made minions. The fact that after only three and a half years he throws off the charade and declares himself to be God will not matter.

> We need to understand that the Antichrist will not demand worship until well after the Islamic world has universally acknowledged and accepted him as the Mahdi.[223] To deny him after this point would be the ultimate shame for Islam.[224] Once the deception has taken place, it will be impossible to undo. The die will have been cast.[225]

Add to all this the fact that the preferred method of execution for Muslims is beheading, the method by which tribulation saints are said to be martyred in Revelation 20:4, and it becomes hard not to imagine them having a pivotal role in the Antichrist's rise to power.

Warning to the Earth Dwellers

> Then I looked, and I heard an eagle flying in midheaven, saying with a loud voice, "Woe, woe, woe to those who dwell on the earth, because of the remaining blasts of the trumpet of the three angels who are about to sound!"[a]

The first four trumpets were directed at damaging the earth, which is bad enough, as that greatly impacts those living on the earth. However, the last three trumpets are focused on 'those who dwell on the earth,' that is, they are directed against humanity itself, which makes them especially woeful. The word used for dwell is *katoikeó*[226] which means 'to inhabit, to settle,'[227] or 'properly, settle *down* as a permanent resident, i.e., in a *fixed* (*permanent*) dwelling place as one's personal residence; (figuratively) 'to be *exactly at home*'.'[228] The target of these three woes – the fifth, sixth and seventh trumpets – are those about whom we could say, 'the Earth is their home.' Christians, who are saved by the free gift of the grace of Jesus Christ, and whose destiny is to be transformed into an incorruptible body, belong to Christ, and so have a home in heaven with Him. The earth dweller is someone who has rejected the free gift of salvation, and whose destiny is bound to his own corruptible, earth-born flesh. The earth dweller views death and decay as a part of the natural cycle of life and so, like a pig wallowing in its own feces, accepts his fate with transcendental ignorance; little does he know, death is not the end. (Tribulation saints, that is, those people that take the name of Christ during this time, will likely be spared these woes to a large extent, though it is said that they will have to endure a different fate; that of being beheaded by the Antichrist and his minions.[b])

The bird that is heard is an eagle, or *aetos*,[229] which is used to refer to 'an eagle or bird of prey.'[230] The eagle is seen in 'midheaven,' or *mesouranéma*,[231] which is: 'mid-heaven, the highest point in the heavens, which the sun occupies at noon, where what is done can be seen and heard by all…'[232] This eagle which speaks of the three woes will somehow be seen and heard by all of the people of the earth. Despite this rather blunt warning, the earth dwellers will still be caught unawares, in keeping with the imagery of the eagle, which relates to how it hunts its prey.

---

[a] Revelation 8:13
[b] Revelation 20:4

> Now my days are swifter than a runner; They flee away, they see no good. They slip by like reed boats, like an eagle that swoops on its prey.[a]

When an eagle attacks, it swoops in from above, catching its prey by surprise. Ironically, since the eagle is announcing its presence to the earth dwellers, they should be on high alert. In their foolishness they will not heed the warning; they will not see these three woes coming. One reason for this may be that the last three trumpets are supernatural in nature. The fifth and sixth trumpet speak of creatures and beings rising up out of the *abusso*,[233] or the bottomless pit, which is a place of spiritual destruction. After the calamity of a tidally disrupted comet crater-chaining across the surface of the earth, people will still be living in the 21st century mindset of positivism,[b] which rejects the spiritual and views the physical as the only cause of the effects that we observe in the universe. The fifth trumpet will change all of that.

It is also interesting to note here how the eagle flying in mid-heaven of Revelation 8:13 is mirrored in the minor prophecy which I call 'the eternal gospel.'[c]

> And I saw another angel flying in mid-heaven, having an eternal gospel to preach to those who live on the earth, and to every nation and tribe and tongue and people; and he said with a loud voice, "Fear God, and give Him glory, because the hour of His judgment has come; worship Him who made the heaven and earth and sea and springs of waters."[d] And another angel, a second one, followed, saying, "Fallen, fallen is Babylon the great, she who has made all the nations drink of the wine of the passion of her immorality."[e]

Again, the message is to those who live on the earth, the earth dwellers, only this time the message is one of redemption and is delivered to them in the form of an angel. While the earth dwellers are being cursed with the three woes announced by the eagle, they are also being blessed with the message of salvation announced by an angel. It is poignant that mankind is exhorted to recognize God as the Creator of all things, especially in consideration of the philosophy of modern times, where mankind denies God's hand in creation.

---

[a] Job 9:25-26

[b] Positivism holds that every rationally, justifiable assertion can be scientifically verified.

[c] See outline in the introduction.

[d] It is interesting here how the angel mentions the 'sea and springs of waters,' as, on our timeline, the sea has just been struck with a mountain and the springs and waters have been poisoned per the second and third trumpets.

[e] Revelation 14:6-8

The word for judgment here is *krisis*,[234] which means 'a decision, judgment,'[235] and also: 'to separate, distinguish, judge.'[236] We derive the English word crisis from this Greek root, which in essence refers to a turning point.

> The Greek word Krino meant separate, judge or decide, and from it came the nouns krites "judge" – from which we get critic, and kriterion, a test to judge by. The related word "krisis" signified the preference of one alternative over another. The Day of Judgment is hemera kriseos, in the Greek New Testament – truly a crisis for those at risk of damnation.[237]

We usually equate judgment with punishment, that is, one's just deserts for bad behavior, but once we dig into the Greek, we find that the last week of Daniel is more of a process of weeding out the good from the bad, the believers from the unbelievers. Each person must be brought to a point of decision. In our time, this process of judgment is conducted over the course of a lifetime, with each individual being responsible for making the most of the life they have been given. However, once the 70th week starts, a strict, end-times schedule comes into play. Everyone on the earth will be required to make a decision for or against God during this seven-year time frame; and not all will have the whole allotted time, as many will perish before the conclusion of judgment. Will the earth dweller recognize God as the Creator-King of the universe, or will he turn away? Will it be heaven or will it be hell? Everyone must decide. We know from the myriads of tribulation saints before the throne in heaven in Revelation 7 that many will respond positively to the message of the eternal gospel. Those who reject it will fall into destruction with Babylon.[a]

---

[a] As we come to understand judgment in its proper context, that is, as a process of separating the good from the bad, it becomes apparent that the church need not be present at this time. If one has accepted Jesus Christ as their Savior, they are the wheat that has already been separated from the chaff; it doesn't make sense to doubly thresh the wheat. This constitutes another talking point for a pre-judgment rapture

The Fifth Trumpet

> Then the fifth angel sounded, and I saw a star fall from heaven which had fallen to earth; and the key of the bottomless pit was given to him. He opened the bottomless pit, and smoke went up out of the pit, like the smoke of a great furnace; and the sun and the air were darkened by the smoke of the pit.[a]

In my timeline of the blowing of the trumpets, I have the fifth trumpet sounding right on the heels of the first four, with little or no pause. The reasons are several. First, we have the rapture, where the Restrainer is taken away, which is a game changer in how the universe works. Supernatural entities hostile to mankind, which up until this point have been operating under strict limitations, are suddenly given free rein over the earth for a short period of time. The proverbial lid has been removed from the mouth of evil, as we discussed earlier about the two women who take the ephah of wickedness to Babylon in Zechariah's night visions. Second, we have a star from heaven, which had fallen (past tense) to earth. This star, which is described with the personal pronoun 'he,' is given a key, and takes action. Knowing that angels are referred to as stars in Scripture,[b] and the fact that this angel has already fallen to the earth, gives the information we need to deduce that this 'star' is a fallen angel. Which particular fallen angel may be up for debate, but I have a strong suspicion that this fallen star is the devil himself. Why would God give Satan the key to the bottomless pit? The answer is simple: so he can open it![c] During the 70th week, God will exert maximum pressure on the earth dwellers via the spiritual entities and principalities that hate mankind most in order to wring the last of the believers out of their number; thus we have the first of three woes.

It is interesting to note that what rises out of the pit darkens not only the sun, but also the air, or *aer,*[238] which not only refers to 'air, the lower air we breathe,'[239] but also 'signifies the 'ruler of the powers in the air', i. e., the devil, the prince of the demons that, according to Jewish opinion, fill the realm of air.'[240] In other words, there is a spiritual manifestation to this darkness, as indicated by the darkening of the *aer*, as well as a physical manifestation, as

---

[a] Revelation 9:1-2

[b] Revelation 12:4 - '...[the dragon's] tail swept away a third of the stars of heaven and threw them to the earth.'

[c] I don't really know how it works, but Satan doesn't get to keep the key; he later gets tossed in himself for 1,000 years.

represented by the darkening of the sun. I think it seems logical that we carry forward this interpretation into our thinking about the locusts which come out of the smoke of the pit, or perhaps, because of their sheer numbers, are described as smoke because they have a similar appearance.

> Then out of the smoke came locusts upon the earth, and power was given them, as the scorpions of the earth have power. They were told not to hurt the grass of the earth, or any green thing, nor any tree, but only the men who do not have the seal of God on their foreheads. And they were not permitted to kill anyone, but to torment for five months; and their torment was like the torment of a scorpion when it stings a man.[a]

To the locusts that rise up out of the abyss, physical power or authority *(eksousia*[241]*)*[b] is given that is comparable to a scorpion. The venom of scorpions worldwide varies greatly in potency and effect, but some have poisons that act as neurotoxins.

> Renowned as one of the deadliest scorpions on the planet, the Deathstalker inhabits the scrublands and deserts of the Middle East and Africa. It has a distinctive yellow color along the legs and tail and a darker body and grows to 3 inches (7.6 cm) in length. The sting from one of these stalkers is excruciating and increases the heart rate and blood pressure. Muscle convulsions and comas are also known complications from the sting from a Deathstalker.[242]

To this we can add respiratory complications and paralysis.

> The Arabian Fat-Tail's sting attacks the central nervous system and results in respiratory collapse and paralysis.[243]

Neurological problems and paralysis are notable characteristics attributable to scorpion venom, which has implications for the rest of the passage. Also, it should be mentioned that scorpions can sting over and over again, limited only by the need to replenish their venom.[244]

The interesting thing about these locusts/scorpions in particular, is that they are given specific instructions as to the scope of their mission. The word used here, which indicates a literal, verbal exchange and is defined as '(denoting speech in progress), (a) I say, speak; I mean, mention, tell, (b) I call, name, especially in the pass., (c) I tell, command', is *ereo*.[245] They are given

---

[a] Revelation 9:3-5
[b] See this word used above in reference to Death and Hades, the fourth apocalyptic rider.

specific directives: do not harm any plant, and do not harm any human with the seal of God on their forehead. Everything and everyone else is fair game. The word used for seal, *sphragis*,[246] '...is often used metaphorically'[247] so it can be taken as literal or symbolic. I personally imagine it to be both; there may be some type of indelible mark made upon the forehead of believers during this time, whether it is a tattoo or a brand or other, that will be an outward sign of faith. This mark will protect followers of Christ from the first woe, but will make it easy for the armies of the Antichrist to identify them and round them up for execution. Hence, the first woe, scorpion locusts, may be used as a part of the process of separating the believers from the earth dwellers; the wheat from the chaff.

The word used for 'torment' in verse 5, *basanizo*,[248] means 'I examine, as by torture; I torment; I buffet, as of waves,'[249] or 'universally, to vex with grievous pains (of body or mind), to torment.'[250] All of this gives the impression that these creatures will attack with intelligence. They have a sting that causes pain and paralysis, but will know when to stop short of killing you. Once they have you down, they will keep you down, stinging you over and over again, acting out a macabre torture scene.

> And in those days men will seek death and not find it; they will long to die, and death flees from them.[a]

The word here used for 'seek' is *epithumeo*,[251] which means '[to] desire, [or] lust after,'[252] '.. what a person truly yearns for; to 'greatly desire to do or have something – to long for, to desire very much.'[253] The word for 'death' is *apothnesko*,[254] a verb which means 'to die,'[255] '...focusing on the separation that goes with the 'dying off (away from).'[256] From the Greek we see how the text is saying that men will long desperately for death as an end to their torment but will be unable to find it. Kept alive by these nasties, only to be stung repeatedly, is a kind of torture that I imagine would drive people mad. Certainly, one would desire to die rather than continue on in a semi-catatonic state, being re-injected with venom at intervals, just enough to immobilize, but not enough to put individuals out of their misery.

---

[a] Revelation 9:6

> The appearance of the locusts was like horses prepared for battle; and on their heads appeared to be crowns like gold, and their faces were like the faces of men. They had hair like the hair of women, and their teeth were like the teeth of lions. They had breastplates like breastplates of iron; and the sound of their wings was like the sound of chariots, of many horses rushing to battle. They have tails like scorpions, and stings; and in their tails is the power to hurt men for five months.[a]

This section describes the locusts in detail, and they sound like nothing mankind has ever seen upon this earth. The word for 'appearance' is *homoioma*,[257] which refers to 'a likeness, or rather: form; a similitude.'[258] '[it]...does not require one element of a comparison to be derived from the other; indeed, it can be wholly separate from it. Rather, it refers to a basic analogy (resemblance), not an exact copy.'[259] What this means for the rest of the passage above is that, where we shouldn't interpret this section literally, that is the locusts don't actually have the faces of men, or the hair of women or the teeth of lions, but that they have characteristics that are similar, such that, if we actually saw one of these creatures, we would agree to the comparison.

It is possible that John was thinking of a cataphract when he wrote of the locusts appearing like 'horses prepared for battle.'

> A cataphract was a form of armored heavy cavalry that originated in Persia and was fielded in ancient warfare throughout Eurasia and Northern Africa. Historically, the cataphract was a very heavily armored horseman, with both the rider and mount almost completely covered in scale armor, and typically wielding a kontos (lance) as his primary weapon.[260]

This would imply that perhaps these creatures have a growth of scales along their faces, or all over their bodies. It is also possible that they might be *wearing* some type of armor instead, and as unnatural as that sounds, it fits the description.

These locusts may also have a yellowish coloring to their head region, potentially lined with spikes, so as to resemble a crown. They also may have markings that resemble a pair of eyes, a nose, and a mouth, so they exhibit what looks like a human face. From the passage we also gather that they have a feature that resembles long strands of hair. It is hard to come to any concrete solutions to some of the aspects listed in the description, but we can imagine the horrific spectacle they might present. Having teeth like lions, however, seems to have ominous implications.

---

[a] Revelation 9:7-10

> Lions possess one of the strongest bites in the animal kingdom. With a bite force of around 650 pounds per square inch, a lion can easily crush the bones and flesh of its prey. A lion's canine teeth can reach a length of up to 3 inches. These massive canines are used for biting, gripping, and tearing apart the prey.[261]

Whereas I do not expect these creatures to have tusks 3 inches long, or a bite force of 650 pounds per square inch, I think what this passage is telling us is that these locusts have teeth that are capable of tearing flesh; perhaps even powerful enough to excise a sizable chunk of meat. If you consider that their mandate is to refrain from killing, yet they have license to torture, then you must allow that disfigurement of face, hands, and other body parts is a distinct possibility. Between their tails and their teeth, you can imagine that one might be scarred for life after an encounter with one of these denizens from the abyss… both physically and mentally. The mention that they have breastplates of iron could be literal or figurative, but perhaps it just means that these bugs are well armored and particularly hard to kill.

Some point out that the sound these locusts make as they fly through the air is comparable to the sound that helicopters make in flight, and so come to the conclusion that this is what is meant. While I admit that this is a possibility, I am persuaded that, considering the balance of the passage, what John is describing is creaturely, not mechanical. Helicopters carry antipersonnel weapons which are specifically designed to kill, which would violate the mandate given to the demon locusts. Helicopters also would not be able to effectively differentiate between those protected by the seal of God and those who were not. One could argue that helicopters might be able to dispense some type of debilitating neurotoxin out of their 'tails' into the air above their targets, but again, this lacks the ability to differentiate between individuals or control dosage so as to render people immobilized, but not dead.[a] It also would not explain their stinging capabilities. If indeed these locusts do turn out to be the biological oddities that I imagine them to be, the fact that the beating of their wings produces such a low frequency as to be compared to the galloping of horses would suggest that they are a fair bit larger than any insect with which we are presently familiar.

The last bit of verse 10 asserts that the power of the locusts resides in their tails, which would make sense if their venom affects the nervous system

---

[a] Possibly, some kind of modern, diabolical flying drone could also be imagined to account for this creature.

and causes paralysis. If these creatures are the result of biological experimentation involving chimerical life forms[a], they may only have a lifespan of five months, and would be similar to typical locusts which live three to five months.[262] Demons that rise up out of the pit might then conceivably use these hybrid lifeforms as avatars. If the locusts emerge straight from the abyss in physical form, then perhaps they are sent back where they came from after five months. Either way, this will not be a pleasant time for the earth dwellers.

> They have as king over them, the angel of the abyss; his name in Hebrew is Abaddon, and in the Greek he has the name Apollyon.[b]

The abyss, or *abussos*[263] is, in Jewish conception, 'an unfathomable depth… the home of the dead and evil spirits.'[264] Also: '…a very deep gulf or chasm in the lowest parts of the earth:… both as the common receptacle of the dead, and especially as the abode of demons.'[265] We learn about the *abussos* from Luke 16:19-31, which describes a paradisaical side and a hellish side to Sheol. Between the two sides 'a great chasm is fixed'[c] which is impossible to cross, and separates the good from the bad. Some scholars take this gulf to be the *abussos*, or bottomless pit. As such, we could think of the abyss as the deepest, darkest place in the underworld. In fact, we learn from Luke 8:31, when Jesus heals the demoniac and sends the evil spirits into a herd of swine, that the abyss is a place that even demons loath to go.

The angel of the abyss has two names. *Abaddon*,[266] which means 'Destroyer' or place of destruction (personified)[267] and *Apollyon*[268] which can be interpreted as 'the destroying one,'[269] or 'cause to perish, be ruined.'[270] It is also interesting to note that the Greek word for 'name' here, *onoma*[271] not only means name, but also 'character, fame, [or] reputation.'[272] More specifically, it can imply '…the manifestation or revelation of someone's character, i.e. as distinguishing them from all

---

[a] Human liver and heart cells have already been grown in mice and pigs for years in order to test experimental medicines. Also, in 2021 US and Chinese researchers jointly announced that human and chimpanzee embryos had been combined in a chimerical hybrid that reportedly lived 20 days before being destroyed. However the article only mentions the one, and in a laboratory setting you never only create one culture or sample for observation. No mention is made of the fate of the other hybrids they indubitably created. If this much has been made public, one can only imagine what is going on behind closed doors.
[b] Revelation 9:11
[c] Luke 16:26

others.' 'According to Hebrew notions, a name is inseparable from the person to whom it belongs, i.e., it is something of his essence.'[273] This is to set up what follows, as the name of the 'angel of the abyss' means destruction. In the Old Testament the abyss (*Abaddon*) is associated with destruction,[a] and is in fact called a 'place of destruction.'[274] The question that remains is this: Is the abyss named *Abaddon* after the dark angel that lives there, or is the angel named *Abaddon* because of the place in which he resides? I suspect the reasons are both, as destruction captures the nature and character of the pit *and* the dark entity which will emerge from it.

On balance, not many angels are mentioned by name in the Bible, fallen or otherwise. This one has two names: *Abaddon* in Hebrew and in the Greek, *Apollyon*. The implications of this may be further-reaching than I imagine, but my personal theory is that the significance of having both a Hebrew and a Greek name is that this prophecy applies to both Jews and Gentiles. This is in contrast with much of Old Testament prophecy and a significant portion of Revelation for that matter, where prophecy has a central focus on Israel.

At any rate, his name means destroyer and he may have already made a few appearances on earth in the Old Testament. The first of these we find in Exodus.

> For the Lord will pass through to smite the Egyptians; and when He sees the blood on the lintel and on the two door posts, the Lord will pass over the door and will not allow *the destroyer*[b] to come into your house to smite you.[c]

Subsequently, the firstborn of every house in Egypt that did not display the blood of a sacrificed lamb on the lintel and doorposts was struck, and among the Egyptians 'there was no home where there was not someone dead.'[d] The identification of an individual in this passage as 'the destroyer' is ominous because we already know of someone who goes by that very appellation. The Hebrew word used here for 'destroy' is *shachath*,[275] the definition for which is given as: 'perhaps to go to

---

[a] Job 31:12, Job 26:6, Job 28:22, and others.
[b] Italics mine.
[c] Exodus 12:23
[d] Exodus 12:30

ruin.'[276] This word carries with it the connotations 'to ruin, or spoil'.[277] This suggests that this destroyer gets his name from his method of killing, which is to corrupt or spoil the flesh, which is then interpreted by man as some form of pestilence. The reaction of the Egyptians seems to corroborate this, as when they see the death of their firstborn, they urge Israel to leave in haste, remarking: "We will all be dead."[a] Perhaps it was the fear of so much sudden death that prompted them to say that; then again, perhaps they were also fearful of contagion deduced from the state of the bodies left behind.

We see the appearance of 'a destroying angel' in other places as well.

> So the Lord sent a pestilence upon Israel from the morning until the appointed time, and seventy thousand men of the people from Dan to Beersheba died. When the angel stretched out his hand toward Jerusalem to destroy it, the Lord relented from the calamity and said to the angel who destroyed the people, "It is enough! Now relax your hand!" And the angel of the Lord was by the threshing floor of Araunah the Jebusite.[b] Then David spoke to the Lord when he saw the angel who was striking down the people, and said, "Behold, it is I who have sinned, and it is I who have done wrong; but these sheep, what have they done? Please let Your hand be against me and against my father's house."[c]

King David had conducted a census to count the strength of his army, which was in disobedience of a direct order from God; thus God reduced the strength of his military force. God gave him a choice of one of three things for his punishment: 7 years of famine, 3 months of being pursued by his enemies, or 3 days of pestilence. David chose not to fall into the hands of his enemies, but let God choose between the other two. God chose pestilence, and a destroying angel was charged with carrying out His order. This angel is also referenced above as 'the angel of the Lord,'[d] and where the Lord stopped him was the threshing floor of

---

[a] Exodus 12:33

[b] The threshing floor of Araunah was located on Mount Moriah, immediately north of David's city and overlooking it. - NASB study Bible note on II Samuel 24: 16

[c] II Samuel 24:15-17

[d] You could argue that 'the angel of the Lord' is different from the destroying angel, but it seems to me from the context that they are one and the same. First the destroying angel is mentioned, then the angel of the Lord is by the threshing floor – which is symbolic of judgment (separating the good from the bad). Then David sees the destroying angel. This is

Araunah the Jebusite. (The term 'the angel of the Lord' appears in several different contexts in the Bible: angel means messenger, so in a general sense, it could just mean 'one who carries out God's will.') The truly amazing thing about this passage is that this destroying angel had to be commanded *twice* to stop. Almighty God is speaking when He first says 'enough!' and then speaks again, saying, 'relax your hand!' It is astounding to consider the need for a second spoken command when you realize that it is the very spoken word of God which brought the universe into existence. One has to wonder if the destroying angel was on the verge of disobeying the first command, something which in the angelic realm would be unthinkable.

Another passage in Scripture where the angel of the Lord is mentioned in a very similar context was when Sennacherib, the king of Assyria, was threatening Jerusalem.

> Then it happened at night that the angel of the Lord went out and struck 185,000 in the camp of the Assyrians; and when the men rose early in the morning, behold, all of them were dead.[a]

The Greek historian Herodotus wrote about this event some 300 years later as seen through the eyes of the Egyptians.

> The next king, I was told, was a priest of Vulcan, called Sethos. This monarch despised and neglected the warrior class of the Egyptians, as though he did not need their services. Among other indignities which he offered them, he took from them the lands which they had possessed under all the previous kings, consisting of twelve acres of choice land for each warrior. Afterwards, therefore, when Sannacherib, king of the Arabians and Assyrians, marched his vast army into Egypt, the warriors one and all refused to come to his aid. On this the monarch, greatly distressed, entered into the inner sanctuary, and, before the image of the god, bewailed the fate which impended over him. As he wept he fell asleep, and dreamed that the god came and stood at his side, bidding him be of good cheer, and go boldly forth to meet the Arabian host, which would do him no hurt, as he himself would send those who should help him. Sethos, then, relying on the dream, collected such of the Egyptians as were willing to follow him, who were none of them warriors, but traders, artisans, and market people; and with these marched to Pelusium, which commands the entrance into Egypt, and there pitched his camp. As the two armies lay here opposite one another, there came in the night, a multitude of field mice, which devoured all the quivers and

---

more like a variation in describing the same thing as opposed to introducing a new character in the middle of the narrative.

[a] II Kings 19:35

bowstrings of the enemy, and ate the thongs by which they managed their shields. Next morning they commenced their fight, and great multitudes fell, as they had no arms with which to defend themselves. There stands to this day in the temple of Vulcan, a stone statue of Sethos, with a mouse in his hand, and an inscription to this effect – "Look on me, and learn to reverence the gods."[278]

The discrepancy in place, that is Pelusium instead of Jerusalem, more than likely points to the probability that Herodotus used Egyptian sources, which may have been a case of conveniently repurposing some of the details. By Sennacherib's own admission, Jerusalem was not sacked during this campaign.

> As for Hezekiah, the Jew, who had not submitted to my yoke, 46 of his strong, walled cities and the cities of their environs, which were numberless, I besieged, I captured, I plundered, as booty I counted them. Him, like a caged bird, in Jerusalem, his royal city, I shut up. Earthworks I threw up about it. His cities which I plundered, I cut off from his land and gave to the kings of Ashdod, Ashkelon, Ekron and Gaza; I diminished his land.[279]

Sennacherib highlights his successes, while marginalizing what was left undone. The fact of the matter is, his campaign was indeed cut short, and although Jerusalem is directly on the way from Nineveh to Egypt, it was left virtually untouched. This is a stunning omission, as it was the refusal of Hezekiah to, as Sennacherib puts it, 'submit to my yoke' that had caused him to initiate the campaign in the first place; it is a mystery of history why he stopped short.

It is likely that calamity struck before the Assyrian army ever reached Pelusium. The mention of field mice many scholars take to be a direct reference to a plague of some kind.

> Although Herodotus never mentions plague, the scholarly consensus is that this was what he was in fact referring to, due to the presence of mice in the story. In his commentary on this account, Robert B. Strassler, editor of The Landmark Herodotus, stated: "This is Herodotus' version of the Jewish story of the pestilence which destroyed the Assyrian army before Jerusalem. Mice are a Greek symbol of pestilence; it is Apollo Smintheus (the mouse god) who sends and then ends the plague in Homer, Iliad I."[280]

Two salient points come to the fore from the Egyptian version of this historical account. First, that the mechanism for death was something that presented symptomatically like that of plague, and second, that the ruin of the army was brought about in a single night. It is unlikely that a plague in the natural sense would prove so fatal over such a short period of time. In any event, the method of the destroying angel in these three instances in Exodus, II Samuel, and II Kings is consistent, though I would propose that the pestilence that he brings is supernatural. At the end of the day, it is debatable whether the angel(s) spoken of in these passages directly refer to Abaddon or not, but mass killing and pestilence would certainly fit the modus operandi of someone referred to as 'the destroyer.'

Many have surmised that the destroyer is the devil himself. I am persuaded otherwise, as Satan throughout Scripture has been portrayed as a very tactful liar and a deceiver, whereas this guy seems to be more of a brute, having the unique ability to corrupt mortal flesh. Abaddon seems more like an attack dog, such that when he is set loose upon humanity, he goes on a rampage and has to be warded off (as in the Hebrew houses of Egypt) or forcefully commanded to cease and desist (as on the threshing floor of Araunah the Jebusite). If the abyss is his realm, this would mean that he is a resident when Satan comes to open it, and as such, he would represent a separate spiritual entity so disruptive that he's kept locked up, and only loosed upon the earth on limited occasions.

> For if God did not spare angels when they sinned, but cast them into hell and committed them to pits of darkness, reserved for judgment;[a]

Taking all of this into account, Abaddon's role in Revelation becomes somewhat of a curiosity. For here we have the manslayer of old showing up at the end of days, taking a back seat to the Antichrist and the false prophet and others, relegated to the unenviable position of playing king over a bunch of creepy bugs, and to top it all off, he isn't even allowed to kill anyone. Given his capabilities, he is definitely being underutilized. If he killed 185,000 people every night, it would take him about 88[b] years to purge the world of its billions, but then again, we have no indication that this represents his peak capacity. Perhaps he is *too* powerful, *too* disruptive. Perhaps the reason for his limited role is that if

---

[a] II Peter 2:4

[b] This is figured on a population of 6 billion, assuming the conditions of the Pale Horseman have already reduced the population of earth by roughly 25% or more. (We aren't given a figure for casualties from the first four trumpets.)

he were set loose upon the earth with no limitations, judgment would be over far too quickly.[a] This also suggests that the 70th week of Daniel is not a death decree for all mankind; rather, it is a threshing floor, where the wheat is separated from the chaff, the good separated from the bad. A time when all the people of the world are going to be called to a point of decision to choose God or choose Babylon.

It also strikes me that, as Apollyon is the king of the demon locusts, he might be one to direct their activities with infernal malice. If God offers protection in the form of His seal upon a person's forehead, Apollyon might offer similar respite for accepting the mark of the beast. There is nothing in Scripture to substantiate this, other than dire warnings against taking the mark,[b] but this would greatly intensify the *krisis* of judgment. Taking the mark of the beast results in the ultimate destruction of those who do so, and as destruction is Apollyon's specialty, this might be something that could become top of mind for him at this juncture.

At any rate, the text below seems to indicate that the first woe will fully come to pass before the sixth trumpet (the second woe) sounds.

> The first woe is past; behold, two woes are still coming after these things.[c]

---

[a] It could also be a form of punishment for not obeying God's first command to stop on the threshing floor of Araunah the Jebusite.
[b] Revelation 14:9-11
[c] Revelation 9:12

The Sixth Trumpet

> Then the sixth angel sounded, and I heard a voice from the four horns of the golden altar which is before God, one saying to the sixth angel who had the trumpet, "Release the four angels who are bound at the great river Euphrates." And the four angels, who had been prepared for the hour and day and month and year, were released, so that they would kill a third of mankind.[a]

The Sixth trumpet is chock-full of numerology. For starters, six is the number for man. The number of the horns of the altar is four, which we have already studied at some length in this book, and it seems to always mean that something is worldwide in scope. In this case, the horns, *keras,*[281] are on the altar, *thusiasterion.*[282] The horns represent 'power and strength'[283] and the altar is 'for the slaying and burning of victims,'[284] and so is probably symbolic of the most powerful or worst period of judgment.[b] Taken all together, we could interpret this section to be stating that what follows is God's final stage of judgment on men that dwell on the earth.[c]

Finally, there are four angels, bound up in the Euphrates, which are to be released. The Euphrates River in ancient times represented the dividing line between east and west. The Babylon of Nebuchadnezzar straddled this river, its fabled waters flowing under the walls and through the city center. The river and the city are closely linked in biblical typology. In such case, there is the implication that these four angels, which presumably will be loosed upon the whole world, have some direct relation to the Babylon of old and the idol worship that promulgated from there. It is also likely that the reference goes much farther back in time, to the first city recorded in the Bible, one located on the same plain as Babylon, called Babel: Babylon being derived from Babel, meaning 'gate of God.'[285] In Assyrian Babel is written as *Bab-ilu*[286] which also means 'gate of God,'[287] and it appears as *Bab-ilium*[288] in Sumarian with the exact same meaning. It is clear in these inferences from three different languages that the Babel of old was a place of religious significance. It is

---

[a] Revelation 9:13-15
[b] Again, the symbolism of the altar suggests bloodshed.
[c] Which has already been announced by the eagle flying in mid-heaven.

quite possible that this means that the Tower of Babel was actually a temple of some sort, that is, a 'gateway to the gods,' and so would represent the introduction of idol worship into the world immediately after the flood. Idol worship has been an integral part of temple pomp and ceremony dating as far back into antiquity as recorded history can tell. The Bible equates idol worship with demon worship.[a] (Since this is the first big construction project that man undertakes after the great deluge, it is quite possible that the worship of wayward spiritual entities was something remembered as opposed to representing a new invention. Thus it may indicate the root of the wickedness that was going on before the flood, but that is a topic for another book.)

If you consider that Babylon, the city of man, is often portrayed in opposition to Jerusalem, the city of God, then this mention of the angels of the Euphrates could also foreshadow how the nations will 'tread underfoot the holy city for forty-two months'[b] during the time of the Antichrist. These four angels may actually be incarcerated in the physical river until the appointed time,[c] which would make the imagery both symbolic *and* literal. In any case, I imagine these beings are released in conjunction with the opening of the abyss and the emergence of the demon locusts and, potentially, a whole host of other nasties:

> The number of the armies of the horsemen was two hundred million; I heard the number of them. And this is how I saw in the vision the horses and those who sat on them: the riders had breastplates the color of fire and of hyacinth and of brimstone; and the heads of the horses are like the heads of lions; and out of their mouths proceed fire and smoke and brimstone. A third of mankind was killed by these three plagues, by the fire and the smoke and the brimstone which proceeded out of their mouths. For the power of the horses is in their mouths and in their tails; for their tails are like serpents and have heads, and with them they do harm.[d]

---

[a] I Corinthians 10:20

[b] Revelation 11:2

[c] Four angels have been bound in the Euphrates until a specific day. Since this 'day' is a part of the cycle of Daniel's 70 weeks, I view it to be measured from the beginning of the cycle, or the declaration of Artaxerxes Longimanus to rebuild Jerusalem in 445 BC (See Appendix A). As the 70th week is currently on hold, this day is also contingent upon the resumption of the prophecy, or when Israel signs a covenant with the Antichrist.

[d] Revelation 9:16-19

At first glance, these horses mentioned above make me think of tanks equipped with flamethrowers and spinning flails mounted in the rear. However, as we consider the context of a world gone mad with a demonic assault, I would not be surprised to find these 'horses' to originate from the abyss, just as the locusts of the fifth trumpet. The same applies for the army; they could be spiritual forces recently emerged from the darkness of the pit, or they could be an army of men, raised up from the earth.

Most scholars look at this passage and conclude that the reference to two hundred million is just another way of saying 'myriads' or of referring to an army too large to count. The problem with this interpretation is that John specifically says that he heard the number – he didn't try to count the number, he *heard* the number. If we presume that God could communicate an accurate vision of the future to John, as evidenced in the book of Revelation, then counting the actual number of the army of horsemen is just a minor detail, even though there weren't nearly that many people in the entire world at the time of writing. I think what the passage is saying here is that God told John the number of the horsemen, for the very reason that they would have been impossible to count. (As in so many cases, I think it is much easier to interpret the Bible when we simply take it at face value.)

The colors of the breastplates are *purinos*,[289] which means flaming, fiery, or of fire,[290] *huakinthinos*,[291] which is 'of hyacinth, of the color of hyacinth, i.e., of a red color bordering on black,'[292] and *theiodes*,[293] which refers to brimstone or sulfur[294] and implies the color yellow. There is a parallelism in the grammatical structure that follows, as out of the mouths of these horses proceed fire and *kapnos*[295] (smoke[296]) and brimstone, and we see still further that these three elements represent a plague upon the earth such that a third of mankind is killed by *purinos* and *kapnos* and *theiodes*.[a]

Between the locusts, Abaddon, and the release of the four bound angels, it is likely that a whole host of other denizens of darkness make

---

[a] *Huakinthinos* is most often translated as dark purple or blue; however, in some instances cited in Homer, Lucian, the Septuagint and others, we have a rendering of this color as more of a dark red or black, per the note in Thayer's. Given the parallelism in the passage, I equate *huakinthinos* with *kapnos*, or smoke.

their appearance at about the same time, which may add some color to a cryptic verse in the book of Daniel, in which an angel describes the end of times kingdom of ten toes:

> "In that you saw the feet and toes, partly of potter's clay and partly of iron, it will be a divided kingdom; but it will have in it the toughness of iron, inasmuch as you saw the iron mixed with common clay. As the toes of the feet were partly of iron and partly of pottery, so some of the kingdom will be strong and part of it will be brittle. And in that you saw the iron mixed with common clay, they will combine with one another in the seed of men; but they will not adhere to one another, even as iron does not combine with pottery."[a]

A common interpretation of this passage is that it is referring to intermarriage between the group of people described as iron and those described as clay. This doesn't really make any sense, however, as with intermarriage the result is that two different peoples merge into one. What is described by Daniel is two totally different classes of 'people' that do not merge – 'as iron does not combine with pottery.' Clinging, or cleaving, is an Old Testament reference to sexual intercourse, so as we consider the phrases 'they will not adhere to one another' and 'in the seed of men,' one way to take this is that it is referring to some kind of procreative act that does not involve a man inseminating a woman. Modern science can provide a possible answer to this riddle in the form of in vitro fertilization. This general process was used in the creation of the human/chimpanzee chimera cultures mentioned in the note above; that is, the embryos were fertilized outside of a living body.[b]

Also, the clay/pottery is in keeping with the biblical image of man. The iron represents something else, possibly something *not-man*. This passage from Daniel could be cryptically referring to some future genetic modification of Earth's biological life forms; not as crazy as it sounds, as the prospect of chimeric fauna has already made the leap from the realm of science fiction to science reality. An animal form that is not created by God may not have His seal of protection on it, and potentially would be fair game for possession to be used as a demonic avatar.[c] The

---

[a] Daniel 2:41-42

[b] As an alternate theory, the 'horses' of the army of 200 million could be advanced machinery; an upscale of the mechanical 'dogs' already being used in police work.

sudden intrusion of hordes of demons and fallen angels into the world fits with this thesis, whether or not they constitute the army of two hundred million. Granted, this all sounds a little far-fetched, but we should not underestimate the technological capabilities of mischievous fallen angels who are much more intelligent than we are, and who have ages of practical experience with arcane concepts about which we can only guess. With the Restrainer gone, they will be able to interact and exchange ideas with mankind freely. As we consider the possibilities, we have to allow that what transpires during this time may be something that we, with our twenty-first century prejudices, struggle to comprehend.

In any event, it may take some time between the release from the abyss of Satan's henchmen until such a large army is raised; we know from other passages of Scripture that the Man of Sin only has a short 42 months to reign, which comprise the last 3 ½ years of the 70th week of Daniel. My guess is that these forces will be used to consolidate his power in the first half of the tribulation and then deployed to destroy every living thing on the earth in the second half. There is a passage in Joel that symbolically refers to a horde of locusts and speaks about an army of which 'there has never been anything like it.'

> A day of darkness and gloom, a day of clouds and thick darkness. As the dawn is spread over the mountains, so there is a great and mighty people; there has never been anything like it, nor will there be again after it to the years of many generations. A fire consumes before them and behind them a flame burns. The land is like the garden of Eden before them but a desolate wilderness behind them, and nothing at all escapes them. Their appearance is like the appearance of horses; and like war horses so they run.[a]

Some scholars associate this passage in Joel with the army of 200 million in Revelation; destruction by fire and the 'appearance of horses' make for a strong correlation. The reference to 'the day of the Lord' a little later in this selection from Joel (verse 11) indicates that these creatures who have the appearance of horses symbolize God's judgment in the last days. As fire, smoke, and brimstone adorn the breastplates of

---

[c] When Jesus exorcised the demoniac, the demons requested permission to enter the herd of swine. Perhaps in the case of a taking possession of a chimera, they wouldn't have to ask first.

[a] Joel 2:2-4

the horsemen of Revelation, and breastplates cover the heart of a warrior, these colors may also symbolically represent their intentions: that is, the extermination of every living thing on the face of the earth – 'nothing at all escapes them.' This would be difficult to believe of a human army, as usually the motivation for service is the booty they gain from killing their enemy; this army keeps nothing for itself and burns everything.

Although war is the only condition specifically mentioned in close association with the four fallen angels of the Euphrates, I suspect that they might be the force behind the Antichrist's rise to power. I think that the four horsemen of the Apocalypse, mentioned in the first four seal judgments, foreshadow the activities of these angels: first they empower the Antichrist for conquest (white horse), then they bring war (red horse), then severe economic oppression[a] (black horse), and finally death (pale horse); the conditions of war and widespread death being realized in the actions of this army of fire, smoke, and brimstone.

You would think that with all of the destruction and mayhem brought on by these supernatural forces, those left on the earth would turn to God. However, the last two verses of chapter 9 reveal some interesting conditions that arise in the hearts of men during this tumultuous time.

> The rest of mankind, who were not killed by these plagues, did not repent of the works of their hands, so as not to worship demons, and the idols of gold and of silver and of brass and of stone and of wood, which can neither see nor hear nor walk; and they did not repent of their murders nor of their sorceries nor of their immorality nor of their thefts.[b]

At face value, it sounds like this prophecy is just a projection into the future of what the original author knew of pagan worship at the time. Our modern sensibilities struggle to apply this description to the lifestyle of the average unbeliever. Some things apply: murders, sorceries (pharmakos[297] – 'used of people using drugs and 'religious incantations'.'[298]), immorality, and thefts. Idol worship, however, seems to be a thing of the past, and the current trend in society is away from a belief in God and the supernatural in general. In the present day, it is not

---

[a] Revelation 13:17, where no one can buy or sell without the mark of the beast.
[b] Revelation 9:20-21

hard to see how the great apostasy, discussed earlier, might be lurking right around the proverbial corner.

Once we take a step back and examine our timeline, however, we see that at this point in the narrative, mankind will have just struggled through a cosmic collision with a comet that has left a third of the earth in ruin. The devastation of our world will drive many to live in fear. Also, at about the same time, creatures from the abyss start to appear and bring torment and misery and pain. The mind of man will be in a very different state when all these things come to pass.

At this juncture, everyone will have converted to some kind of religion: unbelief can only survive in a society that is assured of the comfort and stability of an unchanging world that contains no malicious spirits that go 'bump' in the night. With the rules of the spiritual realm categorically altered, allowing the unrestrained intermingling of the powers and principalities of darkness with the peoples of the earth, atheism will go the way of the dodo bird.[a] There will be two camps: those who come to faith in Jesus Christ through the ministry of the 144,000, and those who turn to the idol worship of Babylon.

---

[a] The Bible often describes idols as blind, dumb, and incapable of movement. But it also refers to them as a habitation for demons or spirits, and as such, fits the model for a proper idol in many cultures the world over. With so many demons running around during the end times, they may be able to infuse these idols with a palpable presence that can be felt by the earth dwellers.

The Seven Thunders, the Angel and the Little Book

> I saw another strong angel coming down out of heaven, clothed with a cloud; and the rainbow was upon his head, and his face was like the sun, and his feet like pillars of fire; and he had in his hand a little book which was open. He placed his right foot upon the sea and his left foot upon the land; and he cried out with a loud voice, as when a lion roars; and when he had cried out, the seven peals of thunder uttered their voices. When the seven peals of thunder had spoken, I was about to write; and I heard a voice from heaven saying, "Seal up the things which the seven peals of thunder have spoken and do not write them."[a]

Revelation 10 starts with this strange scene of a very powerful angel, perhaps even a gigantic angel, coming down out of heaven and placing one foot on the land and one foot on the sea. In biblical terms, the land represents Israel, and the sea represents the Gentiles, so we can be sure that what follows pertains to the whole earth. The Greek word used here for angel is *aggelos*,[299] which can refer to 'a *messenger* or *delegate* – either human or heavenly.'[300] This angel is described as being *ischuros*,[301] which means 'strong' or 'mighty.'[302] 'For the believer, (*isxyrós*) is God's power 'standing by' – ready to *unleash* itself to bring about His preferred-will, through faith. This *engaging* strength is *always and immediately available* from the Lord, which accomplishes *His assignments.*'[303] This same word was used in Revelation 5:2 to describe the 'strong angel' that asks who is worthy to open the Seven-Sealed book. The angel of chapter 10 is clothed with a cloud, *nephelé*,[304] which not only means 'cloud,'[305] but is reminiscent '...of that cloud in which Jehovah is said (Exodus 13:21f, etc.) to have gone before the Israelites on their march through the wilderness.'[306] The rainbow upon his head is described with the same word, *iris*, as the rainbow that surrounds the throne of God in Revelation 4. Also, his face is like the sun, and his feet like pillars of fire; a strikingly similar description is used of Jesus Christ in Revelation chapter 1.[b] These similarities have led some scholars to deduce that this angel is, in fact, Jesus Christ. What seals the deal for me is the oath that this 'angel' swears.

---

[a] Revelation 10:1-4
[b] Revelation 1:15-16

Then the angel whom I saw standing on the sea and on the land lifted up his right hand to heaven, and swore by Him who lives forever and ever, who created heaven and the things in it, and the earth and the things in it, and the sea and the things in it, that there will be delay no longer.[a]

An oath usually has two components. The first component is a divine witness, which is covered here by the appeal to 'Him who lives forever and ever,' or we might say, God the Father. The second component of an oath is a promise regarding one's future action or behavior. And for an oath to truly be viable, the promise of future action must lie within the capabilities of the oath maker, or else it is an empty promise. Here the promise is 'that there will be delay no longer.' As what immediately follows in chapter 11 is the worst of the worst of times, then it makes sense that it is the judgment of God to which He is referring. I would propose to you that only the second person of the Trinity, Jesus Christ, may declare before God the Father that judgment must no longer be delayed. If this were just an announcement, then yes, an angel could convey that message, and they often do so, as we saw earlier in the eagle's announcement to the earth dwellers. It is the swearing of an oath that makes this pronouncement different and identifies this strong angel as Jesus Christ Himself; He is, in fact, the only One who is able to swear such a thing by His own authority/ability. (Jesus also underscores the fact that God is the Creator of all things, yet again decrying the misbegotten philosophies of the modern day from the distance of antiquity.)

If you buy into my thesis that this angel is actually Jesus Christ, then it is the title deed to the earth in His right hand that He lifts to heaven as He swears,[b] which directly implies that it is what is written on the scroll which shall no longer be delayed. In addition, it is this same Seven-Sealed book which He bought with His own blood that gives Him the right of dominion over the earth, and to determine what happens to it. The fact that He is pictured as standing on the land and the sea underscores this authority. The prophecy of the Seven-Sealed book ends with our modern-day chapter 11, so there is but a little bit of it left, hence the book or scroll is described as being little.[c] It is poignant

---

[a] Revelation 10:5-6

[b] Which we have from chapters 4-5.

[c] Some would infer that this speaks to Christ's return to the earth, but I think that the mention of having a foot on both the land and the sea simply portrays Him as having dominion over all

that, when John takes the little scroll from the strong angel, it is already open in His hand,[a] implying that this is something that happens in the midst of ongoing action and, in fact, the scroll has been open and operational since the moment of silence in heaven observed at the beginning of chapter 8.

What has angered Jesus so much that He would swear an oath to the holy Father? I suspect that this interlude in chapter 10 denotes the halfway point of the 70th week of Daniel and represents what is happening between the blowing of the sixth and seventh trumpets.[b] From Daniel we know that at this juncture the Antichrist will break his peace covenant with Israel and commit the abomination that leads to desolation in the temple. Jesus speaks about this time.

> For then there will be a great tribulation, such as has not occurred since the beginning of the world until now, nor ever will. Unless those days had been cut short, no flesh would have been saved; but for the sake of the elect, those days will be cut short.[c]

Most people refer to the seven years of judgment as the tribulation, but technically this term should only be applied to the last 3 ½ years: a period of time that is going to be characterized by the greatest suffering ever witnessed in the history of mankind. It is no wonder that the advent of such tribulation should begin with an oath sworn before God Almighty.

Backtracking a little, we notice that the seven peals of thunder speak out with voices. We do not know what they say, as John is instructed not to write it down. Thunder, in Scripture, is associated with judgment.[d] Most people, when they read this section, come away with the impression that it was just one message that was given, and gloss over the fact that there are seven thunders speaking. Just as there are seven seal judgments, seven trumpet judgments, and seven bowl judgments, here we have seven thunder judgments, so it would be

---

the earth, which meshes well with my theory that the little book is the last bit of the title deed to the earth.

[a] Revelation 10:8

[b] The sixth trumpet chronicles the releasing of the four angels from the river Euphrates and the raising of the army of 200 million. Such a large army would take some time to assemble and ready for war, and this interlude occurs while that is happening.

[c] Matthew 24:21-22

[d] In particular, God's righteous anger, which is a theme in chapter 10.

reasonable to assume that these thunder judgments comprise a fourth set of seven judgments.[a]

Also, when we consider the structure of the judgment sets, we see that there is always an interlude between the sixth and the seventh judgment. Between the sixth and seventh seal we have chapter 7 of Revelation in our modern Bible. Chapter 10 and most of chapter 11 constitute the interlude between the sixth and seventh trumpet. The interlude between the sixth and seventh bowls is just one verse: Revelation 16:15. The point that I am trying to make here is that the seven omitted thunder judgments might well, on the whole, constitute several chapters worth of missing prophecy; that is, the seven thunder pronouncements plus an interlude. One can only guess why John was told not to write them down, but I suspect that these judgments might pertain to the first 3 ½ years of the 70th week of Daniel, and so might contain information that would tip us off as to, perhaps, the identity of the Antichrist, or the Ten Kings, or some other information that might prove untoward if men knew too much about the future. When the time comes, those who have been previously taken up into heaven will have front-row seats to what the seven thunders say, and in that moment we will finally understand.

John is told to take the little book from the angel standing on the sea and on the land.

> So I went to the angel, telling him to give me the little book. And he said to me, "Take it and eat it; it will make your stomach bitter, but in your mouth it will be as sweet as honey."[b]

The contents of the book are revealed as further prophecy a few verses later.

> And they said to me, "You must prophesy again concerning many peoples and nations and tongues and kings."[c]

---

[a] Which is fitting, as we have seen time and time again that the number four often represents the four corners of the earth, and signifies that a particular judgment will have worldwide scope or effect.
[b] Revelation: 10:9
[c] Revelation 10:11

We find from Jeremiah and Ezekiel that the sweetness of eating the word of God represents the calling of an individual to God's service.

> Your words were found and I ate them, and Your words became for me a joy and the delight of my heart; For I have been called by Your name, O Lord God of hosts.[a]

The bitterness that comes later represents God's anger.

> So the Spirit took me up and took me away; And I went embittered in the rage of my spirit, and the hand of the Lord was strong on me.[b]

As such, John is commissioned to prophesy about God's righteous judgment concerning the second half of the 70th week, as this is where we most see the bitterness of God's anger come to the fore; I take this as yet another clue that what comes next pertains to a time of great tribulation.

The Two Witnesses

> Then there was given me a measuring rod like a staff; and someone said, "Get up and measure the temple of God, and the altar, and those who worship in it. Leave out the court, which is outside the temple and do not measure it, for it has been given to the nations; and they will tread underfoot the holy city for forty-two months. And I will grant authority to my two witnesses, and they will prophesy for twelve hundred and sixty days, clothed in sackcloth." These are the two olive trees and the two lampstands that stand before the Lord of the earth.[c]

John is given a measuring rod and told to measure three things: the temple of God, the altar, and the people who are worshiping there. Intuitively, it seems like this work of measuring is representative of judgment, as in comparison to an expected standard, especially given the broader context. While this may be true, if we delve into the Old Testament and look at similar prophecies, in particular Zechariah 2:1 and Ezekiel chapter 40, we find that these instances of measuring are a prediction that something will be built; Jerusalem being rebuilt in the first case, and the millennial temple in the

---

[a] Jeremiah 15:16
[b] Ezekiel 3: 14
[c] Revelation 11:1-4

second. So, even though judgment may be implied (an assumption on my part), the main point here is to prophesy that the temple in Jerusalem will be rebuilt, along with the altar. If there are worshipers in the temple, then that would mean that the sacrifice will also be reinstated by this time.

The identity of these two witnesses has been the subject of much debate. We aren't explicitly told who they are, but if we follow the hints laid out in Scripture, two candidates rise to the top of the list.

> Remember the law of Moses My servant, even the statutes and ordinances which I commanded him in Horeb for all Israel. Behold I am going to send you Elijah the prophet before the great and terrible day of the Lord. He will restore the hearts of the fathers to their children, and the hearts of children to their fathers, so that I will not come and smite the land with a curse.[a]

> Six days later Jesus took with him Peter and James and John his brother, and led them up on a high mountain by themselves. And He was transfigured before them; and His face shone like the sun, and His garments became as white as light. And behold, Moses and Elijah appeared to them, talking with Him.[b]

> And His disciples asked Him, "Why then do the scribes say that Elijah must come first?" And He answered and said, "Elijah is coming and will restore all things…"[c]

We know from Malachi and the words of Christ shortly after the Transfiguration that Elijah is slated to return at some point before Christ's second coming. I subscribe to the theory that if these two witnesses are not a duo of new characters who will be introduced to the world during the 'time, times, and half a time,' that one of them is Elijah. Also, Moses being mentioned in close association with him, both in Malachi (in the last few stanzas of Old Testament prophecy) and then again at the Transfiguration, makes him a good candidate for the other of the two witnesses. The fact that Moses is seen in the company of both Jesus and Elijah, each whose return to Earth at some point in the future is explicitly predicted in Scripture, gives strong support to this theory.

The main reason why I do not think that the Holy Spirit of God will inhabit this last temple built by the hands of man is the judgment prophesied in

---

[a] Malachi 4:4-6
[b] Matthew 17:1-3
[c] Matthew 17:10-11

verse 2. If God were dwelling among His people, He would not bring judgment during this time. Christ spoke about this time of final judgment:

> "Therefore when you see the ABOMINATION OF DESOLATION which was spoken of through Daniel the prophet, standing in the holy place (let the reader understand), then those who are in Judea must flee into the mountains."[a]

> "For then there will be a great tribulation, such as has not occurred since the beginning of the world until now, nor ever will."[b]

This is where scholars derive the term 'Great Tribulation,' and from the context of Daniel, this period of time pertains to the last 3 ½ years of the 70th week. Revelation 11:1 places the completion of the temple as sometime before this halfway mark[c] and, with its direct reference to judgment, places the events of Revelation 11 (that is, the ministry of the two witnesses) as occurring in the second half of this week. The second verse reinforces this idea

> "Leave out the court which is outside the temple and do not measure it, for it has been given to the nations; and they will tread underfoot the holy city for forty-two months."[d]

The court, which was provided for the Gentiles in the layout of Solomon's temple, is not measured, which I take to mean that in the future, when the temple is rebuilt in Jerusalem, it is prophesied to be constructed without such a court. Forty-two months is 3 ½ years, which matches the length of time that Jesus applies to the Great Tribulation.[e] Revelation 11:2 also gives a clue as to what God's judgment on Israel will look like, that is, the holy city will be oppressed by the Gentile nations. More evidence that works to support this proposal surfaces in the following verse.

---

[a] Matthew 24:15-16
[b] Matthew 24:21
[c] In order for the temple to be desecrated it first must be rebuilt.
[d] Revelation 11:2
[e] In other instances in Scripture, whether it is stated as 42 months, 1260 days or 'a time, times and half a time,' the reference is always to the last half of the 70th week. This time frame seems to function as a signal about what Christ calls 'the Great Tribulation.'

> "And I will grant authority to my two witnesses, and they will prophesy for twelve hundred and sixty days, clothed in sackcloth."[a]

When you consider that the Hebrew year is 360 days, then 360 days times 3.5 years = 1260 days = 42 months. Verse 1 implies judgment on Israel, verse 2 says that judgment will last for 42 months, and verse 3 says that two witnesses will prophesy for that same exact period of time. (The prophecy with regard to Israel is measured in days; with regard to the Gentiles, it is measured in months.) The mention of sackcloth relates back to Daniel by way of Joel:

> Gird yourselves with sackcloth and lament, O priests; Wail, O ministers of the altar! Come, spend the night in sackcloth O ministers of my God, for the grain offering and the drink offering are withheld from the house of your God.[b]

If you remember from our study of Daniel 9 earlier, the first thing that the Antichrist does when he comes to power is put an end to the sacrifice and grain offering, which happens at the midpoint of the 70th week. The reference to sackcloth being worn by the two witnesses places their ministry during this same period, as it is an indication that the temple offering is being 'withheld.' This clothing in sackcloth could also represent the mourning of all Israel during this time of intense oppression. We should also note that the phrase '*My*[c] two witnesses' in Revelation 11:3 above identifies the speaker as Jesus Christ, and therefore much of chapter 11 could be viewed as a continuation of, or elaboration on, the oath He made in chapter 10.

Moving on to verse 4, we find more references to Old Testament symbology in relation to the two witnesses.

> These are the two olive trees and the two lampstands that stand before the Lord of the earth.[d]

This refers directly back to the eight visions that Zechariah had in a single night. In the fifth vision he has a conversation with an angel.

---

[a] Revelation 11:3
[b] Joel 1:13
[c] Caps & italics mine. My personal thought is that Christ is speaking here.
[d] Revelation 11:4

> Then I said to him, "What are these two olive trees on the right of the lampstand and on its left?" And I answered the second time and said to him, "What are these two olive branches which are beside the two golden pipes, which empty the golden oil from themselves?" So he answered me, saying, "Do you not know what these are?" And I said, "No, my lord." Then he said, "These are the two anointed ones who are standing by the Lord of the whole earth."[a]

In Zechariah's time, the two olive trees represented Joshua the priest and Zerubbabel (from the royal line of David). The oil symbolizes the anointing of the Holy Spirit. The reference in Revelation 11 to Zechariah signifies how these two witnesses represent the 'Lord of the whole earth' to mankind, and might provide further evidence that the ministry of the 144,000 is over or in decline at this point. Before the tribulation there was the church, with millions of witnesses. Then the church is taken up in the rapture, leaving the job to the 144,000 during the first half of the 70th week of Daniel. Later, in the last 3 ½ years, perhaps there will only be these two. This is the narrative I derive from available sources in Scripture, but the reader should be aware that most scholars would disagree with this viewpoint. I think partly the reason for this disagreement is the mention of the seal that is placed upon the foreheads of the 144,000, signifying protection, and from this it is often conjectured that they will never be harmed. To this I would point out that the two witnesses also enjoy God's protection, as evidenced in verse 5.

> And if anyone wants to harm them, fire flows out of their mouth and devours their enemies; so if anyone wants to harm them, he must be killed in this way.[b]

However, as we see in verse 7, their witness or testimony lasts only for a set amount of time.

> When they have finished their testimony, the beast that comes up out of the abyss will make war with them, and overcome them and kill them.[c]

Likewise, it is quite possible that the 144,000 will have a set length of time for their testimony before they also are martyred. There are several clues for this in Scripture. We see in Revelation 12, which I call the Prophecy of the

---

[a] Zechariah 4:11-14
[b] Revelation 11:5
[c] Revelation 11:7

Woman – and which refers to Israel – where a dragon (Satan) pursues the woman. She is protected from him for 1260 days, or 'a time, times and half a time' in the desert. Seeing that she cannot be harmed, the dragon is furious:

> So the dragon was enraged with the woman, and went off to make war with the rest of her children, who keep the commandments of God and hold to the testimony of Jesus.[a]

The dragon goes off to make war with 'the rest of her children.' If I am correct in my assessment of the woman, these would be children of *Israel* that the dragon persecutes. Not only that, but 'the rest of her children' recognize Jesus Christ as the Messiah. Many of the messianic Jews would have been among those who fled into the desert.[b] Unless the 144,000 are with them, they are going to be among those with whom the dragon makes war. Daniel also speaks to this.

> Then I, Daniel, looked and behold, two others were standing, one on this bank of the river and the other on that bank of the river. And the one said to the man dressed in linen, who was above the waters of the river, "How long will it be until the end of these wonders?" I heard the man dressed in linen, who was above the waters of the river, as he raised his right hand and his left toward heaven, and swore by Him who lives forever that it would be for a time, times and half a time; and as soon as they finish shattering the power of the holy people, all these events will be completed.[c]

First, we notice how the oath taken in this passage is quite similar to the one taken by Jesus Christ in Revelation chapter 10, and continuation into chapter 11,[d] only here the duration of judgment is decreed as 'a time, times and half a time'. (This parallel prophecy provides further indication that the speaker in Revelation 11:1 is the same as the oath taker in chapter 10.) Second, we see how the power of the holy people will be shattered before end time events are completed. As this passage was originally given to God's people of the Old Testament, we can say that it refers specifically to the children of Israel, and

---

[a] Revelation 12:17
[b] See Matthew 24:15-22; Orthodox Jews usually don't mind the New Testament, and so would not be expected to heed this warning.
[c] Daniel 12:5-7
[d] As chapter divisions are a modern convention and not a part of the original manuscripts, you could argue that chapters 10 and 11 should have been one chapter.

can be viewed much in concert with Revelation 12:17 in predicting the destruction of the Jews who do not flee into the desert. I personally suspect that the speaker may be making a direct reference to the 144,000 in the passage above. Regardless, we see by chapter 14 that they are in heaven[a] with their transformed bodies as first fruits of the millennial kingdom.

    I should mention one final note concerning the woman that Satan pursues into the desert: even though there are other children elsewhere that 'hold to the testimony of Jesus,' this does not mean that the ones hiding in the desert all have faith in Jesus. In fact, it would make sense that many of them do not. There is a prophecy in Hosea that foretells the specific condition that will bring about the physical return of Jesus Christ to the earth.

> I will go away and return to My place until they acknowledge their guilt and seek My face; In their affliction, they will earnestly seek Me. Come, let us return to the Lord. For He has torn us, but He will heal us; He has wounded us, but He will bandage us. He will revive us after two days; He will raise us up on the third day, that we may live before Him.[b]

The mention of being raised up on the third day is clearly referring to the resurrection of Jesus Christ. This is a prophecy given to Israel, that when they acknowledge their guilt and seek His face, He will return. It seems to me that they could cut short the 70th week if they would just pray for Jesus to come back early, but at the time when the woman flees into the desert, Jesus has not returned. In fact, Jesus does not return until the very last, at the very end of the 70th week. So, it is at the very end of the week, when all the Jewish nation has been exterminated save those hiding in the desert, that they will finally recognize their guilt as a nation and seek the face of Jesus. Likely, all the remaining Jews will need to do this, unanimously, as a people:

> "It will come about in all the land," declares the Lord, "That two parts in it will be cut off and perish; but the third will be left in it. And I will bring the third part through the fire, Refine them as silver is refined, And test them as gold is tested.

---

[a] The text in Revelation 14:1 mentions Mt. Zion, which is synonymous with Jerusalem; since the rest of the scene, by way of the mention of the throne and the elders is descriptive of heaven, this Jerusalem is widely considered to be the New Jerusalem, the eternal dwelling place of God and His people.
[b] Hosea 5:15-6:2

They will call on My name, and I will answer them; I will say 'They are My people,' and they will say 'The Lord is my God.'"[a]

This passage from Zechariah certainly seems to indicate that the only Jews who survive judgment week will be the ones who have called on the name of the Lord Jesus. Another passage in Zechariah seems to be speaking along these same lines.

> 'For behold, the stone that I have set before Joshua; on one stone are seven eyes. Behold, I will engrave an inscription on it,' declares the Lord of hosts, 'and I will remove the iniquity of that land in one day. 'In that day,' declares the Lord of hosts, 'every one of you will invite his neighbor to sit under his vine and under his fig tree.'[b]

The 'land' spoken of here is referring to the people of Israel.[c] Some see the phrase 'in one day' as referring to Good Friday, when Christ died on the cross. I prefer to see it as a death-to-resurrection cycle; His death on the cross counted as payment for the sins of the world, but it is His resurrection that makes eternal life possible for the rest of us. If Christ did not rise from the dead, we would have no one in Whom to hope for our salvation. We would have no kinsman redeemer to take the Seven-Sealed book from the right hand of the Father and assume stewardship of the earth. Israel, and all mankind, would have been forever disinherited; for even though the title deed would have been paid for in blood, there would have been no one found worthy to receive it. It is the raising of Christ from the dead that makes it possible for us to obtain the salvation for which He gave the ultimate sacrifice.

Even in modern times, Israel as a nation has rejected this salvation, so technically, their iniquity has yet to be removed. This prophecy specifically predicts that the redemption of all Israel will come to pass 'in *one* day.' The reference to the vine and the fig tree is a proverbial picture of peace and contentment, which is indicative of the Day of the Lord.[d] This is usually a reference to the thousand-year reign of the Messiah, but this prophecy is referring to the advent of this epoch as the time of its fulfillment, that is, when all of Jewry will acknowledge and call upon the name of their Messiah. Jesus

---

[a] Zechariah 13:8-9
[b] Zechariah 3:9-10
[c] See NASB study note on Zechariah 3:9
[d] See NASB note on Zechariah 3:10

has promised that He will come when they call on His name, and the very day He returns will mark the establishment of His kingdom on earth, and the reclaiming of all Israel as His people. In fact, you could say that this passage portrays Christ's resurrection, and the Day of the Lord, as the same event, *qualitatively*. Israel will be saved individually and collectively: 'in that day... every one of you.'

Elijah would be ministering to Israel during this time, and this is how he will fulfill the prophecy that he will 'restore the hearts of the fathers to their children and the hearts of the children to their fathers,' and how he will be one who will 'restore all things.' Elijah will lead the children of Israel back to God, and in the nick of time; as their enemies are closing in from all sides, they will finally recognize their sin and cry out to Jesus Christ. Perhaps it is the death of Elijah himself that will be the final straw that moves every single one of them to faith. When Jesus does return to His people, there will be great sadness:

> And in that day I will set about to destroy all the nations that come against Jerusalem. I will pour out on the house of David and on the inhabitants of Jerusalem, the Spirit of grace and of supplication, so that they will look on Me whom they have pierced; and they will mourn for Him, as one mourns for an only son, and they will weep bitterly over Him like the bitter weeping over a firstborn. In that day there will be great mourning in Jerusalem, like the mourning of Hadadrimmon[a] in the plain of Meggido.[b]

When the Jews finally turn to Christ in faith, there will be great sorrow; for not only did their fathers reject their Messiah, but they also pierced (crucified) Him.

Getting back to Revelation 11, the fire that consumes the enemies of the two witnesses (see verse 5 above) potentially alludes to Elijah's encounter with the messengers of King Ahaziah in II Kings 1:10-12, where the king twice sent messengers, and Elijah twice called down fire from heaven to consume them. Furthermore, if we compare the miracles performed by the two witnesses in verse 6 to Old Testament types (that is, extreme drought and water turned to

---

[a] Hadad was a thunder/warrior god worshiped by the Assyrians (Northern Iraq), and Rimmon was a similar god worshiped by the Armenians (Syria). This passage could be speaking prophetically about two of the people groups that will come against Israel in the battle of Armageddon.

[b] Zechariah 12:9-11

blood), these events mirror what happened during the ministries of Elijah and Moses, respectively.

> They have the power to shut up the sky, so that rain will not fall during the days of their prophesying; and they have power over the waters to turn them into blood, and to strike the earth with every plague, as often as they desire.

Again, we are never told explicitly that the two witnesses are Elijah and Moses, but I find the weight of the evidence quite compelling. To top it all off, the prophecy of the seven bowls or vials, Revelation chapters 15 & 16, which I see as a separate prophecy, seems to complement parts of this section, as many of the vials represent the miracles that God wrought through Moses or Elijah in the Old Testament. The first vial, malignant sores, is very similar to the sixth plague of Egypt.[a] The second and third vials, the turning of the sea and the rivers and springs into blood, are similar to the first plague.[b] The fifth vial, darkness over the kingdom of the beast, is like the ninth plague.[c] Finally, the sixth vial, presumably a drought that dries up the Euphrates River, is similar to when Elijah shut up the sky for 3 ½ years.[d] This would be the fulfilling of the line 'they have power… to strike the earth with every plague… '; as such, we can see the seven bowls of wrath as mirroring the plagues that the two witnesses bring on the earth.

The significance of these parallels is twofold. First, it provides further evidence that the two witnesses are, in fact, Moses and Elijah, and second, it strengthens the argument that the ministry of the two witnesses occurs during the second half of the week, as consensus places the seven bowls in that timeframe. In fact, the case could be made that the 3 judgment prophecies that follow chapter 14 (which could be thought of as the midpoint of the 6 judgment prophecies), the prophecy of the seven bowls, the judgment of Babylon, and the prophecy of the coming of Christ, all happen predominantly in the second half of judgment week.[e]

---

[a] Exodus 9:9-11
[b] Exodus 7:14-25
[c] Exodus 10:21-23
[d] I Kings 17 & 18: 3 ½ years; potentially foreshadowing his ministry as one of the two witnesses.
[e] See my outline of Revelation in the introduction.

After the beast kills these two witnesses, verse 8 gives a couple of clues as to where their ministry will end:

> And their dead bodies will lie in the street of the great city which mystically[a] is called Sodom and Egypt, where also their Lord was crucified.[b]

The city is identified as Jerusalem by the mention of the location where Christ was crucified. Also, Jerusalem is compared to Sodom[c] and Egypt[d] in the Old Testament to describe immorality and idol worship, respectively. In essence, Jerusalem is mentioned three times in this verse by way of different imagery/references, which implies an emphatic confirmation. We might even infer that much of Israel will turn once again to idol worship in the last days. The imagery here is that the city of God (Jerusalem) has been defiled and has become like the city of man (Sodom/Egypt).

The bodies of the two witnesses are left unceremoniously lying in the street and denied burial, which is a sign of utmost disrespect. Then the people of the earth go so far as to celebrate:

> And those who dwell on the earth will rejoice over them and celebrate; and they will send gifts to one another, because these two prophets tormented those who dwell on the earth.[e]

In the Old Testament, when the Jews exchanged gifts, it was in celebration of ridding themselves of an enemy.

> Because on those days the Jews rid themselves of their enemies, and it was a month which was turned for them from sorrow into gladness and from mourning into a holiday; that they should make them days of feasting and rejoicing and sending portions of food to one another and gifts to the poor.[f]

By giving gifts at this juncture, those who dwell on the earth identify themselves as enemies of the two witnesses, and by extension, enemies of God.

---

[a] Or spiritually
[b] Revelation 11:8
[c] Jeremiah 23:14-15
[d] Ezekiel 23
[e] Revelation 11:10
[f] Esther 9:22

The section ends with the two witnesses being brought back to life and being caught up in a cloud into heaven. Their enemies witness their ascension and then there is a great earthquake that destroys a tenth of the city. It's possible that this earthquake could be the same one that marks the second coming of Jesus Christ.

> In that day His feet will stand on the Mount of Olives, which is in front of Jerusalem on the east; and the Mount of Olives will be split in its middle from east to west by a very large valley, so that half of the mountain will move to the north and the other half toward the south.[a]

Such a large movement of earth could produce the reaction of the people who 'were terrified and gave glory to the God of heaven.'[b] The end of these events coincides with the end of the second woe.

> The second woe is past; behold the third woe is coming quickly.[c]

Remember, the second woe was the army of two hundred million. It is the third woe that will terminate the second, and in the end be much, much worse for the earth dwellers. It is interesting to note how the first two woes are pointed out explicitly in the book of Revelation, yet the third woe comes with only a warning; it is declared to be 'coming quickly,' with no confirmation as to exactly when it takes place. We are seemingly left in the dark, wondering where the third woe went, as there is no mention of it at all in the rest of the book. You could say that we are woefully uninformed as to when this untoward event occurs in the sequence, and this confusion has given rise to a great deal of speculation about what part of Revelation represents this third woe. I would maintain that it has been hiding in plain sight all along, and that it is exactly what the Scripture says it is.

---

[a] Zechariah 14: 4
[b] Revelation 11:13
[c] Revelation 11:14

The Seventh Trumpet

> Then the seventh angel sounded; and there were loud voices in heaven, saying, "The kingdom of the world has become the kingdom of our Lord and of His Christ; and He will reign for ever and ever." And the twenty-four elders, who sit on their thrones before God, fell on their faces and worshiped God, saying, "We give You thanks, our Lord God, the Almighty, who are and who were, because You have taken Your great power and have begun to reign. And the nations were enraged, and Your wrath came, and the time came for the dead to be judged, and the time to reward Your bond-servants the prophets and the saints and those who fear Your name, the small and the great, and to destroy those who destroy the earth." And the temple of God which is in heaven was opened; and the ark of His covenant appeared in His temple, and there were flashes of lightning and sounds and peals of thunder and an earthquake and a great hailstorm.[a]

Thus ends the prophecy of the Seven-Sealed Book. Christ physically returns to the earth to begin His reign, the nations are judged, the dead are judged, and His faithful servants rewarded. All of the things which have been predicted for thousands of years in Old Testament prophecy will come to a final, world-changing conclusion. I would propose to you that what this passage is speaking of is the day when Christ comes back to establish His millennial kingdom. In short, the seventh trumpet heralds the inauguration of the Day of the Lord, and what follows are things that pertain to this hinge in history. In the warning given that the second woe is over, there is a clue: 'coming quickly' or coming 'as a thief' is how the return of Jesus Christ is described in many places in the Bible,[b] so we could say that He uses this phrase as His calling card.

Perhaps we could say that the Day of the Lord doesn't officially start until Christ comes back, but as the judgment of the nations in Scripture is described as a uniquely horrific time that must begin just before His return, it would be difficult to separate it, qualitatively, from these times. Old Testament references clearly treat it as an integral part of the Day.

> I will display wonders in the sky and on the earth, blood, fire and columns of smoke. The sun will be turned into darkness and the moon into blood before the great and awesome day of the Lord comes.[c]

---

[a] Revelation 11:15-19
[b] Revelation 2:16, 3:11, 16:15, to name a few.
[c] Joel 2:30-31

> Put in the sickle, for the harvest is ripe. Come, tread, for the wine press is full. The vats overflow, for their wickedness is great. Multitudes, multitudes in the valley of decision! For the day of the Lord is near in the valley of decision. The sun and moon grow dark and the stars lose their brightness.[a]

> Wail, for the day of the Lord is near! It will come as destruction from the Almighty. Therefore all hands will fall limp, and every man's heart will melt. They will be terrified, pains and anguish will take hold of them; They will writhe like a woman in labor, they will look at one another in astonishment, Their faces aflame. Behold, the day of the Lord is coming, Cruel, with fury and burning anger, To make the land a desolation; And He will exterminate its sinners from it. For the stars of heaven and their constellations Will not flash forth their light; The sun will be dark when it rises And the moon will not shed its light. Thus will I punish the world for its evil And the wicked for their iniquity; I will also put an end to the arrogance of the proud And abase the haughtiness of the ruthless. I will make mortal man scarcer than pure gold and mankind than the gold of Ophir.[b]

'...The nations were enraged and Your wrath came.' Once you realize that the seventh trumpet announces to the world the Day of the Lord[c], it becomes readily apparent why this trumpet represents the third of the three woes, just as the eagle flying in midheaven proclaimed it so in Revelation 8:13. We should remember that the three woes are directed at the earth dwellers, that is, those who call this fallen and sinful earth home. Earth dwellers are those who have rejected the free gift of salvation of Jesus Christ. Matthew tells us what happens as this last trumpet is blown:

> And then the sign of the Son of Man will appear in the sky, and then all of the tribes of the earth will mourn, and they will see the Son of Man coming in the clouds of the sky with power and great glory. And he will send forth His angels with a great trumpet, and they will gather together His elect from the four winds, from one end of the sky to the other.[d] [e]

---

[a] Joel 3:13-15

[b] Isaiah 13:6-12

[c] Many commentators refer to this section as 'anticipatory', that is, they say it anticipates the day of the Lord, and so the seven bowls are included as a part of the third woe. I would say that the ending to chapter 11 prophesies the actual day of the Lord and represents the end of the Prophecy of the Seven-Sealed Book, which has an independent story line within the greater book of Revelation.

[d] Matthew 24:30-31

[e] Some interpret the larger passage of Matthew 24:29-41 as saying that the rapture and the Second Coming of Jesus Christ will happen at about the same time. My interpretation is that this passage is qualitative, not chronological. I explain what I mean by this in Appendix D, *Qualitative Juxtaposition*.

Why will the tribes of the earth mourn? Because by the time they see the Son of Man in the clouds of the sky with power and great glory, it will be too late to receive forgiveness. For God's people, the Day of the Lord will be a joyous time, where God fulfills all the promises that He ever made to them. For the earth dweller, the advent of Christ's kingdom is a harbinger of doom. Their destiny now is to stand before their Creator at the great white throne, face judgment according to their works, and be thrown into the lake of fire where they will spend eternity in pain, sorrow, and suffering. This is by far the worst of the three woes.

The mention of the ark of the covenant in the temple in heaven tells us about how available God will make Himself during the Millennium. The ark in the Old Testament represented the presence of God. The ark was kept behind a veil in the temple in the Holy of Holies, that is, the most sacred place of all. Here in Revelation 11, the temple is portrayed as being open and the ark in the Holy of Holies is visible for all to see. This means that the veil has been removed; there is no longer a barrier or separation between God and His people. Perhaps this figuratively represents how Jesus Christ, God incarnate, will be living among men upon the earth during His thousand-year reign.

This seventh trumpet also marks the end of prophecy as mentioned back in chapter 10:

> But in the days of the voice of the seventh angel, when he is about to sound, then the mystery of God is finished, as He preached to His servants the prophets.[a]

The mystery of God is a reference to prophecy, and so, the mystery of Revelation 10:7 is finished with the blowing of the trumpet of chapter 11. The sounding of the seventh trumpet also marks the end of the Prophecy of the Seven-Sealed Book, which started with the lengthy process of opening the book (seven seals) and then proceeds with the revealing of its contents (seven trumpets) and ends with the proclamation of the great and mighty Day of the Lord!

---

[a] Revelation 10:7

Practical Tips

Remember the experiment that I proposed in the introduction? Did you read the book of Revelation at least once before starting this book? Has this interpretation and the application of it improved your understanding of this portion of Scripture? If your answer is yes, then it is likely that you have a whole host of different questions than when we started. You may also be wondering: 'Okay, if it is possible that we are currently waiting for confirmation of the running of the black horse on his first patrol, that is, worldwide hyperinflation may be on the verge of rearing its ugly head in the near future, now what?'

The main thing is not to go out and do something drastic like build a nuclear fallout shelter, or immediately convert all your money into gold and silver. There is a saying among traders of the stock market: 'If you are early, you are wrong.' The Bible doesn't tell us when the world is going to end, but there are clues in how it will happen that should give us some insight as to what actions to take as the time gets close. In the meantime, there are some practical things we can do in a measured way that not only can help us prepare, but that also will make life more enjoyable along the way.

For instance, one thing we can do to prepare for difficult times ahead is to start developing some basic skills that will help us in the future. Take a section of rope and learn how to tie a few useful knots. Buy a sewing kit and learn how to mend your own clothes. Learn how to cultivate food crops from seed; it's more difficult than you might expect, but a little experience goes a long way. Buy some basic tools: a hammer, an ax, a spade, a shovel, a hoe, or a wheelbarrow. If you like woodworking, get into that and learn how to make practical things, like chairs, tables, and step stools. A good quality knife can also come in handy in a pinch. The little time and money that it takes to learn and buy a few practical things would be well spent under any circumstances.

Reading a book like this probably brings about some deep introspection of how one leads one's life. Repairing relationships with other people, especially friends and family, is not a bad idea, even if the world is not coming to an end. Taking the first step with someone from whom you are estranged would be advisable, regardless of the circumstances. During the episodes of hyperinflation in Zimbabwe, which began in 2007, people found that the community of their local church proved invaluable for weathering the storms of repeated price devaluations. A diverse group of people are much better at surviving extreme conditions than an individual, as each person brings their own unique skill set to the table. The whole is stronger and more resilient than the parts. So one thing you might think about is how to go about finding a community of people that you can love and trust when times get difficult.

For the here and now, make a bucket list. What are the things you would have wanted to do before you die, and how can you make them happen without breaking the bank? Don't pass up the opportunity to enjoy life because you are too busy worrying about the future. I believe there are still a lot of good times left, especially such as can be had with friends and family.

These are some of the things that you can do to prepare for your physical well-being if times get tough (specifically, I am thinking of the times before the 70th week starts), but to be honest, the most important thing you can do for now and for the future is to figure out your eternal destiny. First, you need to realize that God considers you to be very valuable. The Bible says that God made man in His own image,[a] which means that we are His prized possessions. However, we should also be reminded that being made in His image also comes with a lot of responsibility. If there are beings somewhere in the universe that look like God, but that misrepresent Him and His character through disobedience (in other words, they sin), because God is a just God, those beings must be destroyed, in this case with eternal condemnation and fire. For this reason, the Bible says that the wages of sin is death.[b] Death is what we earn because of our sin. You could say that with the advent of sin, God lost His prized possession.

Man, in this state of being sinful and separated from God, requires some rescuing. The Bible says that 'God so loved the world that He gave His only begotten Son, that whoever believes in Him shall not perish, but have eternal life.'[c] God loves Himself, and is very jealous of Himself; by extension God loves that which is made in His image, and is very jealous of all that has been crafted in His likeness. His desire to recover mankind for the purpose of joining Him in heaven for all eternity is so great, that He sent His Son, Jesus Christ to die on the cross to pay with His blood the death penalty that we

---

[a] Genesis 1:26
[b] Romans 6:23
[c] John 3:16

deserve. How much do you think you would have to pay God to do such a thing? Nothing! '... the free gift of God is eternal life in Jesus Christ our Lord.'[a] When Jesus Christ took the Seven-Sealed scroll from the Father's right hand, He redeemed the earth and claimed His inheritance, and the saints, all the people of the earth who believe in Him, are redeemed as well.

This redemption process is the whole point of the 70th week of Daniel. If God wanted to kill everybody, He could just speak a word and be done with it. In fact, when Jesus does finally come back a second time, that is what He will do; He will dispatch the armies of the Antichrist with the sword that comes out of His mouth. He is God, so there is creative/destructive power in His voice. No, the reason for the last week of judgment is to compel every person living on the earth to decide if they will turn to Christ or not. Everyone must choose. Not only will He go to great lengths to save us, He will also go to great lengths to persuade us. As C. S. Lewis once said: 'Pain is God's megaphone.'[307]

So what will you decide? You can place your faith in Jesus Christ right now by simply praying to Him for forgiveness of your sins and asking Him to come into your heart and make you the person that He wants you to be. It really is that simple to accept this free gift from God. It comes down to a matter of trust. Will you place your trust in Jesus Christ and accept the shedding of His blood to save you from your sins? Or will you reject what He has done for you and depend on your works to justify the life you choose to live? This is by far the most important decision that you will ever make, as it will directly affect where you spend eternity.

As it turns, out there are a few practical advantages to accepting Jesus Christ into your life. Where I can't promise that God will automatically solve all your problems, that is, if you have financial, relationship, or substance abuse issues, etc., those will persist. However, as becoming a follower of Christ also means that your body becomes a temple for the Holy Spirit, that means that all the fruit of the Spirit becomes available to you as you walk with Him.

> But the fruit of the Spirit is love, joy, peace, patience, kindness, goodness, faithfulness, gentleness, self-control; against such things there is no law.[b]

---

[a] Romans 6:23
[b] Galatians 5: 22-23

As you walk with God and allow Him to take control of your life, the Holy Spirit will slowly change your character and make it possible for you to overcome your problems… even and especially the debilitating ones. In addition to this, I can guarantee two more things, based on the many promises included in the Scripture about how Jesus takes care of His own and has a very special place prepared in heaven for every one who comes to Him: Every morning will be new, and every day will be filled with hope. Forgiveness really is something that must be experienced to appreciate the full impact of it in your life. It is my hope that if you are reading this now, you will choose to join me in this grand adventure!

> … let the one who wishes take the water of life without cost.[a]

---

[a] Revelation 22: 17

Appendix A: 70 Weeks of Daniel

In his book *The Coming Prince,* Sir Robert Anderson conducted the seminal investigation on the prophecy of the 70 weeks of Daniel. He first converts years to days using a Hebrew year of 360 days; that is, 483 years (69 weeks) x (a 360-day Hebrew year) = 173,880 days allotted for the first 69 weeks of the prophecy to come to pass. He then takes this allotted time and applies it to known history to see if the timing works out. The 'issuing of the decree to restore and rebuild Jerusalem' is now known as the Edict of Artaxerxes Longimanus on March 14th, 445 BC, a date provided by secular sources. He works from other independent sources to date the coming of the Anointed One on April 6th, 32 AD,[a] which is the day that Christ entered Jerusalem 'lowly and riding upon an ass,' the start of what we now call the Passion Week. 445 BC + 32 AD = 477 years. Then you have to subtract a year, as there was no year zero, that is, from 1 BC to 1 AD is only 1 year not 2, to come up with a total of 476 years. 476 years x (a 365-day secular year) = 173,740 days. Then add 116 days to account for leap years, and another 24 days to include the time between March 14th and April 6th, and you get 173,740 + 116 + 24 equals 173,880 days!

---

[a] Again this date of 32 AD is figured from the fifteenth year of Tiberius Caesar, the beginning of Jesus' ministry, noted in Luke 3:1. Essentially, this date can be deduced by the BC method of rulers and kings, which would correspond to a date of anywhere from 26 – 28 AD. This inaccuracy stems from the fact that the AD calendar was invented somewhere between 521 and 523 years after the birth of Christ, but is recorded as 525 AD on modern calendars. Year 1 was calculated incorrectly, so this throws the whole system off. One might consider it a great historical irony that, in the modern age, with all our technological advancements, we don't even know what year it is!

Appendix B:
Of Monkeys, Typewriters & the Creator

There is an illustration used to communicate the concept of evolution that says if you have an infinite number of monkeys typing perfectly randomly on an infinite number of typewriters, that said monkeys would collectively produce every imaginable work of literature, including such stories as have not yet been conceived by the mind of man, as well as every possible, infinitely long, combination of gobbledygook. And, because infinity is infinite, you would have a never-ending time frame in which to accomplish the 'writing' of all these books.

Evolutionists have latched on to this idea, as it ascribes godlike qualities to this concept of chance, as a way of trying to make the impossible seem possible. They argue that over a very long and unimaginable time, say several billion years, anything even remotely possible not only *can* happen, but that it *must* happen. The problem with this line of reasoning is that it represents a misapplication of the above concept. The last time I checked, 13.8 billion – the accepted age of the universe – does not equal infinity. In fact, a googleplex (10^{100}) still falls *infinitely* short of infinity, because, though it is an unimaginably large number, it is yet finite, and finite numbers do not possess godlike power. Thus, with regard to any question involving the development of life on the earth by 'chance,' we must do the math to determine if 'chance' has had enough opportunities to actually do the job.

As it turns out, the complexity of DNA in even the most rudimentary of one-celled organisms presents a massive barrier to happenstance. Oversimplifying the simplest of these, Stephen C. Meyer, in his book *Signature in the Cell*, calculates the probability of a 150-amino acid protein chain arranging itself at random in an idealized primordial soup in consideration of 3 basic requirements for life: 1) All bonds between amino acids must be peptide bonds, 2) all amino acids must be left-handed, and 3) any amino acid sequence that supports life must form a stable, three-dimensional structure. To find the probability of life arising at random we multiply these three factors together to figure how difficult it is. We start by assuming that the soup exists under ideal conditions; that is, it is chock-full of the correct amino acids that support life, in the right concentrations for the linking up of those building blocks into long chains, and that there is no oxygen present to muck things up. Right off the bat, what follows is a gross underestimation of the actual probability for the undirected origin of life, but it does serve as an instructive illustration.

In laboratory settings, amino acids form peptide and non-peptide bonds with equal probability, thus the occurrence of the bonds that we need, the peptide bonds, happens about 50% of the time, or ½. We can figure the probability of a chain of amino acids, 150 units long, consisting of all peptide bonds as $(½)^{149}$ (we are counting the bonds, not the acids).[308] This works out to roughly 1 chance in 10^{45} (that is a 10 followed by 45 zeros!). But we're only getting started. Likewise, right-handed and left-handed versions of amino acids are generated with 'equal frequency,' so the probability of all left-handed acids in our 150-unit-long protein chain works out to be much the same, that is $(½)^{150}$, or again, about 1 in 10^{45}.[309] Multiplying these two requirements yields 10^{45} X 10^{45} or roughly 1 chance in 10^{90}.

We still have one more to go: the last requirement is that the end result be a stable protein chain, as opposed to just some random assortment of amino acids that just falls apart. Here Meyer relies on a paper published by Douglas Axe in 2004, where the calculated number of functional proteins possible, based on the protein having the ability to fold into a three-dimensional stable structure able to support life, worked out to be 1 in 10^{74}. Multiplying 10^{90} by 10^{74} yields 1 chance in 10^{164} (that is a 10 followed by 164 zeros!).

We're still not done yet! So far we have only calculated the probability, or perhaps we should say the *improbability*, of producing a simple protein chain 150 amino acids long that might have the ability to support life. To build a single-celled organism, you would need hundreds of these protein chains, all pre-programmed with symbiotic cross-functionality to support the complex communication, replication, and finely tuned enzymatic regulation of chemistry within the cell. An estimation of the probability of the complexity of this cooperative balance occurring undirected is left out of the calculation, so again, we are grossly underestimating. Meyer explains.

> If we assume that a minimally complex cell needs at least 250 proteins of, on average, 150 amino acids and that the probability of producing just one such protein is 1 in 10^{164} as calculated above, then the probability of producing all the necessary proteins needed to service a minimally complex cell is 1 in 10^{164} multiplied by itself 250 times, which is $(10^{164})^{250}$ or 1 in $10^{41,000}$. This kind of

> number allows a great amount of quibbling about the accuracy of various estimates without altering the conclusion. The probability of producing the proteins necessary to build a minimally complex cell – or the genetic information necessary to produce those proteins – by chance is unimaginably small.[310]

Meyer apparently has a gift for understatement. Just to underscore the magnitude of his finding, that is a 10 followed by 41,000 zeroes! The copyright on his book is 2009, so undoubtedly significant changes and advancements have occurred in the fields of genetics and biology that may fine tune some of these numbers, but as quoted above, 'a great amount of quibbling' can take place without changing the conclusion.

To bring a little perspective to the unimaginable, Meyer then calls on the work of mathematician Bill Dembski, to assess what they call the 'probabilistic resources' of the universe to determine if, in spite of it all, life might have been theoretically possible to arise at any time, anywhere in the universe. They start with the smallest unit of time.

> According to physicists, a physical transition from one state to another cannot take place faster than light can traverse the smallest physically significant unit of distance (an indivisible quantum of space). That unit of distance is the so-called Planck length of 10^{-33} centimeters. Therefore, the time it takes light to traverse this smallest distance determines the shortest time in which any physical event can occur. This unit of time is the Planck time of 10^{-43} seconds.[311]

Dembski calculated that if there are 10^{80} elementary particles in the observable universe, and the universe has existed for 10^{17} seconds (the amount of time generally accepted since the Big Bang[a]), and all of these particles act as quickly as possible, that is 10^{43} times per second, this fixes 'the total number of events that could have taken place in the observable universe since the origin of the universe at 10^{140}.'[312] The estimated number of elementary particles in the observable universe may have risen since his 2009 publication, but again, as Meyer pointed out so astutely, we're just 'quibbling' about a few zeroes among 41,000. As you can clearly see, the probabilistic resources of the entire known universe are 24 orders of magnitude below the 10^{164} required to guarantee the production of just one 150 amino acid protein chain, and 40,860 orders of

---

[a] I personally do not believe the ages of the earth and the universe to be billions of years old, but I like this argument as it works from widely accepted, though empirically unproven, assumptions.

magnitude below that which would be required to produce a single-celled organism. In other words, this represents an *impossibility*.[a] It is no wonder that we see Jesus Christ rising up from the pages of Revelation to repeatedly stake His claim as the Creator of all things.

And remember: these calculations represent a gross underestimate! These odds only play out this 'favorable' if you assume that molecules obtain perfectly random interaction, which is not a real-world condition. The natural laws of physics prevent this by imposing order on the system. Furthermore, the chances of the requisite number of proteins to self-arrange *cross-functionally* as they form – that is, pieced together such that their chemical interactions are constructive, like software code – is unimaginably prohibitive. At the very least, we can say that, categorically, this sort of thing did not happen by chance.

---

[a] The response of the scientific community to this argument in recent years has been to propose an infinite number of universes, or a multiverse. (This is not a new idea, but its recent rise in popularity is suspect.) Implicitly, this is an admission that one universe simply doesn't provide enough possibilities to make the genesis of life feasible. Meyer does not go so far as to state that undirected creation is an *impossibility*, though if you have any understanding of mathematics and probability, he certainly seems to directly imply it.

Appendix C
The Age of Grace

The absence of the church in Old Testament prophecy is an omission that rings loudly in the modern mind. It raises the question: Why the mystery? What sets the church apart? Are New Testament believers different from Old Testament believers? The Apostle Paul does a good job of addressing this issue.

> What shall we then say that Abraham, our forefather, discovered in this matter? If, in fact, Abraham was justified by works, he had something to boast about – but not before God. What does the Scripture say? 'Abraham believed God, and it was credited to him as righteousness.'[a]

> Is this blessedness only for the circumcised, or also for the uncircumcised? We have been saying that Abraham's faith was credited to him as righteousness. Under what circumstances was it credited? Was it after he was circumcised or before? It was not after, but before! And he received the sign of circumcision, a seal of the righteousness that he had by faith while he was still uncircumcised. So then, he is the father of all who believe but have not been circumcised, in order that righteousness might be credited to them.[b]

Paul is laboring to point out that Abraham is the faith-father of all followers of Christ: Abraham, by faith, trusted that God would provide for his justification in the future, and in the present day we look back to the time when the sin of the world hung upon a tree. Circumcision was a sign that Abraham had been credited with righteousness and, as Paul points out, righteousness came first. (Circumcision was more than a sign for Abraham, as it was a direct command of God, so it was a matter of obedience, as well as a sign.) Our faith is the same as father Abraham in that our trust is in the same Person for the very same thing.

If the means by which we are credited with righteousness is the same today as of old – that is, by believing that God will do what He says He will do

---

[a] Romans 4:1-3
[b] Romans 4:9-11

– then what sets the church apart from Old Testament believers? The key difference in my estimation is the ministry of the Holy Spirit. In reference to the Holy Spirit, our Lord prepared His disciples.

> "But I tell you the truth: It is for your good that I am going away. Unless I go away, the Counselor will not come to you; but if I go, I will send Him to you. When He comes, He will convict the world of guilt in regard to sin and righteousness and judgment: In regard to sin, because men do not believe in Me; in regard to righteousness, because I am going to the Father, where you can see Me no longer; and in regard to judgment, because the prince of this world now stands condemned."[a]

Christ was referring to something new. Up until this point, the dwelling place for the Holy Spirit was in the temple, and typically the Holy Spirit was poured out temporarily on the prophets, the judges, or a king or two. Now the Holy Spirit was coming to dwell in the hearts of *all* believers, to bear witness to the perfect work of Jesus Christ, as the apostle Paul expresses so succinctly.

> Don't you know that you yourselves are God's temple and that God's Spirit lives in you?[b]

The prophet Joel prophesied about this outpouring of the Holy Spirit:

> "And afterward, I will pour out My Spirit on all people. Your sons and daughters will prophesy, your old men will dream dreams, your young men will see visions. Even on My servants, both men and women, I will pour out My Spirit in those days."[c]

Jesus also predicted the effect on His disciples of the giving of the Holy Spirit.

> "But you will receive power when the Holy Spirit comes on you; and you will be My witnesses in Jerusalem and in all Judea and Samaria, and to the ends of the earth."[d]

---

[a] John 16:7-11
[b] I Corinthians 3:16
[c] Joel 2: 28-29
[d] Acts 1:8

These verses underscore the fact that with the advent of the church, God was changing His method of operation with regard to the ministry of the Holy Spirit. All believers would now possess the call and command to be filled with the Holy Spirit and become God's emissaries to the world.

The Apostle Paul expands upon this historic development.

> Now that faith has come, we are no longer under the supervision of the law. You are sons of God through faith in Christ Jesus, for all of you who were baptized into Christ have clothed yourselves with Christ. There is neither Jew nor Greek, slave nor free, male nor female, for you are all one in Christ Jesus. If you belong to Christ then you are Abraham's seed, and heirs according to the promise.[a]

In Christ, the Jew is no longer a Jew, and the Gentile is no longer a Gentile; we are all the Body of Christ, heirs to the promise given to Abraham.

In times of old, the nation of Israel was supposed to be a light to all the people of the world, drawing them to the temple of God, where He would make Himself known, as we learn in Solomon's dedication prayer for the temple.

> "Also concerning the foreigner who is not of Your people Israel, when he comes from a far country for Your name's sake (for they will hear of Your great name and Your mighty hand, and of Your outstretched arm); when he comes and prays toward this house, hear in heaven Your dwelling place, and do according to all for which the foreigner calls to You, in order that all the peoples of the earth may know Your name, to fear You, as do Your people Israel, and that they may know that this house which I have built is called by Your name."[b]

Solomon underscores the fact that the people of God, Israel, and the temple of God, were assembled so that 'the peoples of the earth may know [God's] name.' What was new with the coming of the Holy Spirit at Pentecost is that the believer *became* the temple. By this means, instead of being located in one place on Earth, and drawing all the world to Himself, the Spirit would now empower all believers, spreading His witness with the wanderings of His people, searching out the lost, convicting them of their sin, and bringing them to righteousness.

The time of the church will not last until the end, however.

---

[a] Galatians 3:25-29
[b] I Kings 8:41-43

> For I do not want you, brethren, to be uninformed of this mystery – so that you will not be wise in your own estimation – that a partial hardening has happened to Israel until the fullness of the Gentiles has come in; and so all Israel will be saved; just as it is written, "The Deliverer will come from Zion, he will remove ungodliness from Jacob."[a]

The partial blindness that afflicts Israel will be removed when the 'fullness of the Gentiles comes in.' This means that once that last believer comes to faith in Jesus Christ, the mystery of the church, that is, the fullness of the Gentiles, will be complete, and God will pick up where He left off in His plan for Israel: the 70th week.[b]

---

[a] Romans 11:25-26
[b] In Scripture, the 'fullness of the Gentiles' refers to the Church Age.

Appendix D
Qualitative Juxtaposition

There are qualitative comparisons that appear in Scripture which are more a result of the Hebraic view of time than they are syntax or language. These structures occur in both the Hebrew and the Greek biblical text, though they are strictly indicative of the culture of the former. In presenting this viewpoint, I am making an assumption that the notions of Jewish culture about time in the Old Testament uniquely reflect God's perspective. That is, since I believe that Scripture is inspired by God, who communicates His message to mankind through the culture, personality, and intelligence of the writers of the Bible, then I would expect Him to take such care as to not allow anything to be included which did not reflect His intent or perspective.

As such, the Hebrews had a distinctly different view of time than the Greeks.

> When we study the Old Testament, we find that time is derivative for the Hebrews. That is, the understanding of time in the Old Testament came from how it described the events of human life and God's interaction with people. For example, time was measured from harvest and agricultural occurrences. Ruth and Naomi arrived in Bethlehem at the beginning of the barley harvest (Ruth 1:22). Or, time was referenced to the sacred events of God's interaction in Israel's history. Time was related to an event that took place and how that event was related to something else that had occurred. Time was not an abstract something over and above events. Herein lay the basic difference between the Hebrews and the Greeks.[313]

The Greek view of time – from which we derive our 'modern' view – emphasizes the flow of time in a linear fashion; that is, we think of time as a line that grows ever longer in one direction. But the Hebrew concept of time was arranged in cycles.

> The Old Testament has no general word for "time" in the abstract sense at all. Neither does it have special terms for past, present, and future. The most common word for "time" means the moment or point at which something happened, or will happen, for example, "Behold, about this time tomorrow, I will send a very heavy hail" (Ex. 9:18, *NASB*).[314]

For the Hebrew, time was not a continuum in which events take place; rather, it was a cycle of happenings marked by momentous events.

> Another way of seeing this difference is to notice that the Hebrews developed no idea of eternity as timelessness. This was a Greek notion. The Hebrews had no idea that there could be life and experience without time. For them, life was time, or better, "to live was time." There was no time where there were no life events, and no life events where there was no time. In the Old Testament, life was humanity's form of existence (Job 1:21; Ps. 90:3-12) and this was time.

> One could characterize the difference between how the Hebrews understood time and how we do by saying that time for us is "chronological" and time for them was "qualitative." In the Old Testament, events and persons were differentiated and arranged, not by their position in chronological sequence to each other, but according to the impact of their occurrence.

> The Hebrews were impressed by the weightiness or significance of things and people, not by how many ticks on a clock went by while doing something. This explains why when scholars study the Old Testament, matters that are revealed by their research to be widely separated with reference to time (our definition) can, if their content coincides, be identified and regarded as simultaneous by the Old Testament (because of their view of time). The worshiper experienced past acts of salvation, such as the exodus, as contemporary and happening right then, even if the exodus occurred in the past.[315]

We noticed this cyclical view of time when we studied the gap between the 69th and 70th weeks of Daniel. These two periods of time are separated by thousands of years, but because they are a part of the same cycle of events, they are written just as if one follows directly from the other. We also saw this with Nebuchadnezzar's dream of the statue of different metals,[a] and Daniel's vision of the four beasts.[b] The gap in each of these prophecies is ignored because the important thing is the cycle of events, not the strict timing.

Honestly, I think this flows directly from God's view of time. We should understand that God lives outside of what we call time. From His viewpoint, all of time is laid out before Him like a mural on a wall. When He looks at each of our lives, He doesn't just see us in the present; He sees our whole lives from birth to death, every moment laid out before Him in His eternal present. The past is just as accessible to Him as the future. This is how He can say "Jacob I loved, Esau I hated"[c] before

---

[a] Daniel Chapter 2
[b] Daniel Chapter 7
[c] Romans 9:11-13

they were even born.[a] I imagine that He doesn't see our lives as a slow-moving line; rather, as a collection of high points and low points.

Interestingly enough, this is how our memory works. We don't remember everything; just the good times and the bad times, and some of the quirky times in between. We tend to remember things in association with other memories that are similar, not chronologically but qualitatively. For example, when we reminisce about high school, we have associated memories of friends, proms, and graduations; rare would be the fellow that would remember the whole of his first week in the order that it happened! And thus, as God composes His message to mankind, He doesn't mention everything, just the important bits, and those by association (or cycles), and not necessarily in order of occurrence.

The examples I have pointed out so far are instances of what I call a qualitative series or cycle of events. There is a gap in each of the prophecies, but otherwise, all the foretold events are arranged in the order in which they occur. Once you figure out that there is a gap in the sequence, everything starts to make sense. There is another form which I call qualitative juxtaposition, which has a few unique distinctions from the serial form, but reflects the same perspective of a qualitative view of time. It appears as a set of two ideas or events which are reversed in order of time; the most important event is listed first, and the event of lesser importance listed second, though they are usually both quite notable in their own right. This construction is often misunderstood to simply be a restatement of the same, when two different things are meant.

We see an example of this in Matthew 24. In verses 29-35 it says the sun will be darkened, the moon will not give its light, and the stars will fall from the sky, and *then* the sign of the Son of Man will appear in the sky, and all the tribes of the earth will mourn when they see the Son of Man coming in all His glory. Then in verses 36-44 it says that people are eating, drinking, and marrying when suddenly the elect will be taken out of the earth, essentially describing an event that no one sees coming. In the first instance there are terrifying signs in the sky, but in the second people are making merry and carrying on just as normal; the way it is presented makes it seem to the Western mind that it all relates to the same event. How can we explain this? I propose that these are two

---

[a] This passage is specifically speaking to the promises God gave to Abraham about the land and blessings which were passed down through Isaac. Esau spurned this inheritance, while Jacob coveted it. God observes everything from His eternal present, so the birth of these two men is inseparable, qualitatively, from the lives they choose to lead.

separate happenings that describe the return of Christ, arranged in the text *qualitatively*. That is, the more important part of the cycle is listed first: verses 29-35 which describe the second coming of Jesus Christ to the earth to begin His reign as King of kings and Lord of lords, and the also very significant, but somewhat less kingly event, the rapture, where Christ meets believers in the air, listed second, is seen in verses 36-44. Most schools of thought concerning biblical prophecy put the rapture before the Second Coming, so we have a consensus that the rapture happens first. We can assert that the two events are mentioned in reverse order, chronologically; thus, we have a qualitative juxtaposition. (Appendix E, *The Parable of the Rich Young Man*, presents another example of qualitative juxtaposition which appears within the ideological structure of the narrative.)

Genesis chapters 1 & 2 constitute another type of qualitative comparison. We could say that chapter 1 is about the creation of the universe and life on Earth; chapter 2 covers the same creation event in about the same time frame but focuses on the creation of man. There are two cycles or topics here, and they happen at about the same time. Perhaps we could say that chapter 2, the chapter about man, is nested, time-wise, within the larger context of all of creation, which is the focus of chapter 1. At any rate, it is clear to see from the narrative that the flow is not strictly chronological but is arranged topically, or according to cycles of events.

Before I close this section it is worth mentioning that perhaps we could apply a qualitative comparison between Revelation 6 (which speaks about the Seven Seals) and Revelation 8 (which covers six of the Seven Trumpets). A counter-argument to the general thesis of this book could be made that this also might be a nested qualitative arrangement, which would imply that these events all happen within the time frame of judgment, instead of my interpretation that the seals happen before and the trumpets later. While I admit this is possible, we do have between the seals and the trumpets chapter 7 and the first few verses of chapter 8, which constitute a time of transition, that is, the gathering of the 144,000 and the half hour of silence in heaven. In the qualitative juxtaposition above, there is no transition; events are placed in direct succession textually, giving the initial impression that there is no disruption in the timing of the events. In fact, I consider this point to be a sort of signature or tell; in all the examples of qualitative comparison in Scripture that I have observed so far, there is no transition in the text that would indicate a change or break in the timing of events.[a]

Understanding how the Hebrews viewed time, and hence how God views time, is instrumental in understanding Scripture, and especially prophecy. It can be hard, with our Western mindset about time and how we say that we *use* time, to acquaint ourselves with a more Eastern concept about how happenings *are* time. It's not about how much happens in a given amount of time, but more a matter of the quality of what happens; time is not measured, it is recorded. To the Hebrews, life was more about making history than it was about passing time.

---

[a] As such, the three transitions or interludes in Revelation, between the sixth and seventh seals, trumpets, and bowls respectively, would denote continuity.

Appendix E
The Parable of the Rich Young Man

> And someone came to Him and said, "Teacher, what good thing shall I do that I may obtain eternal life?" And He said to him, "Why are you asking Me about what is good? There is only One who is good: but if you wish to enter into life, keep the commandments." Then he said to Him, "Which ones?" And Jesus said, "YOU SHALL NOT COMMIT MURDER; YOU SHALL NOT COMMIT ADULTERY; YOU SHALL NOT STEAL; YOU SHALL NOT BEAR FALSE WITNESS; HONOR YOUR FATHER AND MOTHER; and YOU SHALL LOVE YOUR NEIGHBOR AS YOURSELF."[a] The young man said to Him, "All these things I have kept; what am I still lacking?" Jesus said to him, "If you wish to be complete, go and sell your possessions and give to the poor, and you will have treasure in heaven; and come and follow Me." But when the young man heard this statement, he went away grieving; for he was one who owned much property. And Jesus said to His disciples, "Truly I say to you, it is hard for a rich man to enter the kingdom of heaven. Again I say to you, it is easier for a camel to go through the eye of a needle, than for a rich man to enter the kingdom of God." When the disciples heard this, they were very astonished and said, "Then who can be saved?" And looking at them Jesus said to them, "With people this is impossible, but with God all things are possible."[b]

The parable of the rich young man has befuddled Christians for centuries. On the face of it, there seems to be the implication that riches exclude a man from the kingdom of God, and we should sell everything and live in abject poverty. Furthermore, Jesus seems to be saying that it is impossible for a rich man, *because* of his riches, to enter the kingdom of God. There has long been circulated a legend that there was once a gate in Jerusalem that was referred to as 'the eye of the needle,' through which a camel might pass if it bent down on its knees; thus the reasoning goes, a rich man, if he humbles himself *can* enter the kingdom of God after all. The problem with this interpretation is that it is simply not true; no historical evidence has ever been found to prove that a gate in the walls of Jerusalem ever went by that name. I think that the correct interpretation of this passage is that Jesus is in fact saying that it is impossible for a rich man to enter the kingdom of God. His disciples clearly understood what He meant, and He confirms their understanding when He says, "With people this is impossible…" However, if we approach this

---

[a] CAPS denote a quotation from the Old Testament
[b] Matthew 19:19-26

passage with a perspective gleaned from the greater part of Scripture, understanding that it is through God's grace, given as a free gift, and not by works that we are saved, then the rich young man's encounter with Jesus starts to make sense. The key to understanding the passage is to figure out what Jesus means when He says, 'rich man.'

Right off the bat, the very first words out of the rich young man's mouth establishes his fatally erroneous viewpoint: "What good thing shall I do that I may obtain eternal life?" This seems to indicate that he wants to earn or buy his salvation, that is, he wants to know what course of action he can take that will have the effect of producing eternal life. He's not thinking of accepting it as a free gift, he wants to know what he can do to *deserve* eternal life. Jesus calls him out in his foolhardiness when He responds with: "Why are you asking Me about what is good? There is only One who is good…" In a parallel version of this episode, in Mark 10:18, Jesus is recorded as saying: "No one is good except God alone." If only God is good, then everyone else, including the rich young man, is bad, which means that what he deserves is not the kingdom of God, or sanctification, but condemnation. That is to say, he is already condemned based on prior behavior; anything the rich young man might do to try gain God's favor cannot undo the evil he has already done. The interesting part here is that Jesus *is* God. As such, He is referring to Himself when He says: 'There is only One who is good… '.

Jesus seems to offer a carrot, however; there is one way to please God and that is to "keep the commandments," to which the rich young man responds with a foolish question ("Which ones?"), as if any of the Ten Commandments were discretionary. (Perhaps if he actually did love his neighbor as himself, that would count as extra credit?) At this point, Jesus calls him out for a second time. He could have simply responded with 'All of them,' but curiously, He only names six. The number seven represents perfection in Scripture and thus is the number for God. Six is the number for man, and implies something that is incomplete or that falls short of perfection. Symbolic of all the commandments, with their associated implications of exactitude, Jesus is listing here six ways that this rich young man in particular has fallen short of the kingdom of God.

The young man, however, seems to think he has done an upstanding job of following the commandments. Oblivious, he responds with: "All these things I have kept; what am I still lacking?" I imagine that Jesus may have been rolling His eyes at this point. This poor rich boy just doesn't get it; he's looking for something *else* he can do, besides obey the law. Perhaps he could put Jesus up in a nice hotel, or take Him away from His beggar/prostitute/tax collector/fisherman friends and introduce Him to some of his influential contacts. Perhaps he was thinking of donating some land to the cause, as it was said he owned much property. Being rich, it might just be that he was superficial in his outlook on life, and thought that only his outward appearance or reputation mattered. He obviously did not consider the fact that God knows all about him. He probably reasoned that because he hadn't murdered anyone or slept with another man's wife that he had not sinned; but Jesus sees the desires of the heart, and it is in his heart, at the very least, where the rich young man has fallen short.

So Jesus calls him out for a third time. He tells the rich young man to sell his possessions and give to the poor, and after he has done that, he should come and 'follow Me.' Jesus is challenging the rich young man to either put Him first or his riches first. The young man walks away dejected, representing his choice to serve money over Jesus/God. And what is the first commandment? 'You shall have no other gods before Me'.[a] If the rich young man hasn't followed the first commandment, how can we believe that he has followed any of the others?

It is against the backdrop of this conversation that Jesus presents us with a gem of iconic wisdom: 'It is easier for a camel to go through the eye of a needle than for a rich man to enter the kingdom of God.' However, if we have been paying attention, Jesus has actually identified *two* ways for a rich man to enter the kingdom of God. The first way is to keep the commandments; the second way is for the rich man to give up his riches and follow Jesus. When Jesus appears to repeat Himself describing how to enter the kingdom of God, He is actually differentiating between the two: the second way is hard, the first impossible. As impossible as it was for the rich young man to keep the commandments – as Jesus points out three times – it would have been quite doable for him to give up his property holdings and follow Christ, though admittedly difficult. We could rewrite this passage as: 'Truly I say to you, it is hard for a rich man to enter the kingdom of heaven [that

---

[a] Exodus 20:3

is, follow Christ, because rich men tend to love their riches]. Again I say to you, it is easier for a camel to go through the eye of a needle [impossible], than for a rich man to enter the kingdom of God [by works, i.e., keeping the commandments].'

I would propose that this is another example of qualitative juxtaposition, mentioned in Appendix D. Only here it is not events, but ideas that are being compared. Again, the order of comparison usually describes the most important thing first and the less important thing second. In the passage above, keeping the commandments is mentioned first, and following Christ is mentioned second. However, when Jesus presents the juxtaposition, He mentions following Him first (hard), as that is the part we most need to hear, and the keeping of the commandments second (impossible).[a]

One final thing to note: 'The phrase 'kingdom of God' occurs 68 times in 10 different New Testament books, while 'kingdom of heaven' occurs only 32 times, and only in the Gospel of Matthew.'[316] The Gospel of Matthew is recognized as being written mainly to a Jewish audience,[317] and so the phrase 'kingdom of heaven' or 'kingdom of the heavens' – just as we have seen above – refers to Christ's earthly kingdom, which for the Jews would be the coming messianic kingdom or what Christians refer to as the Millennium. Certainly when Christ spoke of the kingdom of heaven, this is how it would have been understood by His contemporaries.

---

[a] I include an interpretation of this passage here as a second to the example of Qualitative Juxtaposition presented in Appendix D, as any biblical principle that is put forth should have at least two good scriptural references.

Appendix F
The Church Clock

How many times in Hollywood movies have you seen an old homeless man on the sidewalk with a sign around his neck that says: 'The End is Near'? It is kind of a running joke, for as long as people have been predicting the end, people have been making fun of them for doing so. The interesting thing about all of this is that as I have begun to study the Scriptures in earnest, I find myself thinking that the old homeless man of the silver screen may be on to something. For starters, I have found prophecy to be somewhat less deterministic[a] than I had originally expected; certainly the happenings prophecy foretells will occur at some point, but the *when* and the *how* seem at times to be a bit negotiable. God Himself seems to be willing to allow for loose interpretations of His own prophecy, where the welfare of His children is involved. One example is the Old Testament prophecy about Elijah returning to pave the way for Christ.

> "Behold, I am going to send you Elijah the prophet before the coming of the great and terrible day of the Lord. He will restore the hearts of the fathers to their children and the hearts of the children to their fathers, so that I will not come and smite the land with a curse."[b]

This prophecy was very well known in Jesus' time. In fact, the Pharisees and Sadducees were reading Malachi and watching for the coming of Elijah, when they should have been reading Daniel and watching for the coming of the 'anointed one,' since Daniel gives the exact timing for the fulfillment of his prophecy. A prophecy of John the Baptist was given before he was born.

> "It is he who will go as a forerunner before Him in the spirit and power of Elijah, TO TURN THE HEARTS OF THE FATHERS BACK TO THE

---

[a] Deterministic – Relating to the philosophical doctrine that all events, including human action, are ultimately determined by causes regarded as external to the will.
[b] Malachi 4:5-6

CHILDREN, and the disobedient to the attitude of the righteous, so as to make ready a people prepared for the Lord."[a]

From the Scripture we have quoted above, it should be clear that John the Baptist was not actually a reincarnation of Elijah, but that his role is similar: John introduces Christ to the world before His first coming, and Elijah is destined to reappear upon the earth to introduce Christ to the world before His second coming. They both go before, to prepare the hearts and minds of men. It is against this backdrop of prophecy that Jesus later says something rather peculiar:

> "From the days of John the Baptist until now the kingdom of heaven suffers violence, and violent men take it by force. For all the prophets and the Law prophesied until John. And if you are willing to accept it, John himself is Elijah who was to come."[b]

The 'it' to which Jesus is referring is the kingdom of heaven. Here Jesus is saying that IF the Jews are willing to accept the kingdom of heaven – that is, accept Him as their Messiah – THEN John the Baptist would become a substitute for Elijah, and thus play the role of paving the way for the first *and* second coming of Christ. I do not think it a mistake that the first words that John is recorded as saying in the book of Matthew are: "Repent, for the kingdom of heaven is at hand."[c] He is clearly indicating that the advent of the messianic kingdom is nearly upon them. Granted, Christ would still have to suffer and die, and in addition, there are a number of Old Testament prophecies that would still have to come to fruition. Daniel's 70th week was still yet to happen, for one. But as I read prophecy, if one-third of the Jews had repented and accepted Christ as their Messiah,[d] all of history thereafter would have been radically different. There would have been no church as we know it today (as there would have been no gap to fill between Daniel's 69th and 70th weeks), as the messianic kingdom would have been inaugurated probably by the middle of the first century. All the people yet to be born would likely still have come into existence, but in a very different, millennial-type world.

---

[a] Luke 1:17
[b] Mathew 11: 12-14
[c] Matthew 3:2
[d] Zechariah 13:9 & Hosea 5:15 taken together

Of course, God knew the Jews would reject Him; that is why He sent John and not Elijah. However, this did not change the fact that the kingdom of heaven was indeed at hand. Instead of seizing the moment, the Jews took it upon themselves to condemn their Savior/Messiah to a brutal death and plead for the release of a murderer.[a] When Jesus presents the crowd with IF, what He means is that it didn't have to be that way. God did not predetermine that the Jews would reject Him; that was something they did of their own volition. IF the Jews had accepted Jesus, I would imagine that Pontius Pilate would have taken a much more aggressive role in the persecution of Jesus, and that He would have died instead at the hands of the Romans for instigating what would have been viewed as some kind of rebellion as king of the Jews. As it was, the Jewish leadership did their dirty work for them.

The poignant observation that I make here is that God is willing to allow for alternative interpretations of prophecy, especially if it affords Him an opportunity to extend His grace. Many times God's hands are tied ironically by the stubbornness/disobedience of His own people. Sometimes in prophecy the WHAT and WHEN are predetermined, but the HOW is left up to us. And as I see it, the WHEN is not always set according to days, months, and years, but according to the behavior of God's people.[b] All of this brings us to my idea of the church clock.

The seven letters to the seven churches in Revelation chapters 2 & 3 inform my idea of what I am calling the church clock, or the countdown timer. These letters can be understood from at least five different viewpoints. The first viewpoint is that of each of the churches to which the letters were initially addressed. The second viewpoint is that of the whole first-century church. The third viewpoint is that the seven letters can be seen as universal instruction for all churches everywhere, at any time. The fourth viewpoint is that they can be seen as instruction for every individual that is a part of any church, anywhere, anytime. A fifth point of view, however, is a bit different from the first four, which sees these seven letters as prophetic, thus foretelling the history of the church. This is quite a statement to make offhand; the full treatment of the subject could easily fill a book. I will attempt to provide a cursory case for this

---

[a] Luke 23:19

[b] This is not always the case; for example, once judgment starts there will be a strict schedule of events.

view below, but the reader should realize that this position is not accepted by all Christian scholars.

Ephesus

> To the angel of the church in Ephesus write: The One who holds the seven stars in His right hand, the One who walks among the seven golden lampstands, says this: 'I know your deeds and your labor and perseverance, and that you cannot tolerate evil people, and you have put those who call themselves apostles to the test, and they are not, and you found them *to be* false; and you have perseverance and have endured on account of My name, and have not become weary. But I have *this* against you, that you have left your first love. Therefore, remember from where you have fallen, and repent, and do the deeds you did at first; or else I am coming to you and I will remove your lampstand from its place—unless you repent. But you have this, that you hate the deeds of the Nicolaitans, which I also hate. The one who has an ear, let him hear what the Spirit says to the churches. To the one who overcomes, I will grant to eat from the tree of life, which is in the Paradise of God.'[a]

The first church mentioned is Ephesus, which is said to represent the apostolic, or first-century church (32 AD – 100 AD[b]). The first clue that Ephesus represents the apostolic church is the mention that they '... put to the test those who call themselves apostles.'[c] If somebody showed up at church today and claimed to be an apostle, nobody would believe them; an apostle would have to be someone who had the privilege of being tutored personally by Jesus Christ Himself and as such, should be long dead. Likewise, the only church on our timeline that would have to deal seriously with such claims would have been the first-century church, as human lifespans do not allow for any measure of believability at later dates. It is interesting to note that none of the other churches are specifically warned about these false apostles, though they certainly should have been on the lookout for similar deceptions.

---

[a] Revelation 2:1-7
[b] Dates given for the prophetic periods of the Seven Churches are approximate. Different scholars give different dates; for instance, many present a significant overlap for the times of the apostolic church and the suffering church, whereas I do not.
[c] Revelation 2:2

Christ provides another clue when He says, '... you have left your first love.'[a] It is clear from the epistles of the New Testament that the first-century church had a serious problem with legalism.[b] Many of the first Christians were Jews who were accustomed to following the Mosaic law, and so had a hard time giving up the old ways. We see many times in the epistles the churches being exhorted that salvation is through God's grace alone, and not a result of works. Where we see these exhortations, it seems that these churches had started down the road to a works-based faith and needed to be reminded of their first love: Jesus Christ and His abundant grace. And finally, Ephesus was a church which figured prominently in the ministry of Paul the apostle, warranting a letter that was to become widely recognized as inspired Scripture, the epistle of Ephesians, giving it a strong association with the first century. The other six churches did not figure quite so prominently in the church of the first century, and so therefore would not be suitable to represent that era.

It is interesting to note that Christ's warning to the church at Ephesus is: 'Therefore remember from where you have fallen, and repent and do the deeds you did at first; or else I am coming to you and will remove your lampstand out of its place....'[c] 'Coming quickly,' or 'like a thief in the night' is biblical code for the return of Christ. Paul warns us that the apostasy will come before the day of the Lord (and the rapture);[d] this tells us that even at this early date, the church had succumbed to a state of corruption that warranted a warning from the Lord Himself. Apostasy is the state of having turned away from Christ, so inasmuch as the apostolic church had turned to works (or the law) for salvation, this represented a rejection of the perfect work Christ had completed on the cross, an offense that Jesus takes personally. One gets the sense from this letter that His coming could happen at any time; the very mention of it here implies that if events had played out a bit differently, that is, if the apostolic church had not repented, church history might have been very short indeed!

---

[a] Revelation 2:4
[b] Acts 15:1-12; Romans 3:20-28; Galatians 2:16, 3.2-5, 10-14; Colossians 2:16-23
[c] Revelation 2:5
[d] II Thessalonians 2

Smyrna

> And to the angel of the church in Smyrna write: The first and the last, who was dead, and has come to life, says this: 'I know your tribulation and your poverty (but you are rich), and the slander by those who say they are Jews, and are not, but are a synagogue of Satan. Do not fear what you are about to suffer. Behold, the devil is about to throw some of you into prison, so that you will be tested, and you will have tribulation for ten days. Be faithful until death, and I will give you the crown of life. The one who has an ear, let him hear what the Spirit says to the churches. The one who overcomes will not be hurt by the second death.'[a]

The second church on our prophetic timeline is Smyrna. Smyrna represents the persecuted or suffering church (101 AD – 325 AD); the name is derived from the perfume myrrh, which was used in embalming the dead. Myrrh must be crushed in order to release its fragrance, and so it has long been regarded as a symbol of pain and suffering. Christ calls attention to their suffering throughout the short letter, even mentioning that they would 'have tribulation for 10 days'.[b] Some scholars point to 10 of the Roman emperors, starting with Nero, who can possibly account for the 10 days mentioned, but this doesn't really work because 1) Nero was a first-century emperor (54 AD – 68 AD), so the timing is wrong and 2) the persecution initiated by Nero, though grotesque and intense, was mainly prosecuted in the vicinity of Rome, and was not a campaign that could be said to be empire-wide or church-wide. Instead, I would point out a period of time from 303 AD to 313 AD, where, by official decree from the emperor Diocletian, every Roman citizen and slave in the empire, from the east to the west, was compelled, upon pain of death, to participate in the sacrifice. This decree was ostensibly not directed against any one group, though everyone knew the Christians worshiped Jesus Christ alone, and not Caesar, or Roma, or Victory, or any of the other Roman gods or goddesses. The result was an empire-wide pogrom against Christians that lasted for 10 years. Eusebius, a Christian historian, says of the tribulation brought about by this decree: 'By the grace of God, the persecution came to a complete end in its tenth year, though it had begun to die down after the eighth.'[318] It really is not hard to make the case that Smyrna represents the suffering church.

---

[a] Revelation 2:8-11
[b] Revelation 2:10

Pergamum

> And to the angel of the church in Pergamum write: The One who has the sharp two-edged sword says this: 'I know where you dwell, where Satan's throne is; and you hold fast My name, and did not deny My faith even in the days of Antipas, My witness, My faithful one, who was killed among you, where Satan dwells. But I have a few things against you, because you have there some who hold the teaching of Balaam, who kept teaching Balak to put a stumbling block before the sons of Israel, to eat things sacrificed to idols and to commit *acts of immorality*. So you also have some who in the same way hold the teaching of the Nicolaitans. Therefore repent; or else I am coming to you quickly, and I will make war against them with the sword of My mouth. He who has an ear, let him hear what the Spirit says to the churches. To him who overcomes, to him I will give *some* of the hidden manna, and I will give him a white stone, and a new name written on the stone which no one knows except he who receives it.'[a]

The third letter was to be sent to the church at Pergamum, which represents the marriage of the church to the world (326 AD – 600 AD). Again, meaning can be found in the name. Pergamum, likely because the city was located on a hill, has come to mean 'elevation.'[319] Another interpretation of the name Pergamum could be rendered as 'high place,' which was associated in biblical times with pagan temples and idol worship. Alternately, if we dive into the morphology[b] of the word, examining its Greek roots, we come up with '*per*,'[320] which means 'fully concerning; wholly, very, really'[321] and '*gamos*,'[322] which means marriage.[323] Putting this together, we can come up with a meaning of 'concerning marriage,' 'by means of,' or 'through marriage.' This is especially poignant when we consider our previous discussion in the body of this book. When Theodosius I decreed that Christianity should be the official religion of the Roman Empire, there were no pagan martyrs; the pagans simply assimilated into the new world order, bringing their beliefs with them, and the result was the transformation of festivals like the winter solstice and spring equinox into Christmas and Easter respectively. In many and significant ways, pagan idolatry had entered the church. After spending a few hundred years trying to forcibly destroy Christianity, the Roman elite changed their tactics and

---

[a] Revelation 2:12-17
[b] Morphology is the study of the forms of words.

married/joined themselves to the church. What they failed to change as outsiders would be easier to manipulate as insiders. The mention of the diviner Balaam in the letter further cements this outlook as, in the Old Testament, it was his advice to Balak, king of Moab, to incite God's anger against Israel by seducing her sons to marry the daughters of Baal worshipers.[a] The children of Israel subsequently fell into idol worship *through marriage* as a consequence.

Christ issues a similar warning to Pergamum as He did to Ephesus: 'Therefore repent; or else I am coming to you quickly....'[b] The warning here conveys a greater sense of urgency: 'coming to you quickly' as opposed to simply 'coming.' The church had again replaced Christ, this time with pagan[c] idolatry. With the prophecy of Pergamum, we see that the church had already committed apostasy twice on a significant enough level to warrant a warning (this time an urgent admonishment), but not full-scale judgment.

At this point, it might be pertinent to speak to perspective. Because this is prophecy, it would be tempting to say, since Pergamum is not the last church mentioned, that is, since we already know the outcome, the church at Pergamum was never in any danger of bringing judgment upon themselves and putting an end to the church age because of their behavior. The fact that it's prophesied ahead of time makes us feel like it was always a one-hundred percent probability that things would work out the way they did. However, in hindsight, we can say that just because something didn't happen, this doesn't mean that it didn't *almost* happen. A narrow escape is a narrow escape, whether viewed in hindsight or as something revealed ahead of time. Some say that the Nazis in World War II were only six months short of developing a functioning nuclear bomb. New evidence has recently come out that they weren't actually that close,[324] but the mere prospect of the Nazis in possession of a nuclear device is quite sobering. This would have totally changed not only the course of the war but also all of modern history. The razor's edge of historical caprice shears away any notions of certitude; we can all look back through time and

---

[a] Numbers 22-24 & 25

[b] Revelation 2:16

[c] As mentioned earlier, I use the term pagan to specifically refer to the Roman priesthood; however, we may generally apply it to all forms of idol worship which have their genesis in ancient Babylon. Though the gods which the peoples of the earth have worshiped down through the centuries may be legion, the globally ubiquitous observances of the winter solstice and spring equinox as rebirth and fertility rituals all trace their origins back to Babel (Babylon).

breathe a collective sigh of relief that Hitler did not prevail. Knowing how things will turn out ahead of time doesn't change probability; it was still a close call. Just because the church didn't end with Pergamum doesn't mean that it wasn't close to ending with Pergamum, hence Christ's warning.

Thyatira

And to the angel of the church in Thyatira write: The Son of God, who has eyes like a flame of fire, and His feet are like burnished bronze, says this: 'I know your deeds, and your love and faith and service and perseverance, and that your deeds of late are greater than at first. But I have *this* against you, that you tolerate the woman Jezebel, who calls herself a prophetess, and she teaches and leads My bond-servants astray so that they commit *acts of* immorality and eat things sacrificed to idols. I gave her time to repent, and she does not want to repent of her immorality. Behold, I will throw her on a bed *of sickness*, and those who commit adultery with her into great tribulation, unless they repent of her deeds. And I will kill her children with pestilence, and all the churches will know that I am He who searches the minds and hearts; and I will give to each one of you according to your deeds. But I say to you, the rest who are in Thyatira, who do not hold this teaching, who have not known the deep things of Satan, as they call them—I place no other burden on you. Nevertheless what you have, hold fast until I come. He who overcomes, and he who keeps My deeds until the end, TO HIM I WILL GIVE AUTHORITY OVER THE NATIONS AND HE SHALL RULE THEM WITH A ROD OF IRON, AS THE VESSELS OF THE POTTER ARE BROKEN TO PIECES, as I also have received *authority* from My Father; and I will give him the morning star. The one who has an ear, let him hear what the Spirit says to the churches.'[a]

The fourth church letter is to Thyatira, which has been described as the medieval church (601 AD – 1452 AD). This is the longest of the letters to the churches, and it corresponds to the longest span of time in church age prophecy. Thyatira means 'sacrifice of labor,'[325] which is interesting to note as the one commendation that Jesus gives this church is: 'I know your deeds, and your love and faith and service and perseverance, and that your deeds of late are greater than at first.'[b] This one positive thing that Christ says about the church at Thyatira stands in stark contrast to the criticism in the rest of the letter, the mention of Jezebel standing out as particularly incriminating. Jezebel in the Old Testament was the daughter of Ethbaal, which means 'Baal's man [or] with

---

[a] Revelation 2:18-29
[b] Revelation 2:19

Baal.'[326] As this indicates, Jezebel's father was a Baal worshiper, and she followed closely in her father's footsteps. King Ahab married Jezebel, and together they led all of Israel into idol worship, elevating the religion to official status in the Northern Kingdom.[a] Jezebel went so far as to have the prophets of the Lord executed.[b]

At this point, it would be prudent to remind ourselves that this letter is addressed to the whole church during this time, regardless of denomination or creed. The whole church is made up of those who take the name of Jesus Christ, officially recognized as such or not. Between the commendation, those whose deeds 'are greater than at first,' and the criticism, those 'who tolerate Jezebel,' it seems clear to me that Jesus is referring to two distinct groups of people within the church at large. By the same token, there is also a distinction here between those who tolerate Jezebel and those who represent Jezebel herself, who is steeped in idolatry and guilty of murder. To be clear, the way I read Christ setting up the logical flow of this letter, Jezebel would represent a third party to the church, that is, *outside* the church. There can be no commendation for those who tolerate the conduct of a Jezebel.

The balance of history betrays the truth of the matter. From violence, intrigue, simony, sexual perversions involving prostitutes,[327] and murder,[328] the papacy must be considered far and away the frontrunner for the appellation Jezebel. It was during this age of the prophesied church that the papacy can be said to have consolidated her power with the sole claim to popery:

> The claim was finally made to stick in the West 19 years after the Great Schism, when, in 1073, Pope Gregory VII forbade Catholics to call anyone pope except the Bishop of Rome. ... in actual fact this title was not commonly accepted in its present meaning prior to 1073.[329]

The seat of power was transferred from the Emperors of Rome to the church over the course of centuries, culminating in 1073 AD with the formality of the title pope solely to be conferred upon the Bishop in Rome. This is a significant point to make, as it was during the period of the prophesied church of Thyatira that the papacy rose to power. It was the papacy that introduced the

---

[a] I Kings 16: 32-33
[b] I Kings 18:4-13

church to the worship of images and relics such as holy water, the worship of Mary, worship of saints and angels, and the adoption of transubstantiation (the belief that the bread and wine of communion are the actual body and blood of Christ, not just representative).[330, a]

Unfortunately, the comparison to Jezebel does not end with leading the church into idol worship:

> Failure to give wholehearted allegiance to the pope was considered treason against the state punishable by death. Here was the basis for slaughtering millions. As Islam would be a few centuries later, a paganized Christianity was imposed upon the entire populace of Europe under the threat of torture and death.
> Thus Roman Catholicism became "the most persecuting faith the world has ever seen… [commanding] the throne to impose the Christian [Catholic] religion on all its subjects. Innocent III murdered far more Christians in one afternoon … than any Roman Emperor did in his entire reign" [331,332]

The biblical Jezebel arranged the deaths of God's prophets; Christians who did not follow the pope were slaughtered by papal decrees upon claims of heresy by the medieval Jezebel. Many of these believers were part of what might be called a primitive church; a church that had no center, no leader except the claim that Jesus Christ was the head of the church, not the pope. Many of them traced their history back to apostolic times, a claim that, ironically, in spite of official 'tradition,' the institutional church cannot truthfully make. These primitive churches were found throughout Europe and Anatolia.[333] They were given many names which, for the most part, they would not ascribe to themselves: they were called Albigensians, Waldenses, Bogomils, Cathars, Patarenes, Paulicians, Poor Men of Lyons, Passagini, Josepini, Arnaldistae, Speronistae, and others.[334]

> The inquisitor, David of Augsburg, admitted that formerly "the sects were one sect" and that now they hold together in the presence of their enemies. These scattered notices, taken from among many, are sufficient to show that primitive churches were widespread in Europe in the twelfth and thirteenth centuries, that in some parts they were so numerous and influential as to have a large measure of liberty, though elsewhere they were subjected to the most cruel persecution, and that, although many names were given to them, and there must have been a

---

[a] Catholics maintain that prayers to the virgin Mary and the saints and relics, etc. only convey honor or veneration and not worship; many Christians, however, define prayer as a form of worship.

variety of views among so many, yet they were essentially one, and had constant communication and fellowship with one another.[335]

The institutional churches of both the east and the west held to the cult of Constantine, that is, the assumption of all the power and authority of Christ Himself. To enforce this, it was claimed by the inquisitors of the Byzantine empress Theodora, that they brought about the deaths of some 100,000 Paulicians between the years 842 and 867 AD.[336] Not to be outdone, Pope Innocent III led a crusade against the Albigensians in southern France (1209 AD), essentially declaring war on his fellow Christians. '...the most beautiful and cultivated part of Europe at that time was ravaged, became for 20 years the scene of unspeakable wickedness and cruelty and was reduced to desolation.'[337]

The institutional church made the claim that these extreme measures were necessary to stamp out heretics. However, those who have read the writings of these primitive churches come to a conviction that these were of a Bible-based faith. Nineteenth-century historian William Jones writes:

> That to justify the Waldenses and Albigensians is indeed to defend the reformation and reformers, they having so long before us, with an exemplary courage, labored to preserve the Christian religion in its ancient purity, which the church of Rome all the while has endeavored to abolish.[338]

The aim of the papal armies during the 1209 AD Crusade was not to reform but to exterminate; the entire populations of some towns were burned alive.[339] This all occurred before the institution of the Inquisition had been established. Accounts of hundreds of people being tortured or burned alive, atrocities prosecuted by papal inquisitors, fill the historical records for some six hundred years. The great irony here is that the sheer number of Christian martyrs executed during the Middle Ages at the hand of the papacy far exceeds that which was done in 300 years by the Roman Empire. Historian John Dowling in 1845 wrote:

> ... it is estimated by careful and credible historians that more than 50 millions of the human family have been slaughtered for crime and heresy by popish persecutors.[340, a]

The question that comes to mind is, was Christ referring to this largely forgotten, primitive church when He says in his letter to Thyatira: 'your deeds

---

[a] This number would include the prophesied times of both Thyatira and Sardis.

of late are greater than at first'? Could He have been referring to martyrdom? This was the fate of those believers who did not tolerate Jezebel, the murderess. It is chilling to realize that the administration of the papacy during the Middle Ages is eerily similar to the prophecy of the totalitarian government of the Antichrist during the 70th week of Daniel.

There is yet another comparison to be made to the biblical Jezebel. She was not only well known for her indulgences in idolatry, leading the children of Israel astray, and the murder of God's prophets, but she also played the key role in securing Naboth's vineyard for King Ahab, an act of particular guile and intrigue that one could say presages the papal inquisitions. It all started when King Ahab approached Naboth and offered to buy his vineyard. Naboth refused on the grounds that the vineyard was part of his inheritance from God, which he had no right to sell. The narrative portrays Ahab as distressed when he returns to his palace and relates the situation to Jezebel. Jezebel tells Ahab that she will take care of the matter. She arranges to have Naboth falsely accused of blasphemy. The punishment for blasphemy was death, and after Naboth was executed – along with his family – Ahab assumed ownership of Naboth's inheritance, vineyard included. As if to go out of her way to aspire to the Old Testament prototype, the Jezebel of the Middle Ages invented the Inquisition, which were orgies of torture and murder where many were falsely accused of – almost exclusively – heresy, and their lands subsequently appropriated by the church.

> Heresy in the Church's eyes was treated as treason against the crown. The Church sought out the heretics, found them guilty, and handed them over to the civil authorities for execution. As its secular arm, the state did the Church's bidding in the execution of heretics, the confiscation of their property, and the enforcement of the Church's decrees against them and their heirs.[341]

These were not one-off occasions, but a modus operandi; it is estimated that at some point, the church owned as much as 25% of the land in Europe.[342] The Old Testament Jezebel was a murderous, idol-worshiping, thieving witch. The Medieval Jezebel took it a step further: even the dead were not immune.

> The property of heretics was confiscated and divided between the inquisitors and the popes. That the corpse of Pope Formosus had twice been disinterred, condemned and excommunicated set a pattern. In 680, the Sixth General Council decreed that even dead heretics should be tried and condemned. Corpses that had

lain in the grave for decades were dug up, tried, and found guilty. At that point the past assets of the deceased were confiscated, causing their heirs to lose everything, including, in many cases, all civil rights.[343]

What did Christ say in Revelation 2:22-23 would be the consequences of sharing a bed with Jezebel? 'Behold, I will throw her on a bed of sickness…And I will kill her children with pestilence, and all the churches will know that I am He who searches the minds and the hearts; and I will give to each one of you according to your deeds.' The Black Death of 1346 to 1353 (during which it is estimated that half the population of Europe perished) looms large in history as a possible fulfillment of this part of the prophecy.[a] What will be the eventual fate of Jezebel and her followers? The second half of verse 22 speaks of being thrown into 'great tribulation,' a direct reference to the end of times; a stark warning for those who tolerate the modern-day Jezebel.[b]

Sardis

To the angel of the church in Sardis write: He who has the seven Spirits of God and the seven stars, says this: 'I know your deeds, that you have a name that you are alive, but you are dead. Wake up, and strengthen the things that remain, which were about to die; for I have not found your deeds completed in the sight of My God. So remember what you have received and heard; and keep *it*, and repent. Therefore, if you do not wake up, I will come like a thief, and you will not know at what hour I will come to you. But you have a few people in Sardis who have not soiled their garments; and they will walk with Me in white, for they are worthy. He who overcomes will thus be clothed in white garments; and I will not erase his name from the book of life, and I will confess his name before My Father and before His angels. He who has an ear, let him hear what the Spirit says to the churches.'[c]

The fifth letter is addressed to the church at Sardis, which has often been identified prophetically as the church of the Reformation (1453 AD – 1750 AD).[d] On the subject of this church in particular, my view diverges from

---

[a] It is estimated that about 50 million died from the Black Death in Europe alone.
[b] Four of the letters (Thyatira, Sardis, Philadelphia, and Laodicea) contain references to what can be interpreted as the great tribulation. Some have proposed that this means that the last four churches represent the spectrum of people present in the church in the last days.
[c] Revelation 3:1-6

many of those who ascribe to the prophetic nature of the seven letters. As I read this letter, Sardis appears to be a predominantly pagan church, the Reformation being its one saving grace. Remember as we get into this, that Christ is writing His letter to the *whole* church, not just one branch or sect. To claim that this letter is addressed prophetically only to Protestants would be a grave indiscretion in my estimation. As we shall see, I call Sardis the zombie church.

Sardis means 'Prince of Joy'.[344] The key to understanding the letter to Sardis is to understand the phrase: 'I know your deeds, that you have a name that you are alive, but you are dead.'[a] Christ states that the church has 'a name;' in particular, a name that is not *His* Name. If you do a study of what it means to take the name of the Lord in the Old Testament, or what it means to gather in the name of Jesus Christ in the New Testament, you will discover a wealth of meaning. Taking the name of the Lord for Abraham was a lot like what a woman used to do when she got married. Traditionally, when a woman married a man, she would take her husband's last name, which represented not only submission, but was a statement of fealty, which implied allegiance, devotion, fidelity, and loyalty. When Abraham called on the name of the Lord, it was a statement of faith; Abraham took God as his God, to follow and be faithful to for the rest of his life. Thus, the statement that Sardis has 'a name' other than that of Christ, is an accusation that the church has fallen so far into pagan idolatry as to constitute an entirely separate religion, *apart* from Christ. The church has a veneer of Christianity (the appearance of life), but has actually turned away from Christ and is apostate, or dead. Death could be viewed as the antithesis of life. Likewise, we should note that if Sardis literally means 'Prince of Joy,' then the real state of the church at Sardis would be the antithesis of this name, and so should be interpreted as something like 'Prince of Sorrow' when taken in context.

The specific phraseology of 'a name' has occurred before in the Old Testament. Shortly after the flood, when the residents of Babel gathered together to form a city and build a tower, they said: "Let us make for ourselves a name."[b] Most scholars posit that this means that the people wanted to be famous and remembered for all time. This sounds plausible, but I would

---

[d] Again, the periods stated are approximate, and if you read other sources on the matter, they will give slightly different dates.
[a] Revelation 3:1
[b] Genesis 11:4

suggest a deeper meaning. The word Babel means 'gate of God'.[a] Viewed in this light, the tower they were building was probably a ziggurat, a stepped pyramid which was to be used as a temple. Closely associated with temples not dedicated to the God of Abraham was the worship of idols. And so Babel came to represent a system of idol worship in the postdiluvian age, which is why subsequent references to Babylon in the Bible, whether it is the historical Babylon that is mentioned, or Nineveh, or Rome, or a city of the end times (such as we see in Revelation), all mention idol worship. 'Babylon' is used as code for a system of pagan mysteries with origins that go all the way back to Babel. Thus, when Christ says of Sardis 'you have a name,' this is especially damning, as it not only calls out their idol worship, but it is a direct reference to Babylon, the mother of harlots.

'What's in a name?' you might ask. I would make the case that when the popes of Rome took on the mantle of Pontifex Maximus, this represented the attitude of an apostate church:

> In the 15th century, when the Renaissance drove new interest in ancient Rome, *pontifex maximus* became a regular title of honour for Popes. After the fall of the Eastern Roman Empire with the fall of Constantinople to the Ottoman Empire and the death of the final Roman emperor Constantine XI in 1453, *pontifex maximus* became part of the papacy's official titulature of the Bishop of Rome.[345]

In ancient Rome, 'The Pontifex Maximus was the president of the [pagan] college, and acted *in its name*,[b] whence he alone is frequently mentioned in cases in which he must be considered only as the organ of the college.'[346] 'The Roman pontiffs formed the most illustrious among the great colleges of priests.'[347] 'The college of pontiffs had the supreme superintendence of all matters of religion, and of things and persons connected with public as well as private worship.'[348] 'As to the rights and duties of the pontiffs, it must be first of all be borne in mind that the pontiffs were not priests of any particular divinity, but a college which stood above all other priests, and superintended the whole external worship of the gods.'[349] I would suggest to you that the assumption of the titulature 'Pontifex Maximus' by the papacy represents much more than a mere title; it is *a name* that not only embodies the rejection of Christ as head of the church, but that also represents a turning away

---

[a] See notes on Babel in the Sixth Trumpet section.
[b] Italics mine

from the teachings of Christ and toward acceptance of idol worship. For this reason, I place the beginning of the prophetic church of Sardis around 1453 AD, where others place its beginning a bit later, around 1500 AD.

The Council of Trent was a series of church conventions held from 1545 to 1563. It was during this time that the papacy cemented its theology as something other than that which is outlined in Scripture. The assertion was made that: 'The church is the ultimate interpreter of Scripture. Also, the Bible and church tradition (the tradition that composed part of the Catholic faith) were equally and independently authoritative.'[350] Officially, this proclamation placed the authority of church tradition on par with Scripture; practically speaking, however, church tradition superseded and directly contradicted Scripture in many instances. The Council of Trent even went so far as to deny that faith alone was enough to justify forgiveness of sins.

> If anyone says… that men obtain from God through faith alone the Grace of justification… let him be anathema.[351]

I would make the case that with the assumption of the pagan priestly title Pontifex Maximus, and a counterfeit version of Christianity as defined by the Council of Trent, most of the prophetic church of Sardis had turned away from Christ and was at this time fully apostate.

What does Christ say in His letter to Sardis about these developments? He says: 'Therefore if you do not wake up, I will come like a thief, and you will not know at what hour I will come to you.'[a] He doesn't say that He will come quickly, but that He will come like a thief; that is, when no one is looking for Him. This third and final warning to the church is the most urgent of all. I would suggest that during the time of Sardis, Jesus Christ came very close to blowing the final trumpet that will be heard at the rapture. The Seven Letters to the Seven Churches came within a hair's breadth of being the Five Letters to the Five Churches.

But the letter goes on to mention a few of those who: 'have not soiled their garments; and they walk with Me in white, for they are worthy.'[b] Contrasted with those who have *a name*, are those who walk with Christ. Having faith in idols is equated to 'soiled garments'; having faith in Christ is

---

[a] Revelation 3:3
[b] Revelation 3:4

associated with being worthy and clothed in white. Who during this time had faith alone in Scripture and faith alone in Christ?

It is more than a quirky coincidence of history that the centerpiece of the Protestant Reformation was *Sola Scriptura:*

> Sola Scriptura is one of the five solae, considered by some Protestant groups to be the theological pillars of the Reformation. The key implication of the principle is that interpretations and applications of the Scriptures don't have the same authority as the [S]criptures themselves; hence, the authority of the church is viewed as subject to correction by the [S]criptures, even by an individual member of the church. Martin Luther, 16th-century monk and figurehead of the Protestant Reformation, stated that "a simple layman armed with [S]cripture is greater than the mightiest pope without it." The intention of the Reformation was thus to correct what he asserted to be the errors of the Catholic Church, by appealing to the uniqueness of the Bible's textual authority. Catholic doctrine is based on sacred tradition, as well as [S]cripture. Sola Scriptura rejected the assertion that infallible authority was given to the magisterium to interpret both [S]cripture and tradition.[352]

Sola Scriptura represented a return of a few in the church to the *name* of Christ, as opposed to the name that the magisterium or priests or popes promoted. The letter to Sardis goes on to state that those clothed in white – that is those who cling to the name of Christ – will not have their names erased from the book of life.[a]

Martin Luther posted his 95 Theses in 1517:

> The *Theses* is retrospectively considered to have launched the Protestant Reformation and the birth of Protestantism, despite various proto-Protestant groups having existed previously. It detailed Luther's opposition to what he saw as the Roman Catholic Church's abuse and corruption by Catholic clergy, who were selling plenary indulgences, which were certificates supposed to reduce the temporal punishment in purgatory for sins committed by the purchasers or their loved ones. [353]

Plenary indulgences and purgatory are artifacts of church tradition. The very idea that money could pay for sin is in direct contradiction to Scripture where, concerning atonement for our transgressions, only the blood of Christ is acceptable. Furthermore, purgatory is never mentioned in the Bible.

Three years after Luther posted his 95 Theses on the door of that church in Wittenberg, Germany, he expanded his stance beyond just a rant against indulgences:

---

[a] See Revelation 3:5

In 1520 Luther further consolidated his program of reforming the Church "with a direct appeal to the German people to take the initiative." People in Luther's day knew [S]cripture—even more so because the invention of the printing press less than a century before had given everyday Christians unprecedented access to the Bible in their own language. Combined with the "humanists'" cultural push ad fontes (which means "to the sources"), Luther and others were returning en masse to the words of [S]cripture and the writings of early Church leaders. This return to the original sources of the Christian faith empowered Luther to challenge the pope on the doctrine of salvation, interpretation of [S]cripture, and the significance of Church tradition. And so the 5 Solas of the Reformation were birthed.

- **Sola Scriptura**, or "God's Word alone," maintains that the Bible is the highest source of authority in a Christian's life, the final court of appeal (though not the only authority: the Bible itself mentions governmental and other authorities).

- **Sola fide**, or "faith alone," affirms that justification—being made right with God—comes only through faith in Jesus.

- **Sola gratia**, or "grace alone," says sinners are saved as an unearned gift of God's grace, "not as a result of works, so that no one may boast" (Eph 2:8–9).

- **Sola Christo** ("solus Christus"), or "Christ alone," emphasizes the exclusivity of Jesus' role in salvation: "No one comes to the Father except through Me" (John 14:6).

- **And soli Deo gloria**, or "to the glory of God alone," says that the purpose of creation, salvation, and everything—including our goal as Christians—is the glory of God, "that God may be all in all" (1 Cor 15:28).[354]

I would submit to you the idea that these 5 Solas, though they took some time to fully develop into the statements of faith as we know them today, represent the return of the church to the *name* of Jesus Christ. This was the path that those who walk with Christ in white took: not the path of self-betterment through works, but the path of simply accepting God's free gift of salvation as outlined in the Bible. To do any less is to reject the perfect work of Christ's accomplishment on the cross. These Solas were not drawn up in a vacuum; these issues were raised – unfortunately – in opposition to the religious status quo. Sacred tradition opposed every single one of them, if not in word, most certainly in deed. History seems to confirm this viewpoint that the Reformation arose in response to a dead church:

> The Jesuit Cardinal Bellarmine was later to admit: "For some years before Luther and Calvin there was in the church almost no religion left. The papacy", he said, "had almost eliminated Christianity."[355]

'Trent consecrated medieval theology, thus ensuring that Catholicism would be narrow and backward-looking for centuries to come.'[356] It also brought about a fundamental change in the institutional church; a change one might say that was noteworthy of describing the new age of Sardis: 'After Trent, Rome's enormous power was confirmed, bishops so lost their independence that no council was held for more than three hundred years.'[357]

You may have noticed that the Reformation was launched well before the Council of Trent, which began in 1545. This is because the Council of Trent was convened in order to formulate an official response to the Reformation. You could say that the reformers forced the church's hand to explicitly state their stance on tradition, among other things, thus formalizing heresy/apostasy. If the order of events had been switched, that is if the Council of Trent had concluded by 1517 and the masses not caught on to Luther's Theses by, say, 1545 or so, perhaps the Reformation would never have happened, and Christ would indeed have come like the thief in the night and swept the various 'proto-Protestant' groups away to heaven, leaving the rest to endure the Great Tribulation. Three times in the Letters to the Seven Churches we have seen Christ give the warning 'repent, or I am coming…'; there will not be another.[a,b]

Before moving on, it is worth noting that if you buy into my theory that the horsemen of the Apocalypse conduct two patrols, one before judgment and one after judgment, then the rider of the white horse, who is unleashed with the advent of the age of European Conquest, begins his first patrol around the advent of another significant prophetic event: the church at Sardis. It would seem that, even though Sardis did not quite bring about the end of the church age, it did, however, represent enough of an apostasy to set in motion the machinery of Armageddon. The conqueror who rides the white horse, bent on conquest, seems to capture the voracious appetite for power exhibited by the

---

[a] I do not mean to imply here that the Reformers represented the perfect church; far from it. I merely point out that they got right the one thing that was needful; to return to the *name* of Jesus Christ.

[b] Twice in the Seven Letters (to Thyatira and to Philadelphia) Christ urges the church to 'hold fast until I come' and 'I am coming quickly; hold fast…'. In both of these instances, the reference to Christ coming is presented not as a warning but as encouragement.

papacy during this time. In our discussion of the first seal, I made the comment that I did not think that the initial patrol of the rider on the white horse represented the Antichrist, with a capital 'A.' On second thought, as the term 'Vicar of Christ' refers to the belief that the pope stands in the place of Jesus Christ and possesses His authority on the earth, the rider of the white horse well may represent a league of antichrists, denoted with a lowercase 'a.'[a]

Philadelphia

> And to the angel of the church in Philadelphia write: He who is holy, who is true, who has the key of David, who opens and no one will shut, and who shuts and no one opens, says this: 'I know your deeds. Behold, I have put before you an open door which no one can shut, because you have a little power, and have kept My word, and have not denied My name. Behold, I will cause *those* of the synagogue of Satan, who say that they are Jews and are not, but lie—I will make them come and bow down at your feet, and *make them* know that I have loved you. Because you have kept the word of My perseverance, I also will keep you from the hour of testing, that *hour* which is about to come upon the whole world, to test those who dwell on the earth. I am coming quickly; hold fast what you have, so that no one will take your crown. He who overcomes, I will make him a pillar in the temple of My God, and he will not go out from it anymore; and I will write on him the name of My God, and the name of the city of My God, the new Jerusalem, which comes down out of heaven from My God, and My new name. He who has an ear, let him hear what the Spirit says to the churches.'[b]

The sixth church on the list is Philadelphia, which prophetically is described as the church of revivals and missions (1750 AD – present). Most scholars place the end of this era around 1900 AD, but I carry it right up until the present for reasons which I will delineate below. Philadelphia means 'brotherly love,'[358] which seems to fit well with this theme. Christ says to this church: 'Behold, I have put before you an open door which no one can shut, because you have a little power, and have kept my word, and have not denied *My name.*'[c, d] During this time, Christians zealous to share the name of Jesus Christ were swept through that open door on the tides of Colonialism and

---

[a] Matthew 24: 23-24
[b] Revelation 3:7-13
[c] Italics mine.
[d] Revelation 3:8

Imperialism to literally every corner of the world, the vestiges of which have lasted until the present day.

Christ says of Philadelphia that 'you have a little power.' He doesn't say that they are strong; rather, He implies that they are weak. I think this may be because the Reformers, after breaking away, then proceeded to return to much of the 'churchy-ness' that had characterized the institutional church. In many ways, they re-institutionalized, with an emphasis on the church building and a certain attitude of 'clubby-ness;' that is, an overt expectation to belong to an official, recognized denomination as opposed to the biblical model of the house church that had prospered so well in the first few centuries, and, as mentioned above, during the time of the primitive churches in the Middle Ages. The motive for institutionalization was to promote good teaching and stamp out heresy. However, the same old problems arise; the heretics simply get absorbed into the congregation and slowly corrupt the church from the inside. Also, with institutionalization comes a tendency to trust the organization to head the church instead of our living Lord, Jesus Christ.

But there was one thing that the Reformers did get right: Christ says they did not deny '*My name,*'[a] which is a grand compliment. For this reason, Christ has opened up the world to them/us as His representatives. In retrospect, the prophetic churches of Sardis and Philadelphia, taken together, seem to mesh well with my ideas about the breaking of the first seal: the white horse representing the pure message of the gospel, and its rider, a power-mad papacy. Also, where Christ says 'I will keep you from the hour of testing,' I take this to mean that the rapture happens at the end of the church called Philadelphia.

Laodicea

To the angel of the church in Laodicea write: The Amen, the faithful and true Witness, the Beginning of the creation of God, says this: 'I know your deeds, that you are neither cold nor hot. I wish that you were cold or hot. So because you are lukewarm, and neither hot nor cold, I will spit you out of My mouth. Because you say, "I am rich, and have become wealthy, and have need of nothing," and you do not know that you are wretched and miserable and poor and blind and naked, I advise you to buy from Me gold refined by fire so that you may become rich, and

---

[a] Italics mine

white garments so that you may clothe yourself, and *that* the shame of your nakedness will not be revealed; and eye salve to anoint your eyes so that you may see. Those whom I love, I reprove and discipline; therefore be zealous and repent. Behold, I stand at the door and knock; if anyone hears My voice and opens the door, I will come in to him and will dine with him, and he with Me. He who overcomes, I will grant to him to sit down with Me on My throne, as I also overcame and sat down with My Father on His throne. He who has an ear, let him hear what the Spirit says to the churches.'[a]

The seventh and final prophetic church is Laodicea, which represents the apostate church. Many scholars place the beginning of this church around 1900 AD, but to me this dating seems arbitrary.[b] I think this date is adopted because that seems to be the time when the missionary movements of the 1800s began to wane; however, this does not mean that the epoch of Philadelphia is over, it just means that it is in decline. If we look at the churches of Thyatira and Sardis, the case can easily be made that these churches were not considered totally apostate because there was enough of a remnant of true believers to be found who clung to the name of Jesus Christ. It is not the majority that determines the definitive state of apostasy; it is the *minority*. Abraham bargained with God over the destruction of Sodom; if there had been found ten righteous men in the city, God said, "I will not destroy it on account of the ten."[c] Likewise, it seems God is extremely patient with His church. It is almost as if God is procrastinating, looking for any and every reason to put off judgment, keep the church in the game, and save more people. As such, I do not see the prophetic age of Laodicea as having started yet.

All this being said, the church at Laodicea is as bad as it is going to get – for the church, that is. It is not a morally corrupt society that defines the end times; since the fall of Adam the world has always been corrupt. No, it is the state of the church that will determine when judgment begins. In the introduction to this final letter, Christ assumes the title 'the Beginning[d] of the creation of God.' The only place in all of Scripture where Christ takes this title is where He introduces Himself to the apostate church. His reminder to them that He is the Creator comes across as especially poignant in regard to our modern, evolution-saturated culture. He is making a statement that He, not

---

[a] Revelation 3:14-22

[b] Granted, much of this dating is indeed approximate.

[c] Genesis 18:32

[d] Alternately, *Origin* or *Source*

evolution or chance, created the universe. Remember: the book of Revelation was written over two thousand years ago. How is it that Jesus could frame His letter in such a way as to be so relevant today?

He invites the Laodiceans to 'Buy from Me... white garments so that you may clothe yourself, and that the shame of your nakedness will not be revealed.'[a] This brings to mind a scene from Genesis in one of the opening chapters of the Bible. Right after committing the first sin recorded in the Bible, Adam and Eve became aware of their nakedness:

> Then the eyes of both of them were opened, and they knew that they were naked; and they sewed fig leaves together and made themselves loin coverings.[b]

Sin has been associated with nakedness from the very beginning.[c] God replaced the fig leaves with animal skins, the first sacrifice mentioned in the Bible, to show that only blood can atone for or cover sin. Christ is saying to the church of Laodicea that they are naked, with no clothes. This implies that they are yet to receive atonement for their sin; or more directly, the church, which should be the representatives of Christ, do not know Christ as their Lord. Jesus also says:

> Behold, I stand at the door and knock; if anyone hears my voice and opens the door, I will come into him and will dine with him, and he with Me.[d]

Jesus is saying that He is standing at the door, trying to get in; at the end of the Church Age, Jesus isn't even in the church! From the imagery of these two verses, it is clear that the apostate church is no longer Christian, i.e., followers of Christ. They have given themselves over to something else, another *name* perhaps.[e] Laodicea is the end of the line. There are no more churches prophesied, and no further call to repentance will be offered.

I think the age of Laodicea is what Paul is referring to when he speaks of the apostasy in II Thessalonians.

---

[a] Revelation 3:18
[b] Genesis: 3:7
[c] This is a typological construction: when you see the word 'naked' in the Bible there is often some association with sin.
[d] Revelation 3:20
[e] I do think there will be a significant number of Christians left at the end, however; just enough to be missed after the rapture.

> Now we request you, brethren, with regard to the coming of our Lord Jesus Christ and our gathering together to Him, that you not be quickly shaken from your composure or be disturbed either by a spirit or a message or a letter as if from us, to the effect that the day of the Lord has come. Let no one in any way deceive you, for *it will not come* unless the apostasy comes first, and the man of lawlessness is revealed, the son of destruction...[a]

Apparently, a letter had been circulated among the Thessalonians saying something to the effect that Jesus had already come back. Paul is writing to reassure them that this is not the case: he says look for the apostasy to happen first. Apostasy means to turn away; an alternate translation is 'falling away from the faith'.[359] Thus, what Paul is speaking of is the turning away from the faith *of the church*. If you want to know when the day of the Lord will come, to gather us together to Him, watch what is happening in the church. Putting all of this together, I see what has sometimes been called The Great Falling Away as the precursor of the age of Laodicea. When you see the church turn away from God, that is the sign that tells you that the rapture is near. Jesus tells the Philadelphians, who inhabit the times just prior to Laodicea: 'I am coming quickly; hold fast what you have.'[b] Jesus communicates urgency in stating that He is 'coming quickly.' He is basically saying: 'Hang in there, it won't be long now.' The assurance given to Philadelphia is the warning for Laodicea.

After the rapture, then judgment, or the 70th week of Daniel, will quickly follow. I believe the church of Laodicea will be left behind and thus will live to see this time. This is why Jesus says 'I advise you to buy from Me gold refined by fire so that you may become rich;'[c] again, fire is symbolic of judgment. Judgment will come upon the end times church like a thief in the night, without warning – there is no such warning in the letter to Laodicea! The missing people of the rapture will capture their attention, but it will already be too late. Judgment will have already begun. Hence, as the star called Wormwood of the third trumpet falls from the sky, it will fall on Laodicea. We will see God's chastisement of the apostate church in the pollution of the waters and springs. How much more poignant if it falls on North and South America, where so many pay tribute to the institutional church for salvation, as well as

---

[a] II Thessalonians 2:1-3
[b] Revelation 3:11
[c] Revelation 3:18

belong to various deviant pseudo-Christian sects, such as the Jehovah's Witnesses, Mormons, and all others who pollute *the name* of God.

Three times over the course of the past two thousand years the rapture has come close to occurring, a singular event which will presage judgment. The first time was very early, in the first century in fact, when the church started to replace the work that Christ had done on the cross with legalism. It happened again during the age of Pergamum, when idol worship was introduced into the church. Then we have the near miss with Sardis, the zombie church, where but for the faith of a few 'clothed in white' (that is, a few who still believed in Jesus Christ alone for salvation), the world would have been plunged into tribulation, a time of trouble the like of which has never been seen. The message is clear: Jesus is the head of the church, and He does not approve when it tries to replace Him with something else.

From this, we can see that the doctrine of the imminent return of Christ has been playing out over the centuries. This doctrine is derived from the many places in Scripture where we are exhorted to look for the return of Christ at any moment.[a] The fact that Christ has not returned in over two millennia has presented no small amount of consternation for Christians. However, when viewed in light of the church clock, it becomes apparent that not only could Christ have returned at any moment, but that He almost pushed the rapture button no fewer than three times. Matthew 24:36 says that only the Father knows the day or the hour of the rapture, but I don't think that the eternal Father measures the timing of this prophecy in days and hours; I would propose that He measures the ticking of the church clock according to spiritual vitality. Once the church bells ring for apostasy, it's game over.

Once judgment starts, events progress along a well-defined timetable. The 70th week is 7 years, or 2,520 days.[b] The Antichrist will have 42 months, or 3½, years or 1260 days to have his way on the earth. We get these precise predictions from the book of Daniel in the Old Testament and the book of Revelation in the New. The Apostle Paul tells us that the 7 years of judgment will start[c] after the removal of the 'restrainer,' that is the Holy Spirit, and I suspect that His removal will coincide with the rapture. However, before this

---

[a] Philippians 3:20; Titus 2:13; Hebrews 9:28; I Thessalonians 1:10, and others.

[b] Using traditional Jewish years of 360 days per year.

[c] I place the start of the 70th week coincident with the revelation of the man of sin, or the Antichrist, by way of the covenant he makes with Israel.

happens, the apostasy, or great falling away, must happen first. So when will the apostasy occur? This will happen when the hearts of people attending church have grown so cold that they no longer expect the return of the Lord Jesus Christ. They will have come to the point where they believe that the exhortations of Scripture to look for Christ's return at any moment are merely symbolic of traditional belief, and not to be taken seriously. And thus, He will come like a thief in the night, when no one is looking for Him.

  I think what the Holy Spirit is getting at with encouraging us to look for the imminent return of Christ is not so much time-oriented as it is faith-oriented. When we stop looking for the return of Christ, we become complacent; complacency leads to unbelief, and unbelief to apostasy. It is a slippery slope that can happen to a congregation in as little as a generation. In this way, we have shed some light upon a curious riddle of Scripture: how, on the one hand, we are exhorted to expect the return of Christ at any moment, while at the same time, we are told by Christ Himself that He will return when He is not expected. Or, perhaps we could say, when He is *no longer* expected.

  One man's faith cannot save another. Abraham's faith cannot save you or me; we must each have our own faith. Likewise, our faith cannot save our children; each generation must take up the baton and carry it forward. There will come a time when this will no longer happen. That time will be called Laodicea. Apostasy is ever and only a generation away. That old homeless man we see in all those movies about the apocalypse is quite right; the end is near. *The end is always near.*

       I am coming quickly; hold fast what you have…

Appendix G
The Great Falling Away

On Christmas Eve, 1968, William Anders took a photograph that, in one two-hundred-and-fiftieth of a second,[360] did more to change the mind of mankind than any other piece of creative art in all recorded history. It was to become the featured photo on the cover of Life Magazine's special edition: *100 Photographs that Changed the World*. Often referred to as the most influential photograph ever taken, it marked the beginning of the modern environmental movement.

Emerging from around the far side of the moon on Apollo 8 around 16:00 Coordinated Universal Time on their fourth trip around Earth's largest natural satellite, Anders snapped the shot, NASA image AS08-14-2383.[361] Rising over the gray, featureless moonscape, half swallowed in the oblivion of ultimate night, floated a preciously pearled blue world; small, fragile, alone. At that distance, no cities, no borders, no boundaries of any kind were visible. Walter Cronkite said of the image, which was later to be named *Earthrise*:

> "How is it possible for humans to live in enmity on this incredible island, instead of [an] understanding of brotherhood of all of us together there, alone in the universe?"[362]

The banning of DDT and leaded gasoline, the Clean Air and Clean Water acts, the hole in the ozone, global warming, the establishment of Earth Day, and much more, were engendered by this one meaningful photograph. Anders later commented:

> "We set out to explore the moon and instead discovered the Earth."[363]

That which before had seemed boundless was succinctly quantified in a single image that encompassed the entirety of it in one frame. For the first time, man gazed upon his ancestral home from a God's-eye view… and grew afraid.

Earthrise exacerbated the existential crisis that arose out of the nuclear arms race of the fifties and sixties, and expanded it into a full-blown religion centered on environmentalism: *The earth is not so big as we thought; will humans survive as a species?* This one image has acquired the specter of a global paradigm shift in human thinking; it has fundamentally altered how society perceives itself. Like a scene out of Aldous Huxley's *Brave New World*, seeds have been sown that would surrender personal individuality in the name of the coperate collective.

At this point, I would be remiss if I did not acknowledge that being a good steward of our planet is important. We live in a world where entropy is a powerful force of chaos and decay, meaning that preservation must be pursued vigorously and diligently. Conservation does a lot of good for obvious reasons, and if we can curb our consumerism to contribute to the cause, we should do so. However, our stewardship should be born out of a sense of responsibility, not a spirit of fear.

Anders remarked years later about his experience as an astronaut.

> "It really undercut my religious beliefs. The idea that things rotate around the Pope and up there is a big supercomputer wondering whether Billy was a good boy yesterday? It doesn't make any sense. I became a big buddy of [atheist scientist] Richard Dawkins."[364]

Anders' conclusion is specious. The sight of the immovable, seemingly unbounded earth as small and insignificant, a gleam of marbled azure shining brightly out of the immensity of absolute black, should call to mind the opening stanzas of Genesis, where God speaks life out of the darkness. If a man had any faith at all, the sights and wonders of the cosmos should inspire a deepening conviction in the existence of an almighty Creator. Such is the deception of the times, like the seeds that the birds steal away in the parable of the sower. I imagine that the great falling away that Paul talks about in II Thessalonians will likely be the result of a paradigm shift of even greater magnitude.

> Now we request you, brethren, with regard to the coming of our Lord Jesus Christ and our gathering together to Him, that you not be quickly shaken from your composure or be disturbed either by a spirit or a message or a letter as if from us, to the effect that the day of the Lord has come. Let no one in any way deceive you, for *it will not come* unless the apostasy comes first, and the man of lawlessness is revealed, the son of destruction.[a]

---

[a] II Thessalonians 2: 1-3

It could be that what is described as 'The rebellion' (some translations interpret it as 'the Great Falling Away') is something that will simply happen over time; mankind has never needed a reason to be wicked. What seems to be implied here, however, is that a tectonic shift in human thinking will precipitate a historic walking away from belief in God.

> For since the creation of the world His invisible attributes, His eternal power and divine nature, have been clearly seen, being understood through what has been made, so that they are without excuse.[a]

Here we find a scriptural assertion that God has placed in even the meanest of mankind faculties capable of grasping a sublime logic that speaks to the existence of a Creator – a spiritual truth that leaves men without excuse if they choose to ignore it. If we consider that Scripture is inspired by the Holy Spirit, we could take this as a proclamation that God *reveals* Himself to mankind through His creation; that is, everyone at some point in their life, even in a state of being dead to God, receives a divine unveiling of His invisible qualities such that evidence, not only of His existence, but also of His character, can 'be clearly seen' and 'understood.'

Evolution, which makes the audacious claim that chance (or aliens) conspired to author life on planet Earth, represents an apostasy or turning away from this truth. Jude, the one book in the Bible totally dedicated to apostasy, has this to say about the end times:

> But you, beloved, ought to remember the words that were spoken beforehand by the apostles of our Lord Jesus Christ, that they were saying to you, "In the last time there will be mockers, following after their own ungodly lusts." These are the ones who cause divisions, worldly-minded, devoid of the Spirit.[b]

Following one's natural instincts (i.e., sin nature) at the expense of a God-given conscience is a direct philosophical implication of evolution – it involves rationalizing one's sin/unbelief. If chance is God, then chance likely doesn't care if 'Billy has been a good boy' or not. Jesus, in His revelatory letter to latter-day church generations, seems to be looking all the way down through history when He says:

---

[a] Romans 1:20
[b] Jude 17-19

> "To the angel of the church of Laodicea write: The Amen, the faithful and true Witness, the Beginning of the creation of God, says this:"[a]

Jesus refers to Himself as 'the Beginning of the creation of God,' reminding us that God is the Creator and is responsible for all things in existence. The only place in Scripture where Jesus is thus named is in the context of speaking directly to the end-of-times apostate church. It is uncanny how these words echo through the ages to grate against the rationalism of the present day! The letter to the church of Laodicea also includes an admonition for those who fall away:

> Because you say 'I am rich, and have become wealthy, and have need of nothing,' and you do not know that you are wretched and miserable and poor and blind and naked, I advise you to buy from Me gold refined by fire so that you may become rich, and white garments so that you may clothe yourself, and *that* the shame of your nakedness will not be revealed; and eye salve to anoint your eyes so that you may see.[b]

What does God say to the apostates of the last days? Literally, try my fire! Implicit in the advice that Jesus gives to 'buy from Me gold refined by fire' is a ticket to ride right into the tribulation. Jesus won't give up on you, but once judgment starts, it is kind of touch-and-go as to whether you will live long enough to repent. If you do repent, your head will be chopped off… literally! If you don't repent, then your destiny lies in the lake of fire after the Great White Throne judgment. Neither choice sounds very good, but if you choose option number one, you get to live with God for eternity, and He'll give you a brilliant, white robe to cover your nakedness.

The social and philosophical ramifications of evolution may very well fully account for the 'rebellion' mentioned in II Thessalonians. I am persuaded, however, that there are too many lukewarm pretenders left in the church today for what is called the Great Falling Away to already be in progress. Once it gets started in earnest, being seen in church will be considered the politically incorrect thing to do, and Easter Sunday Christians will depart in droves. Our surprise at who walks away from the faith will be equaled only by our surprise

---

[a] Revelation 3:14
[b] Revelation 3:17-18

at who turns to faith, though the implication is that people will walk away in much greater numbers. It will be a time when only those who have truly taken God at His Word will be left in the pews.

Logical Positivism[a], ironically, has become the religion of the age. There is a manic search on for alien life – they're spending billions to send probes to Mars for that very purpose. A host of atheists posing as leaders in science and technology are desperately seeking that one discovery that will prove – at least in their minds – that 'life is not a miracle.' Notwithstanding the fact that God could have peppered life all over the universe as much as He pleased, many in the scientific community believe that the discovery of extraterrestrial life would provide penultimate proof of evolution and signify the death of God. Predictions abound that we'll detect a signal from an advanced alien civilization by 2030, simply because we're monitoring more wavelengths for signal activity, with exponentially greater computing power; Moore's Law and all that. We may not have to wait that long.

There have already been a number of false alarms concerning the detection of a signal from E.T. Each time a narrow band signal of unknown origin is detected by the S.E.T.I. (Search for Extraterrestrial Intelligence) Institute, there is a waiting period that ensues to eliminate all of the terrestrial possibilities. Sometimes the source is a military satellite, or an airport radar installation. If such a signal were to be found to be repetitive, where it could be heard by multiple sources and verified as originating from outside the solar system, perhaps by triangulation employing a satellite around the orbit of Jupiter for example, that would be taken as proof of intelligent life out in the universe. Narrow band radio signals are widely regarded by the scientific community as 'engineered' and 'not naturally occurring,' whereas biological computers (single-celled organisms), which are astronomically more intricate and complex, are declared to be random products of chance.[b] Where such colossal exploits of denial abound, anything but the truth becomes possible in the mind of the apostate.

---

[a] Logical Positivism emphasizes empirical evidence and logical analysis as the basis for meaningful knowledge.

[b] I've included in Appendix B a proposal as to why life cannot arise as a product of chance, as well as an explanation how the probability of life has been calculated, per a book called *Signature in the Cell* by Stephen C. Meyer.

Enter Cassini. At the outset, I must assert that this is just a prognostication on the part of the author. The intent here is to provide an educated guess at what may happen, not an assertion of what will happen, though it must be admitted that, at the present time, this idea does technically fall into the category of a conspiracy theory, so... reader, be warned.

Cassini was a space probe launched in October of 1997.[365] Due to its size and weight, the craft first executed two flybys around Venus, using the planet's gravity to pick up speed – gravity assist is cheaper than fuel – before passing close to Earth again, outbound. Then in December of 2000, Cassini whipped past Jupiter for one last boost before continuing on its way, completing insertion into the Saturn system in June of 2004.[366] The mission was a resounding success. Over the next 13 years, Cassini sent back 635 gigabytes of data[367] in pictures, readings, and measurements, which will take decades to decipher. The probe traveled over a total of 4.9 billion miles[368] and completed 294 orbits of the ringed planet during its tour, detecting organic molecules ejected from the ice world of Enceladus,[369] landing a probe on the largest moon, Titan, and, in general, greatly increasing our knowledge of the solar system. Cassini performed so well that mission objectives went through multiple extensions.

It's not until the very end, in a maneuver touted as 'The Grand Finale,' that things start to get weird. With its fuel supply running low, the assertion was made that Cassini 'must' be destroyed to eliminate the potential of accidentally contaminating one of Saturn's moons with life from Earth:

> In order to avoid the unlikely possibility of Cassini someday colliding with one of these moons, NASA chose to safely dispose of the spacecraft in the atmosphere of Saturn. This ensured that Cassini could not contaminate any future studies of habitability and potential life on those moons.[370]

This strikes me as an odd comment to make, especially after NASA had already intentionally landed the Huygens probe on Titan, Saturn's largest moon. If the imperative was not to take any chances with contaminating one of Saturn's moons with Earth life, then why did they send a probe halfway across the solar system just to take the chance of contaminating one of Saturn's moons with Earth life? And then, after landing said probe and making such a big deal about what a great success it all was, why did NASA subsequently feel it necessary to destroy the main craft, Cassini, so that such an event could not possibly happen again? If you think about it, it sounds like a comic excerpt lifted straight from the pages of *The Hitchhiker's Guide to the Galaxy*. This is just the sort of thing that sends my thought processes off in strange directions.

'The Grand Finale' maneuver starts with changing Cassini's orbit so that it plunged into the gap between Saturn and its innermost ring. The craft then made twenty-two dives into this relatively small opening,[371] making a few last observations, traveling between 75,000 – 78,000 miles per hour each time, depending on the specific trajectory.

Cassini's cameras were turned off the day before the final orbit. They were not capable of real-time video, and photos taken from the craft during entry into the upper atmosphere of Saturn would probably not produce viable images as the aerodynamically ungainly craft would destabilize and begin to tumble. Mission Control was able to receive a data stream, right up until a few minutes before the very end, a transmission of instrumentation readings. On the last lap, Cassini's orbit was to be changed slightly so that it would enter Saturn's atmosphere, traveling in excess of 75,000 mph,[372] ostensibly so that it would burn up upon entry.

The really odd bit about all of this is that crashing Cassini into Saturn was not the only option that would have avoided contaminating future studies of the Saturn system. In an official NASA document entitled *Cassini Extended Missions* dated April 1, 2008, at least three viable exit options were proposed for End of Mission: escape to stable orbit around the Sun (heliocentric), escape to a gas giant (Jupiter), or escape to Centaur (small, asteroid-like object in an eccentric orbit).[373] Using gravity assist, they could have escaped Saturn's gravity and gone just about anywhere they wanted, albeit running on fumes. The point I am making is that any one of these options would have held the benefit of gathering a further treasure trove of very useful information about our solar system while eliminating the possibility of infecting one of Saturn's moons with Earth life, if indeed that was a genuine concern. Destroying Cassini was not the only means of achieving the stated goal, contrary to the narrative published to the world.

The very idea that such a maneuver as the Grand Finale would even be undertaken with the end result that all options but one, that of destroying the still functioning craft, are eliminated, goes against the grain of NASA culture, which is always to plan out things 10 steps ahead of any problems that might arise. Engineers knew what they were doing when they positioned the vehicle for this final maneuver. Does it make sense that they would intentionally limit themselves to just one undesirable outcome? Or, could it be that they were lining up the craft for re-routing to an alternate destination?

With Cassini already traveling at 96% escape velocity,[a] [374]it would have been but a technicality to execute one final burn to exit Saturn's gravity well. With the cameras turned off, the data that was received on that last day is really just software when it comes down to it; even a mediocre programmer could have written a subroutine capable of creating output that would look similar to what you might expect from a small spacecraft trying to keep itself upright as it plunges into Saturn's noxious upper atmosphere.

If we entertain for a moment the possibility that Cassini did not come to an untimely end as a fireball over the hydrogen clouds of Saturn, the 'where is it now' part of the question is rather intriguing and also hard to answer, as the field of possibility is rather large. Somewhere in the Southern Hemisphere of the zodiac is a start, as that is the direction in which Cassini would have disappeared if it had picked up one last gravity assist, and would presumably be in the same general quarter of the sky as Saturn was on September 15, 2017. The purpose would be the thing we've been getting at: E.T.

All it takes to fake a signal from E.T. is to surreptitiously send a transmitter into deep space, to the edge of the solar system, without anyone noticing. Or, you launch a craft in broad daylight, and pretend to destroy it (perhaps you really do indeed destroy part of it) and wait about ten years, a good long time for everyone to forget all about it, before transmitting. The implications of pulling off a spoof like this are far-reaching.

If indeed the destruction of Cassini were a red herring, I would expect a counterfeit signal from E.T. anywhere from 2024 to 2032, with 2027 being the sweet spot, ten years after 'demolition.' After another gravity assist, Cassini would be traveling 80 to 90 thousand miles an hour, roughly twice the speed of the Voyager crafts, which took 20 years to exit the solar system, and so would cover a comparable distance in about half the time. The location of an object transmitting from the edge of the solar system could potentially be triangulated between Earth and a satellite around the orbit of Jupiter, as being at a minimum, not from our star, and thus the extraterrestrial origin of the communication would be 'verified.' The space probe dubiously named Lucy[b] will be

---

[a] Escape velocity for the planet Saturn is about 80,000 mph

conducting a survey of asteroids that share the orbit of Jupiter from 2025 until around 2031,[375] so this may be what they intend to use as part of the 'confirmation.'

I can't say for certain that this sort of thing will ever happen, but if an unexplained, narrow-band signal is detected coming from deep space, somewhere in the Southern Hemisphere, between 2024 and 2032 (perhaps broadcasting on the hydrogen line, 1420 MHz, which is the frequency of radio waves created when hydrogen in deep space decays – something that scientists have often hinted at, as if extraterrestrials could be expected to think like we do!), I'm not going to be thinking 'E.T.,' I'm going to be thinking 'Cassini!' In any event, it is easy to imagine the social and cultural upheaval such an event would create. This is the kind of paradigm shift in mankind's thinking, as a social collective, that I think will characterize the Great Falling Away. It will be the day of the atheist; agnostics will have left the building.

UAPs

The US government recently released previously top-secret documents concerning UAPs, Unidentified Aerial Phenomena, formerly known as Unidentified Flying Objects. Most of the footage, provided by the US Navy, is very blurry and pixelated, most likely due to being taken under high magnification. The lack of resolution in these videos makes it impossible to identify the objects being recorded, and in some cases, removes all reference from which motion can be accurately ascertained.

One prominent example is the Tic-Tac video. A black blob being tracked by a Navy pilot seemingly goes flying off at high speed 'to the left' at the end of the clip. The problem is, this video is so blurry, that it provides no reference for movement; the viewer really can't tell if the black blob actually moved out of the frame at unbelievably high speed, or if the camera taking the video was jostled. If you have ever tried to find a planet with a telescope on a starry night, you will be familiar with how, under magnification, small movements can make celestial objects whiz out of the field of view.

---

[b] Lucy literally means 'light bringer', but in a biblical context can also be considered the feminine of Lucifer.

Another well-known example is one named 'Gimbal,' which, ironically, doesn't refer to the fact that most cameras in modern military aircraft are mounted on gimbals – that is, the direction in which the camera is pointed is not necessarily the direction in which the aircraft is headed – but rather, it refers to how the unidentified object seems to roll in midair at the end of the clip. The interesting thing about this video is that it is presented with the horizon at an angle, kind of like a scene from the old Batman television show back in the '60s, when they are showing a scene from the villain's lair. This tilt is indicated by the clouds that swiftly pass by from the upper left down to the lower right of the screen at a 45° angle, and verified by the digital representation of the horizon, which is shown in a position parallel to the clouds. The aircraft is clearly in a banking maneuver, and the camera is turning on its gimbal to follow the movement of the object. This renders the perspective of the camera somewhat misleading. The image is so blurry that the object can't be identified, but most likely, it is another aircraft that performs a banking maneuver at the end of the video, which, due to perspective, gives it the appearance of rotating in midair. There is a halo around the object that is visible in the footage, which is most likely the aircraft's exhaust as viewed from directly behind.

I have only seen a few of these videos, but they all seem to have much of the same elements: very blurry images, presented at a misleading angle, and taken under high magnification. The most likely explanation for every single video that I have seen is that they are a trick of the camera that is recording the footage. They all also seem to try to hide the fact that the direction in which the camera is pointed is independent of the direction of flight for the aircraft on which it is mounted. If the camera were tracking a stationary object while pointed at a right angle to the jet's direction of flight, the object would artificially appear to be moving at high speed relative to the background, which would be moving relative to the jet. Many of these objects appear to be moving very fast, when in fact it is the speed of the airplane on which the camera is mounted that is creating the illusion of movement.

What might be the reason for thus enabling the Ancient Aliens subculture? Perhaps, if you were planning on faking a signal from E.T. in a few years, you might want to create a little hype to increase the expectation in society about such an event in order to prepare the field, so to speak. That way, when something happens, there will be fewer rational, dissenting voices. If you take a step back, however, it really doesn't make any sense; if E.T. already has spacecraft in the vicinity of the Earth, why would they bother sending a signal from so far away? As it turns out, this is exactly the question to ask, expressed in reverse. To explain: In 1950, Enrico Fermi, in light of the assumption that intelligent extraterrestrials should exist in abundance throughout the cosmos, asked the question, 'Where are they?' Given that there are hundreds of billions[376] of planets in the Milky Way Galaxy alone, astrobiologists presume[a] it to be inevitable that intelligent life will emerge on literally thousands of these, and so it would logically follow that we Earthlings should have detected them by now, in the form of radio waves or some other type of synthesized radiation. If E.T. does exist, a modulated signal emanating from deep space should be the very first way in which we become aware of them. However, the fact of the matter is that the universe remains eerily silent.

This brings us to the question at hand: If E.T. has not been detected among the stars, how is it that we have so many eyewitnesses that testify to a close encounter with them on the Earth? Perhaps mass hysteria is an explanation. At any rate, skeptics agree that without the corroboration of deep space detection, the most logical explanation for the UFO question is that it is the result of some type of Earth-born phenomenon, which, I would imagine, is kind of a buzz-kill if you're into that sort of thing. A faked signal from E.T. solves this issue; suddenly, alien abductees become experts as opposed to crackpots.

If there is one thing that *Earthrise* taught us, it is that what was once thought to be limitless, that is, the Earth, is actually quite bounded. As mankind has ventured out into space, the other thing we have learned is that, by sheer dint of distance, we are much more isolated than we ever imagined. Traveling at the speeds of conventional spacecraft, it would take anywhere from 7,000 to 83,500 years[377] to reach the nearest star, depending on how optimistic you are about the development of future propulsion systems: far longer than all of recorded history. Mankind simply does not have enough time to discover another habitable planet before our overuse of this one brings about the collapse of civilization. The physics for overcoming such astronomical distances may

---

[a] As if the term *astrobiologist* were not presumptuous enough.

never prove possible. Despite all the optimistic prognostications to the contrary, spaceship Earth is pretty much all we've got.[a]

So how do you make what little you have last as long as possible? Cooperation. If cooperation fails, as it has so swimmingly for mankind for thousands of years, you resort to coercion. Enter E.T.; where nothing else has managed to unite the people of this planet together under one banner, the detection of a signal originating from an advanced alien culture would suffice. Scientists call this a 'recalibration of our thinking;' at such a time, the call for a one-world government would ring very loudly in the ears of modern men.

So what is wrong with a one-world government? According to Revelation, that is when the real trouble begins…

---

[a] It should be noted that the very same physical constraints would also limit E.T.'s access to Earth.

1. https://biblehub.com/greek/4591.htm
2. Berean Strong's Lexicon, as cited on: https://biblehub.com/greek/4591.htm, Accessed 11/4/2024
3. Septuagint – Wikipedia, Http://en.m.wikipedia.org, accessed 11/24/2022
4. *Food for Thought* by Roy Gustafson
5. Michael S. Heiser, *The Old Testament in Revelation*, Naked Bible Press 2021, p. 153
6. https://en.wikipedia.org/wiki/Clarence_Larkin, last edited on 3 December 2023, at 16:08 (UTC), accessed 6/15/2024
7. Rev. Clarence Larkin, *The Book of Revelation*, Pantianos Classics, first published in 1919, pp. 36-37
8. David M. Levy, *Revelation: Hearing the Last Word* (Bellmawr, NJ: The Friends of Israel, 1999), [p.] 86, as cited on https://israelmyglory.org/article/unsealing-the-title-deed/, July/August 2022, accessed 11/14/2024
9. Larkin, (1919), p. 43
10. From NASB notes on Revelation 1:11, & Exodus 17:14.
11. Berean Strong's Lexicon as cited on: https://biblehub.com/greek/4735.htm
12. Strong's Lexicon as cited on: https://biblehub.com/greek/4735.htm
13. Strong's Lexicon as cited on: https://biblehub.com/greek/1238.htm
14. Strong's Lexicon as cited on: https://biblehub.com/greek/1238.htm,
15. Strong's Lexicon as cited on: https://biblehub.com/greek/3022.htm
16. Strong's Lexicon as cited on: https://biblehub.com/greek/3022.htm
17. NAS Exhaustive Concordance as cited on: https://biblehub.com/greek/3022.htm
18. NAS Exhaustive Concordance as cited on: https://biblehub.com/greek/3022.htm
19. Strong's Lexicon as cited on: https://biblehub.com/greek/7198.htm
20. Strong's Lexicon as cited on: https://biblehub.com/greek/7198.htm
21. Brown-Driver-Briggs Hebrew and English Lexicon, unabridged, as cited on: https://biblehub.com/hebrew/7198.htm
22. Strong's lexicon as cited on: https://biblehub.com/greek/2463.htm
23. Strong's Lexicon as cited on: https://biblehub.com/greek/2463.htm
24. Strong's Lexicon as cited on: https://biblehub.com/greek/5115.htm
25. Strong's Lexicon as cited on: https://biblehub.com/greek/5115.htm
26. E.H. Broadbent, The Pilgrim Church, Martino Fine Books (2018), p. 113
27. Jonathan Bardill, (2012) *Constantine, Divine Emperor of the Christian Golden Age*, Cambridge University Press, p.9
28. Jonathan Bardill, (2012) p.9
29. https://www.dw.com/en/christianity-becomes-the-religion-of-the-roman-empire-february-27-380/a-4602728, last updated 11/16/2009, accessed 12/31/2022
30. As cited on: https://www.reference.com/history-geography/did-christianity-become-official-religion-rome-7742368ae2858587, last updated March 30, 2020, accessed 12/31/2020 (National Geographic cited as original source)
31. Alan Cameron (2011), *The Last Pagans of Rome*, Oxford University Press, p. 13
32. Alexander Hislop (2013: originally published in 1853), *The Two Babylons*, pp. 92-93
33. Hislop (2013) pp. 97-98

34 Larry W. Cockerham (1995), *Revelation: Prophetic Addresses to the Seven Churches*, Brentwood Christian Press, p. 90
35 Dave Hunt, *A Woman Rides the Beast*, Harvest House Publishers, Eugene, Oregon, (1994), p. 124
36 https://en.wikipedia.org/wiki/Silk_Road, last edited on 16 May 2024, at 18:11 (UTC), accessed 5/19/2024
37 Philip T. Hoffman (2015), *Why Did Europe Conquer the World?*, Princeton University Press, p. 2-3
38 John Breuilly, *The Oxford Handbook of The History of Nationalism*, paperback (2016), Oxford University Press, p. 291, *Nationalism in East Asia, 1839-1945*; Rana Mitter
39 Breuilly (2016), p. 291
40 Himanshu Roy & Jawid Alam (2022), *A History of Colonial India, 1757 to 1947*, Routledge, p.1
41 David B. Abernethy (2000), *The dynamics of Global Dominance, European Overseas Empires, 1415-1980*, Yale University Press *New Haven and London*, p. 6
42 https://www.britannica.com/place/India, Last updated 7/6/2022, accessed 7/9/2022
43 https://www.britannica.com/place/India, Last updated 7/6/2022, accessed 7/9/2022
44 Harlow, Barbara & Mia Carter (2003), *Archives of Empire, Volume II: The Scramble for Africa*, Duke University Press. p.1
45 Scramble for Africa picture – Detribalization, Wikipedia, https://en.wikipedia.org/wiki/Detribalization#cite_note-1, last edited 5/28/2022, accessed 5/29/2022
46 Edwin Williamson, *The Penguin History of Latin America, rev. edition* (London 2009), p.89, as cited in Ritchie Robinson, *The Enlightenment, the Pursuit of Happiness, 1680-1790*, (2021), Ritchie Robertson; Harper Collins Publishers.
47 https://www.rcaanc-cirnac.gov.gc.ca, modified 06/11/2021, accessed 8/28/2022
48 https://www.iwgia.org, modified 05/11/2020, accessed 8/28/2022
49 https://theglobalamericans.org, modified 8/31/2016, accessed 8/28/2022
50 https://en.wikipedia.org/wiki/Fall_of_Constantinople, last edited on 18 May 2024, at 11:38 (UTC), accessed 5/19/2024
51 Strong's Lexicon as cited on: https://biblehub.com/greek/2063.htm
52 Strong's Lexicon as cited on: https://biblehub.com/greek/4450.htm
53 Strong's Lexicon as cited on: https://biblehub.com/greek/4450.htm
54 Strong's Lexicon as cited on: https://biblehub.com/greek/4450.htm
55 Strong's Lexicon as cited on: https://biblehub.com/greek/3162.htm
56 Copyright © 2021 by Discovery Bible as cited on: https://biblehub.com/greek/3162.htm
57 Thayer's Greek Lexicon as cited on: https://biblehub.com/greek/3162.htm
58 Strong's Lexicon as cited on: https://biblehub.com/greek/3173.htm
59 Strong's Lexicon as cited on: https://biblehub.com/greek/3173.htm
60 Strong's Lexicon as cited on: https://biblehub.com/greek/1484.htm
61 Strong's Lexicon as cited on: https://biblehub.com/greek/1484.htm
62 Strong's Lexicon as cited on: https://biblehub.com/greek/1484.htm
63 https://www.Albarim-publications.com, updated 05/13/22, accessed on 9/6/2022
64 Table of Nations, NASB study Bible, p. 19

65. The Authorized King James Version, The World Publishing Company, New York, Acts 17:26
66. *The Oxford Handbook of The History of Nationalism*, edited by John Breuilly, paperback (2016), Oxford University Press, p.377: *Latin America: State-Building and Nationalism*, Nicola Miller
67. Breuilly (2016), p. 21: *Nationalism and Vernaculars 1500-1800*, Peter Burke
68. Breuilly (2016), p. 22: *Nationalism and Vernaculars 1500-1800*, Peter Burke
69. Breuilly (2016), p. 22: *Nationalism and Vernaculars 1500-1800*, Peter Burke
70. Breuilly (2016), p. 81: *Cultural Nationalism*, John Hutchinson
71. Breuilly (2016), p. 105: *Independence and Nationalism in the Americas*, Don H. Doyle and Eric Van young
72. Breuilly (2016), p. 105: *Independence and Nationalism in the Americas*, Don H. Doyle and Eric Van young
73. https://en.wikipedia.org/wiki/American_Revolution#cite_note-240, last edited on 25 May 2024, at 11:08 (UTC), accessed 5/25/2024
74. https://en.wikipedia.org/wiki/American_Revolution#cite_note-240, last edited on 25 May 2024, at 11:08 (UTC), accessed 5/25/2024
75. Breuilly (2016) P. 111: *Independence and Nationalism in the Americas*, Don H. Doyle and Eric Van young
76. Breuilly (2016), p. 377: *Latin America: State-Building and Nationalism*, Nicola Miller
77. Breuilly (2016), p. 242: *Nationalism in India, 1857-1947*, Joya Chatterji
78. Breuilly (2016), p. 242: *Nationalism in India, 1857-1947*, Joya Chatterji
79. Breuilly (2016), p. 243: *Nationalism in India, 1857-1947*, Joya Chatterji
80. Breuilly (2016), p. 244-5: *Nationalism in India, 1857-1947*, Joya Chatterji
81. Breuilly (2016), p. 696: *Nationalism and Globalization*, Jurgen Osterhammel
82. Breuilly (2016), p. xxxix, Data from Map. 8: Decolonization
83. Breuilly (2016), p. 311: *Nationalism in Colonial and Post-Colonial Africa*, Bruce J. Berman and John M. Lonsdale
84. Breuilly (2016), p. 366: *Nationalism in Post-Colonial Africa*: Bruce j. Berman
85. Breuilly (2016), p. 264: *The Origins of Southeast Asian Nations: A Question of Timing*, David Henley
86. Breuilly (2016), p. 270: *The Origins of Southeast Asian Nations: A Question of Timing*, David Henley
87. Breuilly (2016), p. 21: *Nationalism and Vernaculars 1500-1800*, Peter Burke
88. Breuilly (2016), p. 22: *Nationalism and Vernaculars 1500-1800*, Peter Burke
89. Breuilly (2016), p. 22: Gellner as quoted in *Nationalism and Vernaculars* 1500-1800, Peter Burke
90. https://en.wikipedia.org/wiki/Industrial_Revolution, last edited on 25 May 2024, at 19:46 (UTC), accessed 5/26/2024
91. https://en.wikipedia.org/wiki/Industrial_Revolution, last edited on 25 May 2024, at 19:46 (UTC), accessed 5/26/2024
92. https://en.wikipedia.org/wiki/Industrial_Revolution, last edited on 25 May 2024, at 19:46 (UTC), accessed 5/26/2024
93. https://en.wikipedia.org/wiki/American_system_of_manufacturing, last edited on 5 September 2023, at 17:02 (UTC), accessed 5/26/2024

[94] Dr Stuart Parkinson, SGR, examines how technological innovation contributed to one of the most devastating wars in human history – and asks what lessons we should take from this, Article from SGR Newsletter no. 44; online publication: https://www.sgr.org.uk/resources/industrialisation-war-lessons-world-war-i, 5 April 2016, accessed 5/26/2024

[95] https://www.europeana.eu/en/blog/progress-in-war-making-the-industrialisation-of-world-war-1, Published November 13, 2019 by Ad Pollé (Europeana Foundation), accessed 5/26/2024

[96] Dr Stuart Parkinson, SGR, examines how technological innovation contributed to one of the most devastating wars in human history – and asks what lessons we should take from this, Article from SGR Newsletter no.44; online publication: 5 April 2016, accessed 5/26/2024

[97] Breuilly (2016), p.414: *Nationalism in Europe, 1918-45*, Oliver Zimmer

[98] Breuilly (2016), p.353: *Nationalism and Imperialism, c.1880-1940*, John Darwin

[99] https://en.wikipedia.org/wiki/Military–industrial_complex last edited on 20 April 2024, at 20:44 (UTC), accessed 5/26/2024

[100] Breuilly (2016), p.365: *Nationalism in Post-Colonial Africa,* Bruce j. Berman

[101] Breuilly (2016), p.706: *Nationalism and Globalization*, Jurgen Osterhammel

[102] Breuilly (2016), p.706: *Nationalism and Globalization*, Jurgen Osterhammel

[103] Strong's Lexicon, as cited on: https://biblehub.com/hebrew/3189.htm

[104] Strong's Lexicon as cited on: https://biblehub.com/greek/3189.htm

[105] Strong's Lexicon, as cited on: https://biblehub.com/hebrew/7838.htm

[106] Strong's Lexicon, as cited on: https://biblehub.com/hebrew/7838.htm

[107] Strong's Lexicon, as cited on: https://biblehub.com/hebrew/7835.htm

[108] Brown-Driver-Briggs Hebrew and English Lexicon as cited on https://biblehub.com/hebrew/7835.htm

[109] Strong's Lexicon as cited on: https://biblehub.com/hebrew/2822.htm

[110] Strong's Lexicon as cited on: https://biblehub.com/hebrew/2822.htm

[111] NAS Exhaustive Concordance as cited on: https://biblehub.com/hebrew/2822.htm

[112] Strong's lexicon as cited on: https://biblehub.com/greek/2218.htm

[113] Strong's lexicon as cited on: https://biblehub.com/greek/2218.htm

[114] Strong's lexicon as cited on: https://biblehub.com/greek/2218.htm

[115] Copyright © 2021 by Discovery Bible, as cited on: https://biblehub.com/greek/2218.htm

[116] Thayer's Greek Lexicon as cited on: https://biblehub.com/greek/2218.htm

[117] Thayer's Greek Lexicon as cited on: https://biblehub.com/greek/2218.htm

[118] Strong's Lexicon, as cited on: https://biblehub.com/hebrew/1220.htm

[119] Copyright © 2021 by Discovery Bible, as cited on https://biblehub.com/greek/1220.htm

[120] New American Standard Bible (1995), Zondervan, note #2 on Revelation 6:6

[121] Strong's Lexicon as cited on: https://biblehub.com/greek/5518.htm

[122] New American Standard Bible (1995) Zondervan, note #1 on Revelation 6:6

[123] Peter Bernholtz, *Monetary Regimes and Inflation, History, Economic and Political Relationships, second edition*, Edward Elgar Publishing, Cheltenham, UK, Northampton MA, USA, paperback 2016, p. 2

[124] Bernholtz (2016), p. 26

[125] Bernholtz (2016), p. 112

[126] Bernholtz (2016), p. 13

127 Steve H. Hanke and Nicholas Krus, *World Hyperinflations,* Institute for Applied Economics, Global Health, and the Study of Business Enterprise, Cato Institute 1000 Massachusetts Avenue, N.W., Washington, D.C., August 15, 2012, p. 1
128 Steve H. Hanke and Nicholas Krus, *World Hyperinflations,* Institute for Applied Economics, Global Health, and the Study of Business Enterprise, Cato Institute 1000 Massachusetts Avenue, N.W., Washington, D.C., August 15, 2012, p.16, see the Hanke-Krus hyperinflation table
129 Bernholtz (2016), p. 112
130 Zweig, Stefan (1944) *Die Welt von Gestern,* Stockholm: Bermann-Fischer, p. 333, as cited in Bernholtz (2016), p. 106
131 Zweig Stefan (1944) p. 333 as cited in Bernholtz, (2016), p. 84
132 Adam Ferguson, *When Money Dies,* (2010), Published in the United States by PublicAffairs, a member of the Perseus Books Group, p. 140
133 Adam Ferguson, *When Money Dies,* (2010), Published in the United States by PublicAffairs, a member of the Perseus Books Group, pp. 200-201
134 Richard Duncan, *The Dollar Crisis* (2005), John Wiley & Sons (Asia) Pte Ltd, P. 8
135 Richard Duncan, *The Money Revolution; How to Finance the Next American Century*, John Wiley & Sons, Ltd. (2022), p. 133
136 Duncan (2022), p.133
137 Duncan (2022), p.134
138 Duncan (2005), p. 8-9
139 Federal Reserve Bank of St. Louis, *The Changing Relationship Between Trade and America's Gold Reserves*, as cited on: https://www.stlouisfed.org/publications/regional-economist/first-quarter-2020/changing-relationship-trade-americas-gold-reserves, May 04, 2020, accessed on 11/23/2024
140 How the US Dollar Became the World's Reserve Currency by Richard Best, https://www.investopedia.com/articles/forex-currencies/092316/how-us-dollar-became-worlds-reserve-currency.asp#citation-6. Updated October 21, 2024, accessed 11/23/2024
141 How the US Dollar Became the World's Reserve Currency by Richard Best, https://www.investopedia.com/articles/forex-currencies/092316/how-us-dollar-became-worlds-reserve-currency.asp#citation-6. Updated October 21, 2024, accessed 11/23/2024
142 *Creation of the Bretton Woods System,* by Sandra Kollen Ghizoni, Federal Reserve Bank of Atlanta, https://www.federalreservehistory.org/essays/bretton-woods-created, November 22, 2013, accessed 6/5/2024
143 https://fortune.com/2021/10/07/dollar-hegemony-reserve-currency-threats-to-dominance/. *The dollar's dominance is far from done* by: PHILIPP CARLSSON-SZLEZAK, PAUL SWARTZ AND PAUL HSIAO October 7, 2021 at 12:30 PM EDT, accessed 6/5/2024
144 Richard Duncan, *The Money Revolution; How to Finance the Next American Century*, John Wiley & Sons, Ltd. (2022), p. 111
145 Duncan (2022), p. 113
146 https://www.economist.com/finance-and-economics/2019/08/15/what-comes-after-bretton-woods-ii, August 15th, 2019, accessed 8/4/2024
147 Fields, D.; M. Vernengo (2011). *Hegemonic Currencies during the Crisis: The Dollar versus the Euro in a Cartalist Perspective.* Levy Economics Institute Working Paper No. 666 as cited on: https://en.wikipedia.org/wiki/Monetary_hegemony, last edited on 13 August 2022,
148 Duncan (2022), p. 354
149 Duncan (2022), pp. 231-233

150 Duncan (2022), p. 233
151 Duncan (2022), p. 217
152 Duncan (2022), p.217
153 Duncan (2022), p.213
154 Duncan (2022), p. 362
155 Duncan (2022), p.362
156 Duncan (2022), p. 340
157 Duncan (2022), p. 340
158 Duncan (2022), p.343
159 Duncan (2022), p. 343
160 Duncan (2005), p.50
161 Duncan (2005), p. 48
162 Duncan (2022), p.245
163 Monetary Base St. Louis Fed. https://fred.stlouisfed.org/series/BOGMBASE, as cited in Duncan (2022) p. 273
164 Duncan (2022) p. 273
165 Friedman, Milton, Counter-Revolution in Monetary Theory, Wincott Memorial Lecture, Institute of Economic affairs, Occasional paper 33, 1970, p.11 https://miltonfriedman.hoover.org/friedman_images/colletions/2016c21/IEA_1970.pdf
166 Duncan (2022) p. 352
167 Chained Explained - *A more accurate inflation adjustment could cut $300 billion from the deficit*, by Brooks Jackson, posted on December 11/2012, https://www.factcheck.org/2012/12/chained-explained/, accessed 11/23/2024
168 *How official Statistics Underestimate Inflation*, By William Levin, https://www.nationalreview.com/2021/04/how-official-statistics-underestimate-inflation/, April 8, 20216:30 PM, accessed 11/23/2024
169 http://www.shadowstats.com/alternate_data/inflation-charts, data published June14, 2023, accessed 6/7/2024
170 *Why Is the Consumer Price Index Controversial?* By Barclay Palmer, published December 02.2023, accessed 6/7/2024
171 https://www.investopedia.com/terms/c/chain-linked-cpi.asp, Chain-Weighted CPI: What it is, How it Works, Example, by Will Kenton, Updated August 15, 2022, accessed 11/21/2023
172 Richard Duncan, *The Dollar Crisis, Causes, Consequences, Cures*, John Wiley & Sons (Asia), Ltd, (2005) p. 251
173 Duncan (2005) p.251
174 https://en.wikipedia.org/wiki/Great_Reset#cite_ref-RC_DeRosa_20201118_18-1, last edited on 9 May 2024, at 07:15 (UTC), accessed 6/5/2024
175 https://en.wikipedia.org/wiki/Great_Reset#cite_ref-RC_DeRosa_20201118_18-1, last edited on 9 May 2024, at 07:15 (UTC), accessed 6/5/2024
176 https://en.wikipedia.org/wiki/World_Economic_Forum, last edited on 2 June 2024, at 14:34 (UTC), accessed 6/5/2024
177 Strong's Lexicon as cited on: https://biblehub.com/greek/1849.htm
178 Copyright © 2021 by Discovery Bible, as cited on: https://biblehub.com/greek/1849.htm
179 Strong's Lexicon as cited on: https://biblehub.com/greek/1093.htm
180 Thayer's Greek Lexicon as cited on: https://biblehub.com/greek/1093.htm
181 Strong's lexicon as cited on: https://biblehub.com/greek/5515.htm

182 Strong's lexicon as cited on: https://biblehub.com/greek/5515.htm
183 Thayer's Greek Lexicon as cited on: https://biblehub.com/greek/5515.htm
184 https://en.m.wiktionary.org > wiki, accessed 11/23/2022
185 Strong's Lexicon as cited on: https://biblehub.com/greek/4501.htm
186 Copyright © 2021 by Discovery Bible as cited on: https://biblehub.com/greek/4501.htm
187 Thayer's Greek Lexicon as cited on: https://biblehub.com/greek/4501.htm
188 Strong's Lexicon as cited on: https://biblehub.com/greek/4501.htm
189 Evan Barrett, *India and China Fight over Kashmir's Natural Resources*, https://www.americansforkashmir.org/post/ india-and-china-fight-over-kashmir-s-natural-resources, June 11, 2020, accessed 8/10/2024
190 See date of writing in the introduction to Jonah, NASB Study Bible.
191 https://en.wikipedia.org/wiki/Battle_of_Nineveh_(612_BC), last edited on 25 October 2024, at 07:11 (UTC), accessed 11/24/2024
192 Strong's Lexicon as cited on: https://biblehub.com/greek/2739.htm
193 Strong's Lexicon as cited on: https://biblehub.com/greek/2379.htm
194 Strong's Lexicon as cited on: https://biblehub.com/greek/5590.htm
195 Strong's Lexicon as cited on: https://biblehub.com/greek/5590.htm
196 Strong's Lexicon as cited on: https://biblehub.com/greek/2896.htm
197 NAS Exhaustive Concordance as cited on: https://biblehub.com/greek/2896.htm
198 Copyright 2021 by Discovery Bible as cited on https://biblehub.com/greek/2896.htm
199 Strong's Lexicon as cited on: https://biblehub.com/greek/2795.htm
200 Strong's Lexicon as cited on: https://biblehub.com/greek/2795.htm
201 Strong's Lexicon as cited on: https://biblehub.com/greek/5117.htm
202 Strong's Lexicon as cited on: https://biblehub.com/greek/5117.htm
203 Strong's Lexicon as cited on: https://biblehub.com/greek/1537.htm
204 Strong's Lexicon as cited on: https://biblehub.com/greek/1537.htm
205 Copyright © 2021 by Discovery Bible as cited on: https://biblehub.com/greek/1537.htm
206 Delsemme, Armand H. and Weissman, Paul. *Comet Shoemaker-Levy 9*. Encyclopedia Britannica, 14 Feb. 2019, https://www.britannica.com/topic/Comet-Shoemaker-Levy-9. Accessed 4/20/2023.
207 Delsemme & Weissman, 14 Feb. 2019, accessed 4/20/2023
208 Delsemme & Weissman, 14 Feb. 2019, accessed 4/20/2023
209 Delsemme & Weissman, 14 Feb. 2019, accessed 4/20/2023
210 Delsemme & Weissman, 14 Feb. 2019, accessed 4/20/2023
211 https://ntrs.nasa.gov/citations/19970022199, Document ID 19970022199, published January 1,1996, accessed 4/20/2023
212 The Super Comet: The Impact (1/2) | Full Documentary, Professor Jay Melosh, University of Arizona, Tucson, timestamp: 37:00, https://www.youtube.com/watch?v=V86G03930Nc, accessed 4/26/2023
213 Super Comet: timestamp 37:00
214 https://www.space.com/19855-shoemaker-levy-9.html, published January 23, 2018, accessed 4/20/2022
215 https://pmc.ncbi.nlm.nih.gov/articles/PMC3504143/, 2012 Nov 21, accessed 11/24/2024

216 https://en.wikipedia.org/wiki/Impact_winter, edited 14 November 2024, at 12:06 (UTC), accessed 12/07/2024
217 Strong's Lexicon as cited on: https://biblehub.com/greek/894.htm
218 Copyright © 2021 by Discovery Bible as cited on: https://biblehub.com/greek/894.htm
219 Strong's Lexicon as cited on: https://biblehub.com/greek/3939.htm
220 Brown-Driver-Briggs Hebrew and English Lexicon, Unabridged, Electronic Database. Copyright © 2002, 2003, 2006 by Biblesoft, Inc., accessed 4/30/2023
221 Joel Richardson, *The Islamic Antichrist*, WND Books, Washington, D.C., paperback (2015), p.20
222 Richardson (2015), pp 31-32
223 Richardson (2015) p. 183
224 Richardson (2015) p. 183
225 Richardson (2015) pp183-184
226 Strong's Lexicon as cited on: https://biblehub.com/greek/2730.htm
227 https://biblehub.com/greek/2730.htm, accessed 12/19/2023
228 Copyright © 2021 by Discovery Bible as cited on: https://biblehub.com/greek/894.htm
229 Strong's Lexicon as cited on: https://biblehub.com/greek/105.htm
230 Strong's Lexicon as cited on: https://biblehub.com/greek/105.htm
231 Strong's Lexicon as cited on: https://biblehub.com/greek/3321.htm
232 Thayer's Greek Lexicon as cited on https://biblehub.com/greek/3321.htm, accessed 12/19/2023
233 Strong's Lexicon as cited on: https://biblehub.com/greek/12.htm
234 Strong's Lexicon as cited on: https://biblehub.com/greek/2920.htm
235 NAS Exhaustive Concordance as cited on: https://biblehub.com/greek/2920.htm, accessed 2/10/2024
236 Copyright © 2021 by Discovery Bible. https://biblehub.com/greek/2920.htm
237 https://www.bbc.com/news/blogs-magazine-monitor-34154767, 15 September, 2015, accessed 2/10/2024
238 Strong's Lexicon as cited on: https://biblehub.com/greek/109.htm
239 Strong's Lexicon as cited on: https://biblehub.com/greek/109.htm
240 Thayer's Greek Lexicon as cited on: https://biblehub.com/greek/109.htm
241 Strong's Lexicon as cited on: https://biblehub.com/greek/1849.htm
242 https://outforia.com/types-of-scorpions/, accessed 1/21/2024
243 https://outforia.com/types-of-scorpions/, accessed 1/21/2024
244 https://www.orkin.com/pests/stinging-pests/scorpions/scorpion-stinger
245 Strong's Lexicon as cited on: https://biblehub.com/greek/2046.htm
246 Strong's Lexicon as cited on: https://biblehub.com/greek/4973.htm
247 Copyright © 2021 by Discovery Bible.. https://biblehub.com/greek/4973.htm
248 Strong's Lexicon as cited on: https://biblehub.com/greek/928.htm
249 Strong's Lexicon as cited on: https://biblehub.com/greek/928.htm
250 Thayer's Greek Lexicon, Electronic Database. Copyright © 2002, 2003, 2006, 2011 by Biblesoft, Inc. https://biblehub.com/greek/928.htm, accessed 1/21/2024
251 Strong's Lexicon as cited on: https://biblehub.com/greek/1937.htm
252 NAS Exhaustive Concordance as cited on: https://biblehub.com/greek/1937.htm
253 Copyright © 2021 by Discovery Bible, https://biblehub.com/greek/1937.htm

254 Strong's Lexicon as cited on: https://biblehub.com/greek/599.htm
255 Strong's Lexicon as cited on: https://biblehub.com/greek/599.htm
256 Copyright © 2021 by Discovery Bible. https://biblehub.com/greek/599.htm
257 Strong's Lexicon as cited on: https://biblehub.com/greek/3667.htm
258 Strong's Lexicon as cited on: https://biblehub.com/greek/3667.htm
259 Copyright © 2021 by Discovery Bible, https://biblehub.com/greek/3667.htm
260 https://en.wikipedia.org/wiki/Cataphract, last edited on 23 December 2023, at 21:03 (UTC), accessed 1/27/2024
261 https://facts.net/nature/animals/10-interesting-facts-about-lions-teeth/, Published 01, January 2024, accessed 1/27/2024
262 https://www.hunker.com/12330606/life-cycle-of-locusts, updated Feb 10, 2022, accessed 1/27/2024
263 Strong's Lexicon as cited on: https://biblehub.com/greek/12.htm
264 Strong's Lexicon as cited on: https://biblehub.com/greek/12.htm
265 Thayer's Greek Lexicon as cited on: https://biblehub.com/greek/12.htm
266 Strong's Lexicon as cited on: https://biblehub.com/greek/11.htm
267 Strong's Lexicon as cited on: https://biblehub.com/greek/11.htm
268 Strong's Lexicon as cited on: https://biblehub.com/greek/623.htm
269 Strong's Lexicon as cited on: https://biblehub.com/greek/623.htm
270 Copyright © 2021 by Discovery Bible as cited on: https://biblehub.com/greek/623.htm
271 Strong's Lexicon as cited on: https://biblehub.com/greek/3686.htm
272 Strong's Lexicon as cited on: https://biblehub.com/greek/3686.htm
273 Copyright © 2021 by Discovery Bible as cited on: https://biblehub.com/greek/3686.htm
274 Nelson's (1982) p. 1
275 Strong's Lexicon as cited on: https://biblehub.com/greek/7843.htm
276 NAS Exhaustive Concordance as cited on: https://biblehub.com/hebrew/7843.htm
277 Brown-Driver-Briggs Hebrew and English Lexicon, Unabridged, Electronic Database, Copyright © 2002, 2003, 2006 by Biblesoft, Inc., https://biblehub.com/hebrew/7843.htm, accessed 4/27/2024
278 *The History of Herodotus Translated by George Rawlinson,* https://files.romanroadsstatic.com/ materials/herodotus.pdf, pp. 156-157,accessed 5/4/2024
279 https://cojs.org/sennacherib-_705-681_bce/, accessed 5/4/2024
280 Strassler, Herodotus, p. 184, note on 2.141.5a; cf. Geoffrey Marks and William K. Beatty, Epidemics (New York: Charles Scribner's Sons, 1976), pp. 7-8, 13, as cited in: https://jbqnew.jewishbible.org/assets/Uploads/454/ jbq_454_caesarplague.pdf, accessed 5/4/2024
281 Strong's Lexicon as cited on: https://biblehub.com/greek/2768.htm
282 Strong's Lexicon as cited on: https://biblehub.com/greek/2379.htm
283 Strong's Lexicon as cited on: https://biblehub.com/greek/2768.htm
284 Thayer's Greek Lexiconas cited on: https://biblehub.com/greek/2379.htm
285 Prof. Karl Fayerbend, Ph. D., of Cothen, Germany, A complete Hebrew-English Pocket Dictionary of the Old Testament, third edition, printed by G. Langenscheidt, Berlin-Schonebberg, U. Iv. R., p.34, https://archive.org/details/acompletehebrewe00feyeuoft/page/n5/mode/2up?view=theater&q=gate, accessed online 8/10/2024
286 Brown-Driver-Briggs as cited on: https://biblehub.com/hebrew/894.htm

287 Brown-Driver-Briggs as cited on: https://biblehub.com/hebrew/894.htm
288 https://www.abarim-publications.com/Meaning/Babel.html, Abarim Publications — first published here on 2006-04-19; moved to present location on 2008-05-18; last updated on 2024-06-27, accessed 8/10/2024
289 Strong's Lexicon as cited on: https://biblehub.com/greek/4447.htm
290 Strong's exhaustive concordance, https://biblehub.com/greek/4447.htm
291 Strong's Lexicon as cited on: https://biblehub.com/greek/5191.htm
292 Thayer's Greek Lexicon as cited on: https://biblehub.com/greek/5191.htm
293 Strong's Lexicon as cited on: https://biblehub.com/greek/2306.htm
294 Strong's Lexicon as cited on: https://biblehub.com/greek/2306.htm
295 Strong's Lexicon as cited on: https://biblehub.com/greek/2586.htm
296 Strong's Lexicon as cited on: https://biblehub.com/greek/2586.htm
297 Strong's Lexicon as cited on: https://biblehub.com/greek/5333.htm
298 Copyright © 2021 by Discovery Bible as cited on: https://biblehub.com/greek/5333.htm
299 Strong's Lexicon as cited on: https://biblehub.com/greek/32.htm
300 Copyright © 2021 by Discovery Bible as cited on: https://biblehub.com/greek/32.htm
301 Strong's Lexicon as cited on: https://biblehub.com/greek/2478.htm
302 Strong's Lexicon as cited on: https://biblehub.com/greek/2478.htm
303 Copyright © 2021 by Discovery Bible as cited on: https://biblehub.com/greek/2478.htm
304 Strong's Lexicon as cited on: https://biblehub.com/greek/3507.htm
305 Strong's Lexicon as cited on: https://biblehub.com/greek/3507.htm
306 Thayer's Greek Lexicon as cited on: https://biblehub.com/greek/3507.htm
307 *Reflections: God's megaphone* By C.S. Lewis Institute, https://www.cslewisinstitute.org/resources/reflections-october-2021/, October 1, 2021, accessed 12/7/2024
308 Stephen C. Meyer, *Signature in the Cell: DNA and the Evidence for Intelligent Design* (2009), HarperCollins Publishers, 195 Broadway, New York, NY 10007, p, 206
309 Meyer (2009), p. 207
310 Meyer (2009), p. 213
311 Meyer (2009), p. 216
312 Meyer (2009), pp. 216-217
313 The Hebrew Concept of Time, Ronnie Littlejohn, pp. 53-56. *Biblical Illustrator*, Winter 1999-2000, Nashville as cited on http://www.ovrlnd.com/Eschatology/hebrewconceptoftime.html, accessed 12/20/2023
314 Ronnie Littlejohn, pp. 53-56. as cited on http://www.ovrlnd.com/Eschatology/hebrewconceptoftime.html, accessed 12/20/2023
315 Ronnie Littlejohn, pp. 53-56. as cited on http://www.ovrlnd.com/Eschatology/hebrewconceptoftime.html, accessed 12/20/2023
316 https://www.gotquestions.org/kingdom-heaven-God.html, last updated January 4, 2022, accessed 8/20/2023
317 See introduction to the book of Matthew in the Zondervan NASB Study Bible (1999), p. 1363
318 Paul L Maier, *Eusebius: The Church History*, (2007), Kragel Publications, Grand Rapids, MI p. 278

[319] Nelson's Three-In-One Bible Reference Companion, Thomas Nelson, Inc., Publishers & Guideposts Associates, Inc. (1982) p. 520
[320] Strong's Lexicon as cited on: https://biblehub.com/greek/4007.htm
[321] Copyright © 2021 by Discovery Bible, https://biblehub.com/greek/4007.htm
[322] Strong's Lexicon as cited on: https://biblehub.com/greek/1062.htm
[323] Strong's Lexicon as cited on: https://biblehub.com/greek/1062.htm
[324] *New Evidence the Nazis didn't come close to the bomb*, by Carmen Drahl, https://www.forbes.com/sites/carmendrahl/2015/09/16/new-evidence-the-nazis-didnt-come-close-to-the-bomb/ updated Sept. 16, 2015, 02:17 pm EDT, accessed 12/7/2024
[325] Nelson's Three-in-one Bible Reference Companion, Thomas Nelson Inc., Publishers & Guideposts Associates, Inc. (1982), p. 718
[326] Nelson's (1982), p. 222
[327] Dave Hunt, A Woman Rides the Beast (1994), Harvest House Publishers, Eugene Oregon, pp. 99-107
[328] Dave Hunt (1994), pp. 243-262
[329] Dave Hunt (1994), p. 505
[330] Larry Cockerham, *Revelation: Prophetic Addresses to the Seven Churches*, Brentwood Christian Press, (1995), p. 90
[331] Peter De Rosa, *Vicars of Christ: The Dark Side of the Papacy* (Crown Publishers, 1988) P.180, as cited in Dave Hunt (1994), p243
[332] Dave hunt (1994), p. 243
[333] E. H. Broadbent, The Pilgrim Church, Martino Fine Books, Eastford, CT (2018), p.97
[334] Broadbent (2018), p.97
[335] Broadbent (2018), p. 97
[336] Broadbent (2018), p.52
[337] Broadbent (2018), p.88
[338] William Jones, *History of the Christian Church*, pp.viii - ix
[339] Broadbent (2018), p.89
[340] John Dowling, *The History of Romanism*, (1845) p.541
[341] Dave Hunt (1994), p. 249
[342] Berman, H. J. (1983). Law and Revolution: The Formation of the Western Legal Tradition. Harvard University Press, p. 92, as cited on: https://www.historytools.org/stories/the-power-of-the-medieval-church-a-historians-perspective, May 25, 2024, accessed 8/25/2024
[343] Dave Hunt (1994), p.253
[344] Nelson's (1982), p. 608
[345] https://en.wikipedia.org/wiki/Pontifex_maximus, last edited on 4 September 2023, at 00:12 (UTC), accessed 9/17/2023
[346] William Smith, *A Dictionary of Greek and Roman Antiquities*, Harper and brothers 82 Cliff-Street (1847), p. 792
[347] William Smith (1847), p. 790
[348] William Smith (1847), p. 791
[349] William Smith (1847), p. 791
[350] https://en.wikipedia.org/wiki/Council_of_Trent#cite_ref-CCC_85_22-0, last edited on 13 September 2023, at 12:20 (UTC, accessed 9/17/2023
[351] Council of Trent, Seventh Session, Cannon 4

352 https://en.wikipedia.org/wiki/Sola_scriptura, last edited on 17 September 2023, at 08:15 (UTC), accessed 9/17/2023

353 https://en.wikipedia.org/wiki/Ninety-five_Theses, last edited on 12 September 2023, at 13:34 (UTC), accessed 9/17/2023

354 https://www.logos.com/grow/5-solas-reformation/, *5 Solas of the Reformation—What They Are & Why They Matter,* Karen Engle, October 8, 2021, accessed 11/1/2023

355 Peter De Rosa, *Vicars of Christ, The Dark Side of the Papacy*, Poolbeg Press, Ltd. (1988) p.120

356 Peter De Rosa (1988), p.121

357 Peter De Rosa (1988), p.121

358 Nelson's (1982), p. 525

359 NASB, see note #1 on II Thessalonians 2:3, 'apostasy'

360 https://en.wikipedia.org/wiki/Earthrise, last edited on 30 October 2024, at 03:32 (UTC), accessed 12/7/2024

361 https://www.lpi.usra.edu/resources/apollo/frame/?AS08-14-2384, accessed 12/7/2024

362 Race to the Moon /Image Gallery, *Earth from the Moon*, https://www.pbs.org/wgbh/americanexperience/features/moon-earth-moon/#:~:text=it reflected the brilliance of, Credit: NASA, accessed 1/11/22025

363 50 Years After 'Earthrise,' a Christmas Eve Message from its Photographer, by Bill Anders, https://www.space.com/42848-earthrise-photo-apollo-8-legacy-bill-anders.html, December 24, 2018, accessed 12/7/2024

364 https://en.wikipedia.org/wiki/Earthrise, last edited on 30 October 2024, at 03:32 (UTC), accessed 12/7/2024

365 Timeline, Launch from Cape Canaveral, https://science.nasa.gov/mission/cassini/the-journey/timeline/, accessed 1/11/2025

366 Saturn Orbit Insertion https://science.nasa.gov/mission/cassini/the-journey/timeline/, accessed 1/11/2025

367 Missions: Cassini, https://solarsystem.nasa.gov/missions/cassini-hds/overview/, accessed 1/13/2025

368 https://solarsystem.nasa.gov/missions/cassini-hds/overview/ accessed 1/13/2025

369 *Cassini at Enceladus: A Decade Plus of Discovery,* https://science.nasa.gov/missions/cassini/cassini-at-enceladus-a-decade-plus-of-discovery/ accessed 1/13/2025

370 The Grand Finale, https://solarsystem.nasa.gov/missions/cassini-hds/mission/grand-finale/overview/, updated February 17, 2022, accessed 1/15/2025

371 Halfway Home, https://science.nasa.gov/mission/cassini/the-journey/timeline/, accessed 1/11/2025

372 Cassini's Two Speeds, https://science.nasa.gov/missions/cassini/cassinis-two-speeds/ January 18, 2017, Accessed 1/13/2025

373 Cassini Extended Missions, Linda Spilker, Cassini Deputy Project Scientist, (EOM Options with Science Evaluation): https://www.lpi.usra.edu/opag/march_08_meeting/presentations/spilker.pdf April 1, 2008, accessed 1/13/2025

374 Saturn by the Numbers, https://solarsystem.nasa.gov/saturn-by-the-numbers/?intent=121, last updated May 16, 2024, accessed 1/13/2025

375 https://en.wikipedia.org/wiki/Lucy_(spacecraft), last edited on 17 August 2024, at 21:02 (UTC), accessed 8/25/2024
376 https://nineplanets.org/questions/how-many-planets-are-in-the-milky-way/, September 29, 2020, accessed 8/25/2024
377 Tom Jones, Astronaut Speaker, https://astronauttomjones.com/2024/05/17/how-long-would-it-take-to-reach-the-nearest-star/, May 17. 2024, accessed 1/13/2025

www.ingramcontent.com/pod-product-compliance
Lightning Source LLC
LaVergne TN
LVHW020927090426
835512LV00020B/3238